The Listener's Voice

The Listener's Voice

Early Radio and the American Public

ELENA RAZLOGOVA

PENN

UNIVERSITY OF PENNSYLVANIA PRESS

PHILADELPHIA

Published by
University of Pennsylvania Press
Philadelphia, Pennsylvania 19104-4112
www.upenn.edu/pennpress

Printed in the United States of America on acid-free paper

10 9 8 7 6 5 4 3 2 1

A Cataloging-in-Publication record is available
from the Library of Congress
ISBN 978-0-8122-4320-8

*For my parents
and in memory of Roy*

Contents

Preface

The Moral Economy of American Broadcasting

When *Gang Busters* came on the air Nanny Roy was packing her grand-daughter's suitcase. It was nine o'clock in the evening in September of 1942. It did not take her long to realize that the story concerned her son. Twelve years previously, she sold dresses at a ready-to-wear shop in Cedar Rapids, Iowa, her husband ran electric trains at a foundry, and her son, Virgil Harris, processed corn at a starch factory. Then Harris became an armed robber, was caught and jailed, escaped, died—gunned down by state police—and joined the ranks of Depression-era bandits immortalized by true crime magazines, movies, and radio. Nanny Roy's granddaughter was leaving for college. Protective of her privacy, Roy promptly mailed a complaint to the sponsor, Earl Sloan and Company. The company forwarded her letter to program supervisor, Leonard Bass, whose response can be surmised from Roy's second letter. "I cannot except your regrets," she declared:

> I understand perfectly if I were a mother with high financial standing this would never of happed. you can't deny the crime of all sorts the worst of all the *robbery* that happens every day thru the rich and mighty from the poor. why not expose them. put your investigator at work on the people who are stealing thru their capacity officially. . . . This sort of crime is worse to me than if a person point a gun at me and demand all I have. Yet it goes on. An 18 year old boy steals a sack of feed an inner tube or a tire and he gets sentenced to 20 years in an institution. let the big feller rob in his undermining way there's no publicity he goes on lectures to society and is met by the broadcasters with a hand-shake.[1]

The true crime show had failed Nanny Roy in a variety of ways. Its researchers had pried into her family history. Its writers had omitted aspects of her son's life that drove him to rob banks. Its sponsors and producers had brushed off her point that workers turned to banditry to survive the Great Depression—a recent memory even as the country began to recover during the war. A modern reader might wonder why she bothered to correspond with broadcasters at all, given how well she understood and articulated the complicity of the commercial broadcasting industry in the inequities of American capitalism. Yet she did write, twice, and received a response. Nanny Roy's letter conveys both her sense of social justice and her expectations of reciprocity from the radio industry.

Many Americans shared her sentiments. Between 1920 and 1950, during the "golden age" of radio, they extended communal values to the increasingly complex national economy and politics. Populist movements revolted against the rise of the impersonal bureaucratic nation state and modern industrial society. The union rank and file believed in "moral capitalism," a social order where industrial employers had a responsibility to provide a fair share for workers. Large corporations advertised themselves as friendly neighborhood stores to appease restive consumers. And the expanding federal government had to meet rising expectations of fairness from the loyal citizenry. This moral economy governed the development of radio as an industry and a mass medium.[2] The industry operated on tacit assumptions that held broadcasters responsible to their audiences. Americans looked to radio not only to reflect but to resolve some of the tensions they felt about the nature of big institutions, the location of social power, and the future of both market and political democracy. This book describes how their expectations shaped the medium.

Today, the idea that listeners' sense of justice shaped broadcasters' production practices appears to defy common sense. Once the main ground for scholarly battles over media effects and national culture, in the era of television radio became the province of memorabilia and tape collectors. Ronald Reagan's deregulation policies made it relevant again, inspiring influential studies of how advertising and corporate monopoly stifled programming and technical innovation. Participatory amateur radio in the early 1920s gave place to one-way local commercial, educational, and non-profit broadcasting. Following the Radio Act of 1927 and especially the Communication Act of 1934, national networks dominated broadcasting and consolidated American national culture. After the ratings services appeared in the early 1930s, broadcasters rarely confronted real listeners, only "demographics" classified by gender, race, geography, income, and purchasing habits. Networks, ad agencies, and sponsors erected a self-serving system of pseudoscientific measurement to render audiences into a commodity that could be more easily sold to agencies and clients alike. Despite flawed methods, ratings have persisted as the foundation for commercial broadcasting into the twenty-first century. "Radio," legal scholar Yochai Benkler concluded in 2006, "for a brief moment destabilized the mass-media model, but quickly converged to it." After that, "there were no more genuine inflection points in the structure of mass media."[3] According to this bird's eye view of the industry, listeners had little impact on its everyday organization but bore the brunt of the consequent corporate media system.

To those who take a closer look, however, radio's past seems less decided. Local stations in the 1920s, it turns out, forged symbiotic relationships with their farmer, immigrant, and middle-class neighbors. The networks did not blanket the entire country until the late 1930s. Regional chains and local stations continued to operate alongside the national system. The Federal Communications Commission used antitrust law to break apart the National Broadcasting Company in 1943. Commercials that hailed shopping as a form of citizenship inspired consumer boycotts. Network programs created a sense of intimacy rather than an impersonal national culture. Listeners imagined personal connections with radio characters, and expected scriptwriters, actors, and sponsors to heed their advice. These new accounts amend the tale of network and commercial dominance. They begin to explain why so many Americans—over 80 percent by 1940—owned radios and listened on average for four hours daily, and why in a pinch families would rather give up their furniture, linen, or icebox than their radio set. George Washington Hill, the president of the American Tobacco Company and one of the first radio sponsors, defined radio as 10 percent entertainment and 90 percent advertising.[4] His often-cited quip becomes more programmatic than descriptive once one looks, as this book does, beyond business plans and political debates to the everyday practices and expectations at work in the making of broadcasting.

The Listener's Voice argues that audiences were critical components in the making of radio, the establishment of its genres and social operations. During the Jazz Age and the Great Depression, with no scientific structure yet available to analyze and predict audience response, radio producers created devices and programs relying on individual listeners' phone calls, telegrams, and letters. In their responses, Americans demanded access to radio production, aiming also to reframe the terms on which modern institutions, the radio industry included, structured their lives. In this period, listener response inspired changes in radio technology, genres, and institutions. Writers and stars used their relationship with listeners to gain some creative autonomy from network and agency executives. By wartime, however, the broadcasting industry relied mainly on scientific management of audiences. Ratings and surveys of specialized markets shaped production choices. Radio genres had standardized and producers no longer invited listeners to participate in the creative process, allowing them only to express taste preferences. Networks consolidated their power over programming decisions, edging out input from audiences, agencies, writers, and stars. It also became harder for radio personalities to convince listeners that their individual testimonies mattered. But scientific marketing never triumphed completely—as television producers embraced ratings, audiences gained more control over local radio. By the time postwar prosperity arrived, centralization and scientific methods gave way to local reciprocal forms of radio production.

This book thus uses radio history as a lens to examine the moral economy that Americans imagined for themselves and for the nation. Its chapters proceed chronologically, focusing on key moments of creative, intellectual, and ethical discovery, when certain listeners and broadcasters challenged corporate standards of ownership and control. Radio technology, and the amateurs, hardware bootleggers, and sports fans who influenced its initial development, appear prominently in the Jazz Age. The Federal Radio Commission becomes a key character in 1927, when it destroys popular visions for a decentralized broadcasting system in favor of national networks, leaving it to radio fan magazines to re-educate listeners in living with the commercial network system. Radio serials enter the narrative during the Depression, when scriptwriters and fans negotiate their storylines. Scientific audience research comes into focus on the eve of the war, when German philosopher Theodor Adorno, having just escaped the Nazi brand of scientific management, confronts its authority at the Radio Research Project, at Princeton and later at Columbia University. At the same juncture, true crime shows elicit poor listeners' disenchantment with corporate radio. And the music industry takes center stage in postwar prosperity, when rhythm and blues disc jockeys, in collaboration with fans, challenge established norms of music production and property. Together, all the strands of this story describe how Americans shaped the early broadcasting industry, and, in the process, invented a moral media economy—a set of uncodified but effective assumptions as to what was and was not legitimate in the relationship between the industry and its audiences.

This story matters because it calls attention to the recurring cycles of popular participation and corporate control in modern media. Scholars usually look back to the pre-1920s experimenter era of radio to imagine a utopian relationship between a mass medium and its audiences. According to media theorist Henry Jenkins, when amateurs relinquished control of radio to broadcasting stations, Americans lost "the potential for a broad-based participatory medium" to "corporate interests." Digital media, he suggests, may experience the same fate. More generally, cultural historian Michael Denning notes "the great paradox" of twentieth-century media where "the genuine democratization of cultural audiences required such large capital investment and technical training as to have restricted greatly the production of films and broadcasts."[5] A small community of skilled enthusiasts—radio amateurs or computer hackers, for example—develops a collaborative medium. But by the time wider audiences gain access to it, the gap between corporate producers and mass audiences grows to the extent that collaboration is no longer possible. This book instead explores how mass audiences have applied the participatory ethic of the early experimenter period to their relationship with commercial cultural industries.

To begin with, commercial industries needed audience participation to create and reinvent a mass medium. Sportscasts owed their raucous ambient sound, and soaps their fantastic plot twists, to listeners' demanding enthusiasm. Even after corporations took control of the medium, in periods of crisis industries had to abandon scientific marketing in favor of direct interaction with audiences. When television encroached on radio's dominance, network radio failed because it reused old programs and stars. Local radio survived because it developed new formats in collaboration with local audiences. Histories of sound reproduction technologies have focused on corporate standards for radio sound. *The Listener's Voice* amends these accounts to show how Americans continually reinvented the new sound medium to help them perceive modern structures of power and authority that encroached on their daily lives. Even with wireless technology already in place by 1920, Americans still needed to invent radio broadcasting as a new "medium" in a broad sense suggested by art historian Rosalind Krauss: to discover specific instruments, styles, and business practices that would extract cultural meanings from the technology.[6] In response to listeners' letters, engineers, writers, performers, and managers made specific formal choices. These choices in turn suggested new forms of sound perception and social order.

Precisely because corporate producers wielded more power than mass audiences, these periods of interaction and negotiation raised questions about social justice in media and society. Media scholars have celebrated audiences—from teenage Madonna look-alikes to *Star Trek* fan fiction writers—who refashioned mass culture to fit their own needs. Let us not. Popular critiques of corporate capitalism became most articulate not during the freewheeling experimenter era, but when the industry upset audience expectations of reciprocity—when networks displaced local radio and when scientific audience research made it impossible for individual listeners to affect radio production. Some audiences proved more likely to draw parallels between political, economic, and cultural domains. Ethnic and rural audiences defended local stations more readily than urban middle-class listeners. Down-and-out Americans were more prone to relate radio executives' disdain for listeners to Depression-era economic inequities. Black listeners appreciated some minstrel performers' artistry yet saw race humor as evidence of their second-class status as audiences and citizens. Such moments provide a unique record of the vernacular social imagination—the ways ordinary Americans conceived and enacted their relationship to big institutions. They allow us to trace modern institution building from the bottom up, as political historian Meg Jacobs described state formation. If cultural historians looked for "popular political theory" in Betty Grable pinups and Hollywood films, this book looks for vernacular political economy in ordinary people's own writings to radio producers.[7] When the industry upset audience expectations of reciprocity, it lent listeners modes of perception and argument that enabled them to critique the industry itself, as well as other institutions and the economic, racial, and gender inequities of modern America.

As a historical touchstone for contemporary debates about participatory media and corporate power, early radio serves well to investigate the American economic moral sense. Gifts, trade, consumption, revolts, elections, and law have all provided material for specific studies of reciprocity. Several wide-ranging and influential accounts disagree about its origins, timing, and attributes. French sociologist Marcel Mauss defines "gift economy" as bonds of obligation created by gift exchange in "archaic" societies, from the ancient Romans to the Haïda and Tlingit of the American Northwest. British historian E. P. Thompson considers the "moral economy" of eighteenth-century food riots a prepolitical response to capitalism. Yochai Benkler believes that a new non-market economy of "social production" is inseparable from the digital communication networks. Meg Jacobs places the "pocketbook politics" of consumer entitlement in the early twentieth century, encompassing the welfare capitalism of the 1920s, New Deal social security, and the economic citizenship of the mid-century fiscal state. These scholars describe related concepts and draw on each other's theories.[8] Yet it is hard to grasp a phenomenon described alternatively as precapitalist or consumerist, primitive or digital, prepolitical or fundamental to liberal politics in America. A focus on an emerging medium resolves some of these contradictions. Media innovation requires reciprocity; with each new innovation, moral media economies inevitably resurface, reshaping and occasionally defying established standards of property.

More generally, the history of American radio presents a paradox, where apparently premodern or postcolonial sensibilities permeate modern life in the West. "Modernity," in its multifarious summations, spans Cubist painting and New Orleans jazz; railroads and the assembly line; statistics and sociology; liberal democracy and colonialism; corporations and migrant labor; simultaneity and speed; the popular press, cinema, and radio. Outside of the West, the story goes, these changes in technology, economy, politics, art, and sense perception encounter indigenous practices and worldviews, producing "alternative" modernities. In Nigeria, the domestic film industry thrives on video pirates' expertise and distribution networks. In Egypt, students, shopkeepers, and taxi drivers hear a moral guide to political judgment in the rhythm and tone of Islamic cassette sermons. In Cameroon, the poor use their belief in witchcraft as a weapon in struggles over material and political resources. The West, all but free of these aberrations, enjoys the classic modernity of free market capitalism, instrumental rationality, and disinterested public debate. The story of radio instead suggests that piracy, sensibility, and belief may be fundamental to modern political economy everywhere.[9]

Commercial broadcasters, for one, put faith in modern scientific surveys. American population management projects stretched from the first U.S. census in the 1780s to the opening of the Harvard Bureau of Business Research in 1911, Army intelligence tests during World War I, and Robert and Helen Lynd's quest for average "Middletown" Americans in Muncie, Indiana, in the 1920s. Scientific methods soared in popularity in 1936, when George Gallup's and Elmo Roper's representative sampling polls correctly predicted Franklin Delano Roosevelt's victory in the 1936 presidential election. Surveys of media audiences followed, with mixed results. After several unhelpful pilot studies, Radio-Keith-Orpheum and Walt Disney Studios refused to renew their contracts with Gallup's Audience Research Institute. But broadcast ratings took hold because they helped networks sell potential audiences to sponsors.

Telephone surveys and audimeter machines underestimated radio audience size by up to 20 percent but shared in the egalitarian authority of opinion polls. Gallup and Roper redefined civic participation when they conveyed the nation's opinion on the economy and military intervention. Network statistics departments trumpeted sponsored radio as a democracy when they quantified and categorized listener preferences. After some grumbling and protests, Americans learned to imagine society as a rational system, known and managed through surveys.[10]

Or so it seemed. Radio fans instead relied on what political theorist William Connolly called "visceral modes of appraisal." They argued from the particular—a sack of feed, a tube, a tire—and opted for practical knowledge against the systematic rigor offered by the networks. They patronized the bootleg radio tube industry, dispensed advice to fictional radio characters, and sent them gifts. They favored trenchant language. Nanny Roy, retired saleslady ("you can't deny the crime of all sorts the worst of all the *robbery* that happens every day thru the rich and mighty from the poor. why not expose them"), violated every standard of detachment, diffidence, prosody, and voice evident in the scientific writing of Hugh Beville, NBC research manager ("It must be admitted that there is still some doubt about the general listening pattern of the lowest economic group"). Excitable and unruly, radio fans resemble neither the mass public constituted by ratings or opinion polls, nor the anonymous and impartial citizenry debating politics in the bourgeois public sphere, as German philosopher Jürgen Habermas famously defined it. Their demands for reciprocity seem to confirm a notion, widely shared today, that sentiments make reasoned judgments impossible.[11]

A long view of audience correspondence tells otherwise. Like the popular periodicals of the eighteenth century, broadcasters cultivated exchange with their publics. In 1711, the London *Spectator*, a popular general circulation daily and, by many accounts, the birthplace of the public sphere, invited gentlemen and, less enthusiastically, artisans, shopgirls, and servants to send in reports and opinions as "materials" for the editor's "speculations" on literary style and urban life. The *Spectator* appealed to an imaginary public of disinterested citizens, but published letters to the editor and accounts of coffee shop debates to trace the circulation of opinion among actual readers. Broadcasters, too, addressed an imaginary public of citizen consumers, wondering if their listeners really existed. The earliest radio stations installed telegraph and telephone operators in the studio to report listener responses in real time. Networks organized mail contests and set up departments to process and answer listener mail. To sort and route to the artists, program managers, and sponsors the more than 12,697,000 letters received during 1931, the Columbia Broadcasting System's audience division reportedly trebled its personnel and facilities. In March 1936 alone NBC claimed to have spent more than $300,000 on postage replying to 1,015,372 letters. Radio fan magazines printed readers' opinions in columns entitled "Voice of the Listener" and "The Listener Speaks."[12] Marketing drove much of this, but ideas did circulate, letters were written, sent, read, and answered. Broadcasters did not conjure up their listening public with a throw of a switch. The public participated in its own making.

Like the serial novels of the nineteenth century, radio programs unfolded as if in an intimate conversation with their audiences. Around the mid-nineteenth century, Congress reduced the basic U.S. postage rate to two to three cents per half ounce, where it remained virtually unchanged for the next hundred years. Rural delivery, motorized post carriers, and airmail came in the early twentieth century. In 1861, the U.S. Postal Service carried 161 million letters, or three times more per capita than twenty years earlier. In 1930, it carried 28 billion. As expectations of personal contact expanded beyond one's home and neighborhood, novelists, stage headliners, and movie stars became objects of epistolary affection. Serial narratives especially promoted "communion between the writer and the public," as William Thackeray put it, "something continual, confidential, something like personal affection." Radio, to advertisers' delight, also made "thousands of people feel free to sit down and write a friendly and personal letter to a large corporation." Sensitive microphones, crooning voices, living room radios, protracted storylines, and informal speech amplified the sense of a "personal touch." Commercials used personal appeal to direct consumer desires. Roosevelt, who received more mail from his constituents than any previous president, began his "fireside chats" with a drink of water and an aside, "It is very hot here in Washington." Yet listeners addressed broadcasters as intimate enemies as well as friends, as Roosevelt found out from the angry responses to his short-lived Supreme Court packing plan.[13] Intimacy served as a mode of judgment as well as a persuasion technique.

Far from an aberrant alternative to modern scientific audience research, this epistolary exchange, and the moral economy it sustained, were fundamental to the making of broadcasting. This became clear as I scanned decades of reader columns in nine radio fan magazines, read thousands of fan letters in seventeen archival collections across the United States, and traced their

authors' lives through census records. (Some of these letters, their authors'
bios, and many radio sounds that inspired them can be found at thelisteners-
voice.org.) Over and over, networks and agencies spent millions "educating"
the public on the democratic nature of ratings and sponsored broadcasting,
against the persistent criticism of reformers, scholars, and lay listeners. Their
monumental attempt to produce individualist and property-abiding "citizen
consumers" compares in scale, if not violence, to reeducation projects aiming
to forge new "Soviet persons" in twentieth-century socialist states. Yet with
each creative turn in broadcasting history, the very conditions of production
ate away at their powers of persuasion. Engineers bent patent regulations;
disc jockeys, copyright laws. Early broadcasters listened to local audiences.
Network writers negotiated with fans. These practices embodied the ideas of
reciprocity that listeners articulated when they confronted national corporate networks and the formulaic ratings system. Today, media executives once
more speak of "reeducating" the public on the sanctity of intellectual property. Lawsuits and publicity campaigns presume that file-sharing audiences
will stop and listen, just like Nipper, the fox terrier who forever heeds "his
master's voice" over the gramophone loudspeaker in the HMV trademark,
first used in 1902 by the Victor Talking Machine Company.[14] *The Listener's
Voice* offers reciprocity between speakers and listeners as a persistent counterpoint to the relationship this famed drawing prescribes.

1

At Ringside

On July 2, 1921 Harold Warren, a real estate salesman, arrived at the beach in Asbury Park, New Jersey, with a receiver mounted on a roller chair. He had been entertaining passersby on the boardwalk with his radio for about a year, but on this day he attracted a particularly large crowd eager to hear a blow-by-blow "voice description" of a heavyweight championship match—a Frenchman, Georges Carpentier, challenged an American, Jack "Manassa Mauler" Dempsey, fifty miles away at the Boyles Thirty Acres arena in Jersey City. Carpentier lost. After the broadcast, Warren enclosed a photograph together with his letter to the organizer, Major J. Andrew White, the acting president of the National Amateur Wireless Association. The grainy halftone, published in the amateur radio magazine *Wireless Age*, shows a crowd of men and women of all stripes, huddled around the sign announcing the broadcast. No one but the proud maker of the radio bothered to look at the camera (fig. 1). This collective experience departed from conventional point-to-point Morse code and voice exchanges among amateur builders of transmission sets. Warren reported a "perfect" listening experience, including the announcer's "clear and vivid" descriptions. "The cheering of the crowd could be distinguished," he went on, "and each sound of the gong seemed as though it were but a few feet" from the listening audience. It was not a live broadcast. Announcer J. Owen Smith in Hoboken had read a description wired from the arena, banging a studio bell between rounds. Listeners heard crowds when there were none.[1]

By the time Dempsey set out to fight the "Wild Bull of the Pampas," Argentine Lois Angel Firpo, for the heavyweight title on September 14, 1923,

1. "A novel way of entertaining an audience was worked out by Harold Warren, who had a roller chair equipped and operating on the boardwalk at Asbury Park, N. J." *Wireless Age*, August 1921, 21, Library of American Broadcasting, University of Maryland, College Park.

ringside noises had become a standard in radio. White, who phoned in the description from the arena to Smith during the Carpentier fight, announced the Firpo bout directly from the ringside, accompanied by bells and shouts from the Polo Grounds in New York City. By all accounts, it was an exciting match. Dempsey won in two rounds, but only after Firpo knocked him through the ropes into the press seats. This time, tensions in radio matched the violence in the ring. Corporations duked it out for the right to broadcast. The first fight was set up by NAWA and the Radio Corporation of America, with a General Electric transmitter borrowed from the Navy. The second was broadcast in New York over RCA station WJZ but transmitted with equipment and over telephone wires owned by the American Telephone and Telegraph Company and its outlet WEAF. Stations worked under greater pressure from listeners. The first fight attracted 300,000 listeners from Massachusetts to Maryland. The second reached millions, and aired at once on an East Coast wired network and as a translated "voice description" as far as Mexico and Argentina. In Washington, D.C., listeners prevailed upon the AT&T network outlet WCAP to relay the returns and upon the RCA station WRC to stay off the air. In New York, 300 telephone callers denounced WEAF for refusing to stay silent so not to interfere with WJZ during the fight. Of the eighteen letters preserved in WEAF files, eleven requested the station to stay off the air, two demanded that the WJZ announcer speak with "pep," and seven reported poor sound from the arena, one of them with tips on how to keep ringside spectators continuously on mike. Radio sound became entangled with ideas about media economy and social order.[2]

Radio's moral economy emerged in the early 1920s, when station engineers and managers invented radio technology and programs by trial and error, testing gadgets and ideas with amateurs and listeners. Today listeners know prizefight radio from Depression-era recordings, perhaps the most famous being the second Joe Louis-Max Schmeling match on June 22, 1938. The black boxer's victory over the German champion, in only one round, symbolized the fight against racism at home and abroad. Over seventy million people—at the time, the largest radio audience for a single program—listened to Clem McCartney's rapid-fire blow-by-blow report, accompanied by the ringside gong and the roar of the crowd.[3] Yet the broadcasting style that allowed Depression-era listeners to experience Louis's victory had developed more than a decade earlier, at a time when black fighters were barred from championship matches. In the early 1920s, new radio stations and receiver manufacturers defied corporate property standards governing the use of copyrighted content and patented equipment. It was then that New York broadcasters and boxing fans developed prizefight reporting, a style that transported listeners into the midst of a diverse crowd of spectators, allowing them to "see" and "touch" the referee and the fighters. What follows is a story of how this sound came to signify reciprocity, collaboration, and opposition to corporate control of radio.

When listeners sought to shape radio styles, they challenged corporate broadcasters' authority. While wireless was still a hobby, a few major companies monopolized the radio equipment market. Amateurs' weak crystal receivers, common before World War I, worked only up to 100 miles and required headphones. Taking advantage of the wartime suspension of patent restrictions, engineering labs at AT&T, General Electric, and Westinghouse developed standardized vacuum tube receivers and transmitters descended from the audion invented by an independent entrepreneur, Lee de Forest, in 1907. Tube sets received at greater distances, worked well with loudspeakers, could be mass-produced, and did not require tinkering from novice users. As a result of an agreement signed in 1919 and revised in 1921, General Electric and Westinghouse manufactured transmitters for their own use and receivers for sale. Only the newly formed Radio Corporation of America—formerly American Marconi—could sell these receivers to amateurs. AT&T, and its manufacturing subsidiary Western Electric, had exclusive rights to provide transmitters to all stations except those owned by GE, Westinghouse, and RCA. AT&T also owned the telephone wires, which within a few years became essential for static-free remote pickups, or "remotes," from night clubs and stadiums. By 1921, AT&T, GE, and Westinghouse owned millions worth of shares in RCA and shared ownership of key radio equipment patents. The "radio trust," as critics would label it within a few years, seemed to eliminate all competition in manufacturing.[4]

This consolidation of capital followed the general trend in the entertainment industry. In the 1920s, MGM and Paramount displaced small New York and Chicago movie studios, the Keith-Albee and Orpheum circuits controlled big-time vaudeville, and only a few large recording companies such as Victor and Columbia survived after radio decimated the recording industry. Prizefighting, too, became a big business in the 1920s, controlled by a few entrepreneurs such as promoter Tex Rickard, who organized boxing events in New York, and Dempsey's manager, Jack "Doc" Kearns. Together, Rickard, Dempsey, and Kearns earned $8.4 million from five fights between 1921 and 1927. The intertwined interests and finances of radio corporations and boxing promoters shaped the development of sportscasting from the outset. The Dempsey-Carpentier broadcast, co-organized by NAWA and Rickard, took place because White succeeded in borrowing a transmitter from RCA, but was not live because he failed to secure phone lines from AT&T. Throughout the 1920s, only large concerns could afford exclusive rights for major sports broadcasts, so every broadcast championship bout also pitted boxing fans against the radio trust.[5]

Yet it was not the trust, but amateurs and their startup companies that fed the explosion of set sales, station licenses, and press hoopla in 1922—the so-called "radio craze." A neighborhood experimenter could easily assemble a transmitter with commercially available vacuum tubes. The minute it broadcast entertainment and news, it infringed on AT&T patents according to the letter of the cross-licensing agreement. At the time of the Dempsey-Carpentier broadcast, only Westinghouse station KDKA in Pittsburgh was officially licensed for public broadcasting. By 1923 576 stations operated nationally. Their owners included colleges, newspapers, department stores, city governments, theaters, and banks. Of these, 93 percent, so-called "squatter" stations, operated in apparent violation of AT&T's patents. Only thirty-five stations used Western Electric transmitters; six others belonged to other trust members. By 1925, when bad publicity forced AT&T to abandon its attempts to extract fees from the squatters, most of the densely populated areas of the United States fell within one hundred miles of a radio station. Corporations confronted a growing "pirate" radio industry.[6]

By law amateurs and their independent companies could produce only crystal sets until November 1922, when one of RCA exclusive receiver patents expired and thus allowed them to produce tube radios. Some independents ignored patent restrictions before then; they also stepped in when RCA could not keep up with demand for replacement radio tubes, which needed to be purchased separately. A national "bootleg" tube industry emerged. With a potential market of one hundred million dollars, it was considered nearly as profitable as rum smuggling during Prohibition. From a secret RCA office, a squad of special investigators, known only by code numbers, infiltrated competing factories looking for bootleggers. In 1922 the cheapest set sold by RCA cost $79.50, but independent manufacturers offered sets for as little as $25, putting radios within reach of most low-income households. Receiver sales in the United States reached 1.5 million sets in 1923, 3.7 million in 1925, and 6.5 million in 1926. Squatter stations and bootleg receivers provided the initial infrastructure for early radio.[7]

Early listeners insisted on a familiar relationship with their stations. In 1920, so many amateurs eavesdropped on the first radio telephone service between Los Angeles and Catalina Island that operators elected to replace it with submarine cable. Lay audiences for public broadcasting showed even less deference. KDKA announcer Harold Arlin recounted in 1925 how once a shopper requested his assistance in finding "a package of pajamas" she just left behind on a street car. Another time, when an out-of-town listener arrived at Pennsylvania Station in Pittsburgh not knowing his relatives' address,

he asked KDKA to "please announce over the radio that I am here and waiting for them to get in touch with me." These expectations were not altogether
naive. "I wish to thank you most sincerely for broadcasting the whereabouts
of my son Martin Gardner upon the death of his brother," wrote the wife of a
foreman at a Schenectady electric plant to General Electric station WGY in
1923. "He was located at Lake George, NY and thru your help he returned
immediately home."[8]

Small stations welcomed such requests. After a few newsworthy re-
unions, WHAS, an outlet of *Louisville Courier-Journal* in Kentucky, made
appeals to lost relatives a regular feature. But corporate functionaries found
chummy listener mail "demoralizing." WJZ announcer Thomas Cowan
remembered how in the fall of 1921, ten days into scheduled broadcasting and a few days after trunks of fan letters began to arrive together with
Westinghouse business mail, Newark plant manager Colonel E. F. Harder
demanded that his office radio be moved out of his sight: "Why, we open
an envelope expecting to find a big order for electric fans—and what do we
get? A letter from a silly woman telling us how well some nincompoop sang
last night!" In magazine advertisements, Westinghouse and AT&T posed as
friendly neighborhood stores. As broadcasters, they were not prepared for
audiences to take the ads literally.[9]

Large metropolitan stations soon developed decorous radio formats that
posited a more formal relationship between broadcasters and the excitable
lay audiences. Schedules included educational talks, religious services, homemaking programs, opera remotes, and tightly scripted studio music performances. When WEAF pioneered sponsored programs in 1923, its managers
decided against "direct" radio advertising—plugging the product by name
during breaks in the program—so as not to intrude on intimate family din-
ners. Instead, broadcasters named programs after their sponsors to generate
"good will" among consumers. Magazine ads pictured elegant couples dancing or lounging next to luxurious radio sets. In these drawings, docility and
refinement became interchangeable. An adman recounted in the trade weekly
Printer's Ink how a young female model dozed off while waiting for her partner to don his tuxedo. The resulting magazine ad had been particularly effective, he argued, because the woman "certainly did appear to be enchanted by
the music." A woman asleep served as a visual shortcut for how broadcasters
wished their target female audience to behave.[10]

Sportscasting did not fit the ideal of cultural uplift such genres and ads
projected. Prizefighting especially had not entirely shed its shady prewar rep-

utation, when many states had outlawed boxing matches. The YMCA board in Hackensack, New Jersey, refused to let amateurs receive the Carpentier bout within the institution's walls because it did not approve of "messages describing a prize fight of a professional nature." After attending the contest, a preacher in East Millstone, New Jersey, declared prizefighting "a moral carbuncle." Even less bloody sports like baseball and football reeked of modern irreverent Jazz Age mores, immortalized by John Held, Jr.'s *Life* magazine cover of a unkempt flapper yelling "Hold 'em!" at a football game. Such associations threatened the corporate aura of respectability. Edgar Felix, a radio amateur turned publicity man for WEAF, remembered how on the eve of the penultimate 1923 World Series game between the New York Giants and the Yankees, set to air over the station, someone from the "top-level executive area" of AT&T decreed that "the company would not violate the Sabbath by broadcasting a baseball game on a Sunday." WEAF broadcast an interdenominational church service instead and passed the game to a low-profile temporary AT&T station, WBAY.[11]

Boxing fans who demanded a say in the making of sportscasting stood apart from corporate broadcasters' target audience of refined, well-off, and female consumers. The few letters preserved in the archives, out of several thousand mailed, telegraphed, and telephoned responses to the Carpentier and Firpo fights, point to the traditional constituencies for both prizefighting and amateur radio—middle- to lower-class white men of all ages and ethnicities. Only 138 of the reported 4,000 responses to the Carpentier broadcast survived. Of the 97 writers who could be identified, three-fourths came from families of laborers, farmers, or clerks; two-fifth were first or second generation immigrants from a total of eighteen countries, including Italians, Slovakians, and Polish Jews. The Firpo bout elicited letters from a machinist, an electrician, a government clerk, a German garage manager, and a Russian window glass maker, among others. This largely plebeian sample of the radio public included no nonwhite listeners and very few women, who wrote only three of the extant responses to the Carpentier broadcast, and one to the Firpo report.[12]

These men shared their enthusiasm for the bloody sport with a much more diverse prizefight-going public. World War I established boxing as a patriotic pastime, at the same time as it trained scores of radio operators and allowed for the development of standardized receivers. In the 1920s, women and affluent citizens across racial lines flocked to prizefights, at the same time as they contemplated buying their first radio set. After the Carpentier match, the *New York Times* declared that female fight fans were no longer a "novelty." Two thousand of them attended, and another two thousand showed up for the Firpo bout. The two matches each attracted total audiences of 90,000, surpassed at the time only by Firpo's fight with Jess Willard in July 1923. The *Chicago Defender*, the premiere national black newspaper at the time, sent three correspondents to cover the Carpentier fight, and reported among the spectators black visitors from Baltimore, Cleveland, Detroit, Chicago, Seattle, and San Francisco. Firpo's bout attracted a small but notable group of "South Americans, Spaniards, Cubans, and Latins in general." Letter writers thus sought to shape radio representation of a pastime common to a wide spectrum of the listening public. Deaf to the call of cultural uplift, these men instead drew upon the tradition of cooperative engineering in amateur radio.[13]

Since well before 1921, engineers had designed radio technologies in cooperation with amateur operators. When inventor Reginald Fessenden played a violin, sang, spoke, and spun records over his alternator-transmitter on Christmas Eve in 1906, he asked those who heard his broadcast to write to him before the next one on New Year's Eve. He received several letters, mostly from operators on ships at sea, expressing delight at hearing music instead of Morse code. Ten years later, 10,279 licensed, and hundreds more unregistered, amateur stations operated in the United States. Because of a wartime ban on amateur transmissions, licenses declined to 6,103 by 1920, but rose again to 10,809 within a year. After the war, corporate engineers relied on these "experimenters" in testing new equipment. In the fall of 1919, amateurs reported on a dry run of two 500-watt transmitters, intended for China, between New York and Cliffwood, New Jersey. Around the same time, AT&T engineers, anxious to fix the fading problems with their ship-to-shore short-wave transmissions from Deal Beach, New Jersey, ended up playing phonograph records for thousands of amateurs who responded. To the engineers' dismay, AT&T headquarters forbade them to rely on amateurs once the company joined the radio trust.[14]

Yet trust restrictions failed to eradicate collaborative invention. An engineer employed at a corporate lab more often than not had also been an amateur operator. In 1907, Lloyd Espenschied and two of his amateur friends wrote to Lee de Forest in response to his arc transmitter test in New York. By the early 1920s, Espenschied was in charge of the Deal Beach ship-to-shore tests at AT&T. "In the early wireless companies," he recalled, "people would just build stuff and try it out." In 1914, experimenter Carl Dreher published an article in the *Wireless Age* on using a single-wire antenna for long range reception, a feature he had discovered while hiding his radio wires from jani-tors. By the early 1920s, Dreher was a sound engineer at RCA. Later, at RKO Pictures, he would become a key advocate for trial-and-error mike place-ment. Operators designed the equipment one day, as engineers, and tested it the next, as amateurs. In 1919, Frank Conrad, assistant chief engineer at Westinghouse, played records in his garage over his amateur station 8XK, later licensed for commercial service as KDKA. In 1921, after setting up and announcing the Dempsey-Carpentier fight, J. Owen Smith, also known by his amateur call sign 2ZL, dispensed equipment advice to his fellow experi-menter, an electrician from Red Bank, New Jersey. Wireless technologies thus emerged as a result of exchanges among peers.[15]

When new public stations set up shop, listeners continued to shape trans-mission technologies. White and Smith tested their GE transmitter with ama-teurs for three days before the Dempsey-Carpentier fight. A "land-slide" of responses via telegraph, mail, and phone led them to lengthen their antenna, rewire their transformer, and add a condenser to boost the signal. WHN en-gineer F. William Boettcher remembered how in 1922—the station was then located in Queens—"the nightly telephone calls from listeners increased tre-mendous" when he prevailed on the station's owners, *Ridgewood Times* editor George Schubel and music store manager Joseph Stroelin, to let him modify a 15-watt de Forest transmitter into a "composite type" 50-watt unit. Encour-aged, Schubel and Stroelin immediately ordered Boettcher to rebuild it as a 100-watt model, which, to their delight, brought "listener telephone calls from the Greater NY Area, and complimentary letters from upper New York State, New Jersey, Connecticut and other New England States." WHN was typical in extending its reach according to listener response. Nearly every early U.S. station offered QSL cards—from the Morse code symbol for "I ac-knowledge receipt"—to listeners who reported reception of its broadcasts at their location.[16]

And so, stations rigged factory-made equipment to suit their immedi-ate needs. Up to the late 1920s, WJZ engineer Raymond Guy recalled, "we did everything by 'cut and try' . . . we had to feel our way along and develop all these techniques and try these things out." A radio amateur since 1911, Guy received the Carpentier report as a radio operator on a ship, the *Martha Washington*, about to sail to South America from Hoboken. He started at WJZ in 1922 and was in charge of field operations by the time of the Firpo broadcast. Guy remembered the initial rate of obsolescence to be no more than three years—three times less than it would be in the 1930s. Others reported an even shorter lifespan for devices. "The microphone was changed from week to week," William Easton, WJZ program director, recalled. "First, tomato can type"—a condenser mike enclosed in a brass cylinder—"then the dish pan, in the form of a cone," a carbon mike made like an inverted loudspeaker. General Electric used its station WGY to conduct "continued research and development." Most stations took equipment manufactured by de Forest, GE, Westinghouse, or Western Electric, then "built some stuff and added it . . . modified it and expanded on it as the occasion required."[17]

In theory, every test aimed for a clear and controlled radio sound. Corporate labs, as Western Electric put it, launched a "scientific attack" on reverberation, in auditoriums, phonograph records, talking pictures, and radio. Early studio designers used Wallace Sabine's absorption equation to "cut down sound reflection to the limit," with potato sacks, hair felt, muslin, thick carpets, and cushioned furniture. "The room seemed dead," one tenor described an eerie moment in a broadcasting studio after his aria. "The piano had stopped reverberating and there was not the slightest sound." Balancing clarity, tone, and volume required both research and discipline. The dishpan mike caught more "mellow" bass and midrange tones than the squeaky "candlestick" telephone transmitter. Condenser mikes overcame the hissing noise common to carbons. Musicians played stuck to the floor, with the higher-pitched reeds and violins closer to the mike, trombones and drums farther away. "Artists Are Put in a Musical Straitjacket," *Radio Broadcast* warned radio hopefuls in 1922, "Moving, Whispering, Even Deep Breathing a Crime."[18]

This purified sound, ads and manuals advised, called for private and studious listening. Listeners "needed" a Brandes headset to "shut out the noise in the room," and a Kolster radio to hone their "sense of hearing." Corporations plied exacting aural standards to domesticate consumers and muscle out independent competitors. In 1922, RCA offered its lavish Aeriola Grand receivers to housewives in the booklet *Radio Enters the Home*, while joining the National Dry Goods Association in warning against cheap "inferior" sets. A year later, in a syndicated article, RCA director of research Alfred Goldsmith counseled against "badly designed" stations with noisy "ordinary amplifiers." He lauded WJZ as the better alternative. The RCA Information Bureau offered twenty-three didactic puff pieces by Goldsmith as a "public service" to major U.S. newspapers, to be printed unedited. The *Boston Globe* hailed the series as "highly instructive." Cleaned-up sound for private listening dovetailed with the corporate mission of cultural uplift.[19]

In practice, refined standards gave in to muddled contingencies. On his

1924 radio tour, news commentator H. V. Kaltenborn broadcast from "barns, garages, fraternity headquarters, shops, office buildings, and stores," as well as a private residence, where "the control room was in the kitchen and the studio was in the living room." Metropolitan stations fared not much better. Sopranos blew fuses. Yowling cats invaded studios through open windows. Condenser mikes required an amplifier and batteries within a few feet, a contraption which, according to Guy, "had a tendency to become very noisy at the most inopportune time." On location, theater managers set up broadcasters as a prime attraction, to operate their pickup equipment from the stage, right in front of the audience.[20]

Such unscripted occasions inspired new ways to shape radio sound. When in 1922 Gilbert & Sullivan manager William DeWolf Hopper forbade the WJZ crew to broadcast from the Shubert Theater in Newark, they sneaked in just one mike on the piano in the orchestra and stowed the amplifier under Guy's seat between his feet. "Throughout the performance we had to sit there," he recalled, "not knowing how it was being received because we didn't dare put headphones on." In dire straits, field technicians "built their own fading equipment"—a portable amplifier for theatrical and sports remotes—"and began to use it before it was done in the studio." Corporate ads claimed sound techniques emerged ready-made from the labs; station engineers developed them, as needed, "on man by man basis."[21]

For their part, audiences embraced what experts took for aural junk. After an opera recital, an electrical engineer advised WGI, a small station in Medford Hills, Massachusetts, to "tell the Artists to please stand near the horn, so that if they should cry while doing their stunt we can hear the tears drop." In mid-1920s at WOR in New York a chorus girl put on a refined voice to read a testimonial on a morning exercise program sponsored by Bernarr Macfadden's pulp sheet *Evening Graphic*. Then she stepped just six inches away and exhaled in her own brogue into a live mike, "My *Gawd*, I'm glad that's over!" Technicians panicked. Most listeners thought the contrast between her on- and off-mike personas "really funny." In 1926 engineer Paul Sabine aired an identical program three times over WLS in Chicago, each time increasing sound reflection. Listeners chose the most resonant broadcast. By 1928, broadcasters, too, came to prefer "less deadening" studio acoustics.[22]

Having missed the lesson on clear sound, audiences flunked private listening as well, as jazz pianist Earl Hines and vocalist Lois Deppe discovered when they performed on KDKA in 1921. "A lot of people had crystal sets," Deppe later remembered, "and there was a radio buff on Wylie Avenue"—a thoroughfare in the black Hill District in Pittsburgh—"who had a loud-speaker sticking out his window. The street was all blocked with people and we were just mobbed when we came back." The American Society for Authors and Publishers, a performance rights organization established in 1914, soon declared such music sharing, anywhere except in one's private home, to be copyright infringement. Such thievery abounded. Appalachian miners listened to concerts on porches. Polish immigrants heard them in Chicago barber shops. Announcer Graham McNamee's wife Josephine listened to him officiate WEAF concerts in crowds in front of New York music stores, to gauge audience reaction. An early WEAF audience survey calculated at least five people per every receiver, noting ubiquitous public listening and "radio parties." Experts advised private appreciation of unpolluted sound; audiences heard radio in context and in public.[23]

Despite this mismatch in aesthetic notions, radio stations turned to listeners for advice. WEAF mail grew from 54,815 letters in 1923 to 237,292 in 1926, all "carefully read, classified in various ways and recorded." William E. Harkness, the AT&T vice president in charge of the station, remembered requesting "suggestions" and even inviting some letter writers "to the studio to discuss the matter." One such lay critic convinced WEAF managers to let him serve up a revue "like a table d'hôte dinner, from soup to nuts" with night club performers of his acquaintance. The second installment never aired because of lukewarm audience response. Listeners plugged and scheduled their proposed numbers. A stationery store owner cited the endorsement of "a number of people" when he asked WGI to perform a gospel song "at some noontime broadcast (preferably the latter half)." He offered to provide words and music if necessary.[24]

Small-time broadcasters credited their raucous sound to listener participation. In 1922, to help radio fans who felt "lack of reciprocal contact," and broadcasters short of "spontaneous reaction from their audiences," jazz station WHN installed a telegraph operator in the studio who read wired responses to the evening's program in real time. Those who sent "a criticism or a constructive suggestion," WHN owner George Schubel envisioned, would become "part of a living audience in full co-operation with the station." Corporate stations soon followed. A few months later, WEAF installed a "special switchboard" to handle the many telephone calls it received during broadcasts. By 1924, an RCA engineer referred to live telegraphed and phoned responses as a standard practice. Such participatory program design belied the prescriptive rhetoric of uplift, individualism, and rationality.[25]

Radio corporations integrated public participation in engineering and program design without enthusiasm. GE, Westinghouse, and AT&T benefited from amateurs' inventions and tests but guarded all resulting patent rights. Corporate station managers viewed reciprocal radio production as a stopgap. Yet peer cooperation defied proprietary engineering models, and program producers could not easily ignore audience expectations of coauthorship. The two competing models of production aimed for two kinds of modern radio sound: one rational, individualist, clear, and corporate; another emotional, public, noisy, and populist. The corporate sound was meant to be packaged and consumed; the populist, to be shared.[26]

Prizefight radio represented the populist kind. It fused audience expectations with the imperfections of emerging technologies. In the 1910s, telephones omitted low-frequency signals. (Today, MP3 files likewise compress away many audible frequencies.) In the 1920s and 1930s, many radio loudspeakers transmitted no bass or tenor tones. Listeners' minds, experts believed, "created the missing tones" of male voices and bass strings. This way of hearing is a cultural skill as well as a biological trait. Musician Ingrid Monson once described how her orchestra members reconstructed their parts from a damaged 78 recording, "filling the gap with a continuation that made musical sense." Prizefight audiences also filled gaps in radio transmissions in ways that made sense to them and debated their interpretations with engineers. The distinctive prizefight radio sound, and its attendant social meanings, emerged from such interactions.[27]

Boxing fans moved from describing what they thought they heard to suggesting technical ways to achieve the listening experience they desired. When Harold Warren mentally placed the studio gong and the noise at ringside, he conformed to a common way of hearing the Dempsey-Carpentier fight. "I understand your description of the fight was the sensation of the afternoon," Tex Rickard told J. Andrew White. "They tell me even the gong was audible." So many people reported hearing the crowd noise that the *Wireless Age* offered to "arrange a get-together of the amateurs who heard the crowd cheering" to ponder their amazing auditory experience. In the preceding decades newspapers had described museum visitors agape before P. T. Barnum's half-fish, half-monkey "mermaid," art lovers trying to pry images of newspaper clippings from *trompe l'oeil* paintings, and moviegoers jumping in fear of a train arriving on the screen. Carpentier listeners, too, seemed to fall victim to the "arts of deception."[28]

Yet subsequent broadcasts sought to realize these vivid misperceptions.

After the fight, engineers introduced devices that enhanced the illusion of total aural environment at the stadium. In July 1922, WJZ installed "sensitive pick-up microphones" at ringside for the Benny Leonard-Lew Tendler lightweight championship match, promising, along with a "blow by blow description of the fight," to broadcast "the timekeeper's whistle and the clang of the gong at the beginning and end of each round as well as the cheers and comments of the spectators." A year later, two million listeners to the Jess Willard-Luis Firpo fight heard "the observer's voice, the gong and cheers" over AT&T's three-station wired network equipped with a new "electric wave filter," with a wider frequency range, 100 to 5,000 cycles a second. By 1924, Rickard blamed falling attendance at championship bouts on stations broadcasting "everything except the actual view of the combatants . . . For the past three years title boxing matches have been fought before microphones, the thud of the gloves and the shouts of the fans being plainly distinguishable." The new devices used the gong and cheers as sound effects.[29]

Engineers selected and placed these devices in cooperation with listeners. For the Dempsey-Firpo fight, the equipment at ringside included an amplifier, batteries, and a number of then common double-button carbon microphones for ambient sound:

> . . . type 373W transmitters for "crowd noise," type 371W transmitters mounted on desk stand for announcers' use and a multiple transmitter attenuator for controlling the relative volume of the noise and announcers' transmitters in parallel. One sound transmitter was located in each neutral corner facing the center of the ring.[30]

The setup, elaborate as it was, still required further improvement. Steamship superintendent Edward Hatton and his friends from Montvale, New Jersey, argued that announcer White gave listeners "the noise made by the crowd" between bouts, "but when the fight was in progress this was all eliminated." WJZ, he concluded, "does not seem able" to keep the ringside crowd from going on and off the air. In his report, WEAF chief engineer J. G. Truesdell agreed, but blamed White and WJZ technicians for the crowd noise problems. Adding "a separate 17A amplifier on each transmitting circuit" during the fight seemed to quell the tetchy phone calls, however; Truesdell recommended always adding the amplifiers in the future. Within a year, WJZ pickup crew had set up volume controls and switches on their portable amplifier to bring in crowd noise "as background to the announcing" and afterward "to gradually 'fade in' or 'fade out' the cheering." In this case, hearing the fight from the perspective of the audience established the proper measure of realism.[31]

In boxing remotes, then, engineers sought to control sound not to elicit a private and regimented auditory experience, but to recreate the public participatory experience at the arena. Carpentier listeners placed the radio bell at ringside for the same reason. "Even the gong sounded plainly as could be," a Jewish railroad station agent reported from the Bronx. "Almost thought I was in the front row at the ringside when you counted Carpentier out. It was realistic and impressive to the highest degree." Because "even the clang of the gong at the ringside could be distinctly heard," an elderly lady next to Charles Dugan, a bookkeeper, in South River, New Jersey, got "so wrought up" that she wished she had bet five dollars on the outcome. At the arena, a similar intense ritual involved spectators "in every walk of life"—not only men, "clerks and bankers, crooks and clergymen, lawyers and day laborers, business men and gamblers," but also women "in every section, from ringside seats which sold for $50 to the more plebeian general admission sections." To observers at this and subsequent fights, "each person there seemed to be conscious of the fact that he"—or she—"was forming an important part" of some larger purpose, "alone yet united in a common consciousness, each fiercely kinetic yet keeping its place in a segment." Such reports depicted a spontaneous sensory and social unity at the stadium.[32]

At the same time, the crowd noise effect revealed the artifice of such unity, already obvious to the less affluent majority of boxing spectators. Field glasses sold briskly at the Carpentier fight. At the 1927 Dempsey-Tunney rematch at the Soldier Field in Chicago the cheapest seats were so far from the ring—over 700 feet—that several five-dollar patrons brought their own portable radios to get in on the action. When Rickard died in 1929, the New York press pronounced him "the twentieth century Barnum" who charged "exorbitant prices for exhibitions at which nothing could be seen even when it was worth seeing." Such reports gave the lie to the common sensory experience at the stadium, in fact confined to the privileged few.[33]

Humbugs like Barnum, historians argue, created a modern culture of skepticism. Prizefight listeners combined sensory and social skepticism. Like the turn-of-the-century spectators who did not really mistake painted news clippings for real ones, and did not in fact run at the sight of the Lumière brothers' train, most Carpentier listeners enjoyed the gong's realism while being well aware that it rang at the studio. Because they could hear the bell clearly between rounds, a retired physician from Philadelphia declared the broadcast "a great advance in broadcasting news," and the teenage son of an assistant foreman from Stonington, Connecticut, judged the report "just as good as being at the ringside." Neither explicitly placed the gong at the arena. Awareness of radio's effects carried with it a sense of underlying economic and social tensions.[34]

Like ambient sound, prizefight announcing evolved in response to listener criticism. Several announcers struck out before sportscasters developed a style that addressed the world view and scope of the listening public. At first, sports broadcasts allowed for little stylistic invention. Corporate pundits set precise standards of expertise, diction, and dignity. Studio engineers commanded the announcer to stand exactly fourteen inches away and croon sideways into the mike. Telegraph and phone reports left no room for ad-libbing. At small stations like WHAS, a telegraph operator passed on blow-by-blow reports to the station manager at the transmitter. At WJZ, Thomas Cowan repeated a 1921 World Series account phoned in by *Newark Sunday Call* sports editor Sandy Hunt. "He'd say, 'Ball one.' I'd say, 'Ball one, strike one,'" Cowan recalled. "I used to be so played out when it was over that I couldn't even collect my thoughts enough to tell who had won . . . I was just a parrot all the time."[35]

The live reports that followed required sturdier equipment and reedier voices. WJZ discovered that announcers had to scream into the mike to rise over the noise from the crowd. Engineers devised a special microphone that did not overload when shouted at, with heavier diaphragms. Vocal range also mattered, as WEAF managers found out when they hired newswriter Hector Fuller to announce the Jess Willard-Luis Firpo fight in 1923. Fuller was a hit narrating the musical comedy "Wildflower" from the Casino Theater earlier that year, but his booming voice blended with the ringside rumble. Four thousand outraged callers jammed the station's switchboards within the first five minutes of the preliminary bouts. In desperation, WEAF operators replaced him with the station's commercial manager, George McClelland, who happened to be at ringside and had a higher-pitched voice. Approving phone calls ensued. Fuller gave up radio and later became a master of ceremonies for New York City Mayor and speakeasy patron Jimmy Walker.[36]

Refined manners likewise became a liability. J. Andrew White's live report of the Dempsey-Firpo fight was a "cordial" and "technically correct" dud. For the first hour and a half, through all preliminary and semi-final bouts, the public complained that his voice was "very hard to make out." Over the order wire, station operators suggested that he "change position" and "sharpen up" his voice because it sounded "blurred," "tubby," "stagy," "lifeless," and "dead." Long distance calls denounced him as a "rotten" announcer. White responded, "I never pay attention to these reports." He droned on, too close to the mike, with tidbits from newspaper clippings. The fierce final bout between Dempsey and Firpo took him by surprise. "'He's up! He's down! He's up! He's down!' White shouted," boxing announcer Don Dunphy described listening to the fight as a child, "This would go on and on. White wouldn't say who was up and who was down." Only after three attempts to dislodge White did McClelland replace him, to the relief of New York and Washington station operators. After the fight, McClelland went back to management and later became a vice president at NBC. He resigned in 1934 to start his own network and, after that failed, shot himself.[37]

The spat over reporting methods continued. *Radio Broadcast*, a glossy weekly and a mouthpiece for RCA and AT&T managers, extolled White as "calm voiced and observing." Electric engineer Lewis Dickinson and his buddies from Boonton, New Jersey, disagreed: "In my opinion Andrew White cannot compare with the announcer you had for the Willard-Firpo or Wilson-Greb fight. White talks in a monotonous, expressionless voice which I find very tiresome and even trying. Your announcer on the other hand put pep into his voice and inserted a lot of little gripes and 'asides' into his talk which kept the listener in a good humor." Dickinson's view won out. Andrew White left announcing after the 1926 Dempsey-Tunney fight. He helped found the network that would become CBS in 1927, and retired from broadcasting a year later when tobacco tycoon William S. Paley took over and forced him out.[38]

The Johnny Wilson-Harry Greb announcer, Graham McNamee, used listener response to develop excitable reporting, a recognizable and deliberate technique. "It began, I think, with the fights," he recalled. "We would get communications saying: 'We liked such and such an expression,' or 'the way you handled the job last night'; and we'd think that perhaps we had been a little less stiff on that occasion, and so take the tip." Dignified enough when announcing concerts, McNamee turned on a different, animated persona for sports reports. "My how mixed up and excited the broadcaster of WEAF got last night over the fight!" a reviewer praised his reporting of a lightweight bout. "Fortunately he wasn't as cold and inhuman as McNamee when he broadcast the concert last Wednesday from the same station." McNamee's partner Phillips Carlin, White's recruits Ted Husing and Norman Brokenshire, and others adopted his prizefight patter to convey the country's athletic and political disputes. Brokenshire remembered how during the 1924 National Democratic Convention he gave a "blow-by-blow eyewitness account of one of the finest donnybrooks" among the delegates while filling in for White, the lead reporter at the scene. "I had a ringside seat. I was letting the listening audience in on the fracas when Major White walked in" and killed the mike. The following year, McNamee topped a popularity poll in the fan rag *Radio Digest,* and reported receiving fifty thousand fan letters after the World Series.[39]

The audible emotions announcers adopted carried anxieties about the social roles of their audiences. Admen thought of women as compliant consumers long before 1925, when the first daytime cooking shows aired. These putative women loved crooners' saccharine voices, arranged the dinner table for family listening, and bought sponsors' toothpaste and cereal. Women boxing fans instead adored prizefighters like "matinee idols," to a degree that made even McNamee uncomfortable. Women who "shrieked" at each blow were "not constructed" for prizefights, he admonished, and "should stay away." Such preconceptions also made it difficult for women to become announcers. "The woman announcer," WJZ program director Charles Popenoe declared in 1926, "has difficulty in repressing her enthusiasm and in maintaining the necessary reserve and objectivity." Yet the star sports reporters took up the very same traits. Raymond Guy admitted that early sports announcers—all of them men—used a "technique" of describing "things that never took place." McNamee believed that audiences desired nothing but "honest enthusiasm." When asked why he reported a tepid bout at an uptown boxing club as a breathtaking battle of the century, he replied, "I only tell it the way it looks to me." During the Great Depression, more objective sports reporters would eclipse McNamee in popularity. But in the Jazz Age, reviewers praised his "art" of conveying "vividly a sense of movement and of feeling." When he died in 1942, *Time* eulogized him as the "voice of the 1920s." McNamee mocked impressionable women, but observed and reproduced their sensibilities, to his own acclaim.[40]

Ringside noise and excitable reporting conjured a public beyond both the traditional male amateur constituency and the new genteel family audience cultivated by corporations. While radio manuals prescribed private listening, fight fans described collective experiences. "Mine was not an isolated case," Dickinson justified his advice, "I have talked with a dozen or more fans." Hatton cited "several fans . . . all of the same opinion." News reports, too, pictured boxing fans as the listening masses. The day following the Dempsey-Firpo broadcast both the *Washington Post* in D.C. and *La Nacion* in Buenos Aires published high angle shots of radio audiences in front of their respective buildings: a sea of boaters, derbies, fedoras, flat caps, cloches, and wider-brimmed women's hats; dark as well as pale faces on each continent. While corporate ads featured dignified radio parties, newspapers measured a fight's success by the variety and verve of the listening crowds. Women "let out shrill cries of enthusiasm" for Carpentier at the Times Square bulletin board. Argentines "wept" for Firpo before the loudspeakers at the *La Nacion* building. Blacks formed "a mass of moving humanity" listening to the Firpo report near the *Chicago Defender* office in Harlem. Sportscasters echoed these reactions to convey the shared ringside experience, and listeners approved.[41]

This implicitly inclusive sound emerged amid unease about fair play in boxing and in society at large. Suffragettes, derided like women fight fans for "shrill" and "shrieking" voices, demanded women's vote at boxing venues in the name of "good sportsmanship," and likened attempts to ban women from matches to the notion "that it would not be ladylike for a woman to go to the polls." Yet three years after the nineteenth amendment, one New York boxing club still seated women without a male escort in a separate section. Throughout the decade, black fans demanded that Dempsey fight the black champion, Harry Wills. Yet white audiences protested and governors banned mixed matches, in sync with postwar race riots in Chicago, Omaha, and Tulsa, residential color lines in Detroit, and whites-only night clubs in Harlem. "Nobody wants razors, blackjacks, or fists flying," singer and comic Jimmy Durante opined in explaining admission policies at the Cotton Club, "and the chances of a war are less if there's no mixing."[42]

Buenos Aires servant girls and Harlem residents who saw Firpo as a stand-in for Wills expected a fair fight as they bet their savings on the "Wild Bull of the Pampas." Yet when Firpo knocked Dempsey out of the ring, several people helped him back in. Each time Dempsey knocked Firpo down—eight times in two rounds—he stayed close and punched again as soon as Firpo stirred to get up. These blatant violations, the *Chicago Defender* reported, "caused Latin-Americans to turn up their nose when Americans say anything about 'clean sportsmanship.' " Although fight fans did not explicitly relate corporate broadcasting policies to these practices of exclusion, they appealed to American sense of fairness in the same style others used to demand political rights, decrying corporate stations' "unsportsman like" behavior toward "the great majority."[43]

Today, listeners' belief in the entitlement of "the great majority" may seem just as overblown as Argentines' belief in the power of Firpo. Yet this belief sustained early radio practices. Listeners who participated in the re-making of styles and technologies saw the medium as communal property. In 1921, amateurs relied on neighbors and friends in setting up their infor-mation network for the Dempsey-Carpentier broadcast. Only three of the identified Carpentier letter writers were professional engineers; half were boys between nine and twenty-one years old. The seventeen-year-old son of a building contractor persuaded his neighbor, a fireman, to use his fire-house as an auditorium for the broadcast. From his receiver in West Med-ford, a ticket seller phoned in reports to his coworkers at North Station in Boston, who informed passengers of the score as they handed out tickets. To White and RCA, the experiment proved that broadcasting could be "re-munerative" and a "publicity device;" amateurs imagined radio as a "general public service."[44]

The cooperative production of this early broadcast made it difficult to as-sign, and easy to assume, credit for ideas, organization, and technical work. RCA, keen to cement its dominance of the Argentine receiver market, claimed sole authorship of the intercontinental Firpo broadcast, even though local amateurs co-organized the retransmission in Buenos Aires. One of them, twenty-two-year-old Horacio Martinez Seeber, launched his sportscasting career translating the blow-by-blow account into Spanish. The earliest chron-iclers of the Carpentier fight conveniently forgot that amateurs produced a brand new radio audience when they provided receivers for public listening. Participants disagreed on authorship and other details. In his 1921 report to RCA J. Andrew White thanked J. Owen Smith for "the voice-retransmission from Hoboken." In 1955 in *Reader's Digest* White claimed that his own voice went over the airwaves. David Sarnoff, who directed RCA support, mentioned nothing about his personal participation in the broadcast when he forwarded White's report to RCA and GE officials. He placed himself at ringside in his 1926 interview to *Saturday Evening Post*. Julius Hopp, manager of Madison Square Garden concerts, brought together Tex Rickard and J. Andrew White for the event and coordinated reception of the fight report in public halls and theaters. In 1935 he claimed in a letter to Sarnoff to have originated not just the broadcast, but the entire "present broadcasting system." Hopp, White, and Sarnoff each had to rewrite history to become *the* author. None of them was. It was a collective undertaking.[45]

Fans articulated this sense of collective ownership when they confronted

AT&T and RCA during the Dempsey-Firpo broadcast. These corporations insisted that the nation needed expensive high-quality programming only large companies could provide, implying also that they alone had the necessary expertise on how and when to dish out this programming. Some listeners agreed. In D.C., after a letter campaign to the *Washington Post*, RCA station WRC stayed off the air to allow listeners to receive the fight on the AT&T network. James Massey, a government clerk, did not join the letter campaign because, he believed, "the two stations here already knew the desire of the fans." He congratulated RCA on "a fine piece of cooperation between these two large and important companies." RCA promptly forwarded Massey's letter to the *Post* for publication.[46]

But in New York, most listeners felt that WEAF let them down when it stayed on the air during the fight. The station received 300 phone calls that evening. Of these, 100 callers demanded that WEAF stay off the air for the main bout, 50 asked the station to sign off for the entire night, 20 were "highly indignant" that the station dared to broadcast during the fight, and 130 appreciated WEAF broadcasts in general but that night cared for nothing but reports from the arena. "It seemed unanimous," station manager Mark Woods concluded, "that everybody was in favor of listening to the fight returns only."[47]

Many letter writers could "see nothing very large minded" in WEAF's decision. Protesters rarely spoke for themselves alone, but castigated the station on behalf of neighbors, friends, and sports fans everywhere. "I should [have] thought you would have bowed to the great majority for once," railed Jewett Fisher, a bonds clerk from Brooklyn. "I understand that there [were] hundreds of telephone calls trying to reach you last night to ask you to signoff until after the fight." Fisher could not believe WEAF could be so "unsportsman like" in the face of such a groundswell of opinion. "We were amazed at your attitude of last evening," he wrote of his fellow boxing fans. Others agreed. "There were thousands of fight fans within your broadcasting who were not able to get in WJZ with any degree of satisfaction when you were broadcasting," declared Gilbert Blaker, a diesel engine salesman from Manhattan. He took it as a particular sign of malice that "whoever was responsible for Friday nights program tried to ring in all of the performers with train-caller voices and sledge hammer piano recitations." From now on, he vowed, "when I listen to WEAF again it will be because I cannot help it." Such angry letters came from managers and proprietors—the station's target "high class" audience—but also from men of less exalted professions such as railroad inspectors and clerks.[48] The populist sound of prizefight radio thus signaled a morality divide between collective audience entitlement and the commercial rules of ownership.

Listeners were not alone on their side of the divide. For at least some engineers, their experience of cooperation in the long run bred ambivalence about corporate control of radio. In the 1920s, Carl Dreher glorified RCA policies in his articles in *Radio Broadcast*. In the 1930s, he joined the labor movement, quit his corporate job, and attacked corporate radio in *Harper's* magazine. Dreher remembered that in the 1920s radio engineers had formed a "fellowship . . . developing a new art, broadcasting" and preferred to do things "with [their] own hands." He first doubted his choice of corporate employment when he could not understand why AT&T would not allow other stations to use its telephone wires to get static-free remote broadcasts: "when I spent an evening in a speakeasy with the engineers of the Telephone Company they were obviously just the same as RCA engineers," and yet AT&T cared more about its profits than its listeners and the engineering community. In the late 1920s, Lloyd Espenschied, along with other engineers, convinced the Federal Radio Commission that commercial network radio was the best technical solution for the broadcasting system in the United States. Yet later, in a 1973 interview, he both fondly remembered his contacts with amateurs during the Deal Beach tests and lamented AT&T's first experiments in sponsored broadcasting. "I feel ashamed," he confessed, "of the part the company played in originating commercial radio in this country."[49] Both engineers' belated judgment against corporate radio rested on their memories of the earlier collective invention of the medium. In the late 1920s, this shared sense of fairness informed popular opposition to the rise of corporate network broadcasting in America.

2

Jumping the Waves

In March 1924, WEAF and its owner AT&T sued WHN and its owners, George Schubel, of *Ridgewood Times*, and Marcus Loew, of Loew's theaters, for infringing on the company's monopoly on transmitters and sponsored programming—the first step toward extracting fees from all "squatter" stations. AT&T had legal grounds but no public legitimacy. William Anders, a twenty-two-year-old typist and son of a German iron worker, submitted a petition to the *New Jersey Evening Journal* from "several hundred radio fans" protesting the WEAF lawsuit. New York commissioner Grover Whalen accused AT&T of taking "complete control of the air" because it used its patents to block the construction of a municipal radio station. The Federal Trade Commission charged the four radio trust companies with "restraining competition and creating a monopoly," and a Chicago lawyer likened them to the Four Horsemen of the Apocalypse. Secretary of Commerce Herbert Hoover declared that "it would be most unfortunate for the people of this country to whom broadcasting has become an important incident of life if its control should come into the hands of any single corporation, individual, or combination." AT&T won the battle—WHN paid the licensing fee—but lost the war. In 1926, because of public outcry, AT&T quit the broadcasting field and sold its stations to RCA. In 1932, the Justice Department broke up the radio trust.[1]

At the same time, with new legal regulation of the radio spectrum, corporations again came to dominate the air. The Department of Commerce issued radio station licenses following the Radio Act of 1912. Then in 1926 a Chicago station WJAZ "jumped" from its assigned wavelength to a "pirated" Canadian wavelength. In the case that ensued a federal judge ruled that the

Department of Commerce did not have jurisdiction over station licenses. To control the overcrowded spectrum where over 200 new stations immediately began operation, the 1927 emergency Radio Act of Congress established the Federal Radio Commission. By then, nearly 700 stations were broadcasting in the United States, over 200 of them nonprofit. In 1928, the FRC's General Order 40 gave each of the forty 500,000-watt "clear channels" to only one station nationally, and left the other 600 stations to share the remaining 50 channels. With the blessing of leading engineers, including Alfred Goldsmith and Lloyd Espenschied, and in the name of efficiency, modernity, and the public good, the FRC granted the best frequencies to large commercial stations joining the two recently formed networks. By 1931, the National Broadcasting Company and the Columbia Broadcasting System, established in 1926 and 1927 respectively, accounted for 70 percent of U.S. broadcasting as measured in station numbers, watt power, and hours on the air. By 1934, nonprofit broadcasting accounted for only 2 percent of total U.S. broadcast time, and radio advertising revenues had grown to 72 million from 4.8 million in 1927. The 1934 Radio Act made the renamed Federal Communications Commission permanent. The American listening public, it seemed, had acquiesced to corporate network dominance.[2]

In fact, the twilight of local radio between 1927 and 1929 marked the moment when listeners articulated an anticorporate moral economy implicit in the reciprocal relationships independent stations forged with their audiences. Most stations operating at a power higher than 100 watts attracted both local and national publics, altogether nearly seven million radio set owners and their families. When the FRC began to allocate better frequencies and more power to network stations, independent stations "jumped the waves"—broadcast on unassigned frequencies—to overcome the interference noise of network affiliates. The Commission worked to abolish "wave jumping." Some listeners agreed, favoring the polished commercial programs developed by national networks and ad agencies. Others wrote letters to Congress explicitly supporting educational and nonprofit broadcasting, echoing the arguments of the broadcast reform movement.[3] But a significant number of listeners offered varied alternative visions of a decentralized broadcasting system. Immigrant families in cities, farmers in rural areas, and amateur fans of distant listening for different reasons supported independent stations over networks, aiming to defend local cultures against national standards and small enterprise against corporate industries. They advocated a vision of a modern communication network and a modern system of social relationships simultaneously local and national, interdependent and uncodified.

From its inception, the Federal Radio Commission confronted listeners who defended stations in their own back yards. The FRC allocated frequencies and power based on "public interest, convenience, and necessity." Commissioners interpreted this formula to mean that every station had to appeal to the widest possible audience rather than a particular group. Small stations—those not owned by a big corporation—instead emphasized their importance to their local constituencies. Station managers and owners cited their religious service, charitable service, and educational service. They argued that they lost audiences because of lower wavelength or lower power. The evidence stations presented to the Commission to justify their existence consisted almost exclusively of listener response. Managers cited numbers of phone calls and fan letters received, results of radio magazine polls, and lists of listeners who responded to giveaways and contests. The smaller the station, the more dependent it was on its public. Bigger stations put into evidence letters from prominent members of the community, such as priests or businessmen, while smaller stations brought in a larger number of letters from ordinary listeners.[4]

Residents of urban ethnic neighborhoods, used to listening to an hour of music, news, and jokes from their old country every week, demanded programs culturally familiar to them. Engineer Arthur Faske and his brother Dr. Leo Faske began WBKN in Brooklyn during the "chaos" of 1926, with six employees and a budget of $300 a week, by "wave jumping" to a frequency reserved for Canada. Soon the FRC ordered them to share another wavelength with four other stations, and finally moved them to a "graveyard" frequency, too high for many old radios. In protest, the Faske brothers forwarded to the Commission nearly a hundred letters congratulating the station on its broadcasts of the Jewish hour on Thursday nights. A university student's "education, as far as a knowledge of Jewish Culture is concerned, has been sadly neglected," but a broadcast by the Hopkins theater artists convinced him to "make an attempt to acquaint myself with Jewish ideals and traditions."[5]

At the hearings, the station reported receiving 200 phone calls and 30 letters a day. Many WBKN listeners promised to write directly to the FRC. "I would like the station of WBKN to voice the Jewish nation," a blind accordion player from Brooklyn wrote, "I will send a letter to the Federal Radio Commission in Washington. I will make a protest about it." A foreman at a shoe factory and father of five, who had immigrated from Russia in 1904, assured

the station on behalf of his family, "We expect to write to the Federal Radio
Com. today."[6] The task of writing to influence a federal agency led ethnic stations and their constituencies to articulate their local culture's place in the
nation.

Independent stations and their local and distant audiences sketched an
alternative topography of social relations, blending local and national loyalties and expectations, and deploying political rhetoric much like boxing fans
in the early 1920s. In 1928 Clarence Nelson, a cabinet maker, wrote to WIBO
in support of the station's demand for a permanent high wavelength:

> I hope that our government has a few officials in its employ that are
> broadminded and not politically corrupt to see that [your radio sta-
> tion] is rendering a service and is absolutely necessary to our [city].
> Therefore it should not be abolished but given a permanent wave
> length such as the commercial stations enjoy. I am a young man 27
> years of age of Swedish descent born in Chicago but believe me I wait
> for the 'Swedish Services' every Sunday as [my] mother does . . . I be-
> lieve a government by the people and for the people should cater to
> them and not to commercial projects.[7]

WIBO was actually owned by Alvin Nelson, the president of the Nelson
Brothers Bond and Mortgage Company. Within two weeks, Clarence Nelson's
letter, together with dozens of similar missives, was presented to the FRC as
evidence in support of his bid to restore the higher wavelength.

Chicago radio station WIBO forwarded to the Commission over ninety
fan letters, many of them in Swedish, and all of them accompanied by a no-
tarized signature of the author authenticating the letter. One woman wrote
that the station's Swedish hour "is the only way my mother gets a chance to
hear any Gospel sermons in her own language." A carpenter's wife reported,
"even my *Greek* neighbors"—a butcher shop owner and his family—"tune in
[the station] every Sunday morning as they say they enjoy the singing." Most
letter writers would agree with the fifty-eight-year-old clerk in a dry goods
wholesale company and an immigrant in the US since 1890, who opined, "A
Great Injustice would be done in this way to the Swedish People of this country, as in my opinion this Station has done . . . a lot of good for their race."[8]
Local listeners needed the station's broadcasts as much as the station needed
their patronage.

Stations forged close ties to local communities. Labor station WCFL might have been the only one that made major decisions by vote of its rank-and-file constituency, but most ethnic neighborhoods in industrial cities like Chicago or New York could point to their own radio hour. Brooklyn listeners to WBKN's *Jewish Hour*, many of them residing a few blocks from the station, learned about the show from the *Jewish Forward*'s radio program listings, eagerly accepted free passes to nearby Hopkinson and Liberty theaters, tuned in while working in local Jewish-owned shops, and offered to stop by and perform numbers. "Thursday a week ago," a sales clerk at Fred Eiseman Radio reported, "everybody [at work] was singing in chorus when you played a certain selection." A fourteen-year-old student at the Brooklyn Conservatory of Music asked for "the opportunity of playing at your radio station whenever possible," and requested an immediate response.[9] These requests counted on a give-and-take between performers and listeners.

This participatory culture had its limitations—the upper-crust "Negro Hour" on WSBC in Chicago refused to broadcast the blues, which were relayed instead by labor station WCFL from the Savoy on the South Side. But as a rule, independent stations assumed and granted a limited freedom of speech in their day-to-day operations. The World Battery Corporation had little control over the Bohemian, German, Italian, Lithuanian, Polish, Slovenian, and Yiddish programs broadcast by its station WSBC in Chicago. Labor organizers, corporate executives, blacks, clansmen, and quacks could all rent an hour or two on the air. Station owners spoke freely as well. Upon receiving "a wire heckling him," KWKH owner W. K. Henderson in Shreveport, Louisiana "gave the world a good piece of his mind," and was heard as far away as Michigan saying, "He has the power and the air, and avers that the station will be broadcasting 'till H--- freezes over.' "[10] Most independent stations stood for a radio system that allotted a voice to every ethnic and political group.

Even though the programming of a particular station catered to a local audience more than a distant one, the stations were usually able to construct a community of listeners that extended beyond local neighborhoods. A group of Scots from Wilton, New Jersey, asked New York's *Radio Program Weekly* to report on Scottish programs, citing in particular broadcasts by WEBN in Chicago. A Swedish Westinghouse Electric Elevator employee in Chicago wrote to WIBO, "I have a number of relatives and friends in O'Brien County and Cherokee Country Iowa who listen a great deal and enjoy more than any other station, the programs which come from your station." Such long-distance loyalty was particularly common in powerful Midwestern stations. Station WDAF, Kansas City, Missouri featured a "Night Hawks" orchestra that inspired fans to send in homemade drawings of hawks and other birds. One such drawing came from a resident of Brooklyn, New York.[11] Stations and listeners constructed, and then defended, a national culture not based on the notion of the metropolitan center.

Taken together, local stations' letter campaigns surpassed in volume those organized by educators and networks. During the hearings for station WDWM, Asbury Park, New Jersey, a Presbyterian minister representing the station dumped an entire suitcase of letters on the table to demonstrate audience support. Unfortunately, while stations pinned their hopes on letters, petitions, and affidavits, FRC General Counsel Louis G. Caldwell dismissed "packing cases" of "valueless" listener testimony as lacking "facts." An early study of three thousand listeners' letters by the Department of Commerce concluded that listeners wanted to divide the stations into powerful national and weak local stations; get rid of pirates who "jumped waves;" wanted no direct advertising; and were divided on the subject of the chains, although few wanted to eliminate chain broadcasting. The Commissioners denied licenses to applicants proposing the only black station in Kansas City and the only Japanese-language station in Hawaii, claiming no need for "additional radio service." Many more letters arrived but were not analyzed. By 1929, listener mail had become such a burden that the FRC asked Congress to decree that the accumulated letters be destroyed. A photograph snapped for the occasion portrayed two government workers rummaging through the mass of letters haphazardly stacked on top of filing cabinets (fig. 2). Commissioner Orestes H. Caldwell later admitted that the FRC "did a *great* many injustices to the stations when [it] assigned their relative positions" because it lacked, or rather refused to consider, information on listener popularity.[12] But if listeners failed to convince the FRC, they still articulated political dimensions of cooperation between independent stations and their constituencies.

Early radio practices helped Americans perceive the interdependence of local stations and the federal government. Given the initial popularity of long-distance (DX) reception, maps of radio stations quickly became a key tool and a symbol of radio listening. Contemporaries frequently made analogies between distance listening and modern exploration propelled by sea navigation, the automobile, and the airplane. One listener justified his hobby by arguing that radio hams are "no different from the pioneers of old, except that they may do their exploring from the comforts of an easy chair."[13] In this period, stations frequently went out of business and new ones appeared every month—to keep up, a radio bug would have to update his map regularly or

2. "Fan mail has become so heavy that the Federal Radio Commission has seeked Congress for special legislation to allow the destruction of accumulated letters." February 26, 1929. National Photo Company Collection, Library of Congress.

buy new ones frequently. An engineer and radio hobbyist described one such map in 1923: "The wall map has printed on it a series of bright-red spots and red letters indicating the location and official designation of the radio broadcasting stations now operating . . . In some regions of the map the red spots even crowd each other clear off into the ocean with red extension lines back to the location of the whole bunch, as at New York, Washington, Los Angeles, and San Francisco . . . And the map is already a back number, for we have heard several stations we can't find on it."[14] Ordinary political and geographic maps fixed borders and landscapes. Radio maps invited manipulation. They existed to be marked up, revised and improved upon. Maps made it obvious that along with the initial radio experience of intimacy and presence, radio provided a way to reconsider connections and relations between things, people, and social phenomena.[15]

In their attempt to encompass any and all existing stations, DX listen-

ers envisioned a decentralized broadcasting system where all stations were
equally important. To capitalize on this enthusiasm, an advertisement for a
De Forest radio set featured a map of the United States with arrows, representing radio broadcasts, converging on Wisconsin from different parts
of the country. This ad represented a Wisconsin listener, rather than, say, a
major New York radio station, as the temporary focal center of the broadcasting system. This system could potentially extend beyond national borders.
An eleven-year-old girl, just transplanted from Detroit to a chicken farm outside of the city, boasted to radio vaudevillian Wendell Hall, "My mother and
father heard you sing in Kansas. The first night we got the radio my mother
and father sat up till 3 o'clock in the morning. We can hear Cuba with it."
The fifteen-year-old son of an auto mechanic from West Somerset, Massachusetts, reported to station WGY in Schenectady, New York, that his radio
could tune in "stations as far west as California and as far east as London,
England." Likewise, a given radio station manager could imagine his station
as a temporary center of the system, with radio sets all over the world tuning
in to its programs. To make it easier to locate a station on a map as well as
on the radio dial, station managers added to the announcement of their call
letters distinctive sounds that identified that station to the listener. A locomo-
tive hoot would pinpoint a railroad division point in Georgia; a car horn, an
automobile school in Kansas City; or a bell solo playing "My Old Kentucky
Home," a Louisville station.[16]

The ability of stations and listeners to locate each other in this uncodified
broadcasting system depended on mutual cooperation. As an equivalent of
QSL cards, meant to document listeners' reception of distant stations, radio
manufacturers and station owners produced "applause cards," which asked
for time, place, quality of reception, name of program, and the kind of radio
set used. Listeners could buy a card in a drug store, fill it out, send it to a
radio station and receive a QSL card in return (fig. 3). Applause cards sent to
WGI, a small station outside of Boston operated by students and faculty from
Tufts University, reported that a listener Bridgeton, New York, "heard your
6:45 program and enjoyed it very much," and another in Rhode Island "heard
your station about 7:30 last night and again during intermission in local programs. Very rarely get Boston stations here as you know." WGI operators also
learned that a listener heard them in Indiana "on a single tube set," another
"on D.E.T. and 2 step" in Brooklyn, and a third on "a one tube single circuit
Reg. St." in New Jersey. Newspaper and magazine articles cited these cards as
proof of a station's geographically diverse audience. Station owners printed

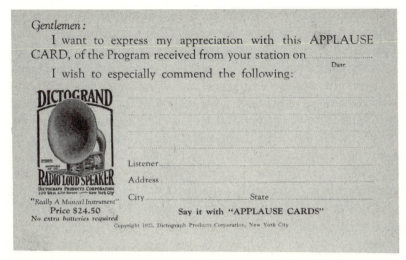

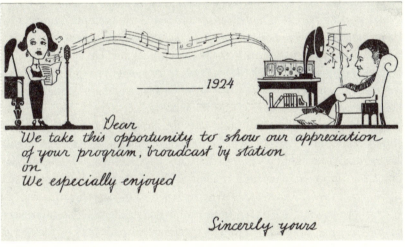

3. Applause cards, 1924. George H. Clark Radioana Collection, Archives Center, National Museum of American History, Smithsonian Institution.

maps marking the areas where their broadcasts could reach to attract advertisers for their programs.[17]

Initially, listeners' cards and letters requesting information about the station were brief and to the point. "Your station has come in very QSA"—strong—"around 6 o'clock lately after a long lapse during the summer," wrote the sixteen-year-old son of an insurance agent from Huntington, New York,

"How are you up there? What's your distance record? Can you give me a description of your station for a little write up in the local newspapers?" Distance hounds wrote to be placed on the mailing list, and to request copies of daily broadcasting schedules, "a letter . . . describing your transmitter and Studio," or "any printed matter relating to your station."[18] Drawing upon Morse code exchanges between their own wireless sets, DX writers used amateur jargon and expected extensive data in return.

Soon the DX audience expanded to include more farmers, workers, and women. "If the store is located in a community most of the inhabitants of which are workmen," one study concluded, "there will be a large proportion of [radio] parts." Indiana worker boasted to an interviewer in 1926 to have captured "120 stations on my radio." Messages and relationships became more personal. "I see no reason why the National shouldn't extend your tour and include some Southern cities," a sugar company employee in New Orleans wrote to vaudevillian Wendell Hall in Iowa, "Hope you have a nice time in Detroit." Hall, a WEAF performer, toured Midwestern radio stations to promote National Carbon Company's Eveready Batteries. "I . . . must be on duty in the early A.M.," wrote a nurse from Baltimore to WGY in Schenectady, "but cannot close my De Forest until you say Good Night . . . this as all previous concerts thoroughly rest me after a hard day with the sick."[19] No longer an obscure technical hobby, DXing became part of everyday life for most listeners.

To help listeners tune in distant stations, broadcasters cooperated to institute "silent nights" when local stations stayed off the air. In 1922, broadcasters in cities including Chicago, Kansas City, Cincinnati, Dallas, and San Francisco instituted silent nights after polling their local listeners. A poll conducted by the *Chicago Daily News* returned 3,700 votes for the idea, 320 against. Newspapers and radio magazines included silent nights and distant stations in program schedules. Radio experimenters made their own powerful sets and competed in radio magazines' DX contests. Casual listeners also benefited. "We followed you back to Chicago," a New York brokerage clerk from Brooklyn wrote to Wendell Hall, "We do not get KYW very good after WEAF closes, so were delighted when you went to WJAZ." An automobile mechanic from Kansas City, Missouri, and his wife reported to WOC in Davenport, Iowa: "We are hearing your Station regularly and appreciate the programs very much, (those after ten o'clock, when our local stations are silent)." Hall's fans asked, "Where do you go from here?" and promised to "keep up," follow him "around via Radio," and "watch for his appearances on other stations." Fans from "as far off as Tulsa Oklahoma" heard him perform in Camden,

New Jersey; from Missouri, "at Chicago, Kansas City and last nite at Jefferson City;" and from Ohio, "at WOS Jefferson City, Mo, WOC Davenport, Ia, & WWJ Detroit, Mich."[20] Before this informal practice died out in 1927, silent nights helped late-night personalities and shows to acquire fans across state and regional boundaries. The ties that Americans formed with far-away stations encouraged them to see the body politic as an invisible social network of distant interdependent relationships. This view shaped listeners' distrust of centralized radio and the networks.

When the Radio Commission began to reallocate frequencies, radio fan magazines provided a public space where DX listeners expressed their distaste of network monopoly. Veteran experimenter monthlies like *Radio News*, published by an experimenter and science fiction pioneer, Hugo Gernsback, had tried since the early 1920s to revise their formats to serve lay audiences as well as hobbyists, but still served experimenters more than the general public. *Radio Broadcast*, the only glossy radio magazine, attempted to reach both trade and general audiences, but with limited success—as late as in 1927 radio dealers, engineers, and technicians made up 60 percent of its readership. These periodicals served the trade more than the fan base. Fan magazines like *Radio Digest* or New York's *Radio Program Weekly*, also launched by Gernsback in 1927, explicitly addressed the "non-technical" listener. *Radio Program Weekly* offered program listings for all of the New York City stations and feature articles on area programs and artists. *Radio Digest*, launched in 1922, switched from technical subjects to entertainment coverage by 1926, offering program listings for all major stations and reporting on local and national programs and personalities. Some of these magazines prospered—by 1930, *Radio Digest* published 100-page issues and had a paid circulation of 100,000.[21]

Like the pulp science-fiction, mystery, and confession magazines, radio magazines often included "Letters from Readers" columns.[22] Judging from these columns, readership for these periodicals remained largely male and hobbyist up to the early 1930s—letters from DX listeners made up half of the published reader mail, with the remainder divided between chain aficionados and defenders of local stations. These magazines published extensive reports on the Congressional debates about the radio system. Editors asked listeners to send in their suggestions for improving the system to be forwarded later to the Commission. Of the readers' letters to *Radio Digest* and *Radio Program Weekly* published between 1926 and 1929, more than half discussed radio legislation in one way or another; of these, half spoke against the chains and the FRC.[23]

Anxious to elicit from the chains the cooperation that the movie fan magazines enjoyed from Hollywood, radio magazine editors supported the networks. They encouraged readers to inform Congress that Americans "do not want education thrust down their throats or in their ears." The radio magazine editors' hopes for network support never entirely materialized. In 1931 *Radio Digest* began a campaign against a proposed Congressional bill that allocated a fixed percentage of airwaves for educational and nonprofit stations. The trade periodicals reported this campaign with enthusiasm and approval. NBC president Merlin Aylesworth even briefly "donated [network] time to the magazine." By 1932, however, network executives decided to "divorce" the *Radio Digest* program announcer "from the Digest and put her on as an NBC or ostensibly a freelance observer" so not to favor this particular magazine "with so many radio publications on the market."[24]

Most fan magazine editors failed to impress the networks. In the early 1930s, *Radio Stars* editor Curtis Mitchell organized writing campaigns in favor of the chains, assured commissioners that the "overwhelming majority of listeners" approved of networks' dominance, and forwarded to the Commission readers' letters such as, "I wish to say that I, one of thousands of middle classed radio listeners, want entertainment and not too much education over the radio and its networks." Yet as of 1934 Mitchell could not secure NBC airtime for his talks, and in vain asked Aylesworth for "the same degree of cooperation that he had previously extended to a radio magazine called 'Radio Digest.'"[25] Possibly miffed at the networks, and probably mindful of the entertainment value of readers' columns, editors constructed from readers' letters a more equitable debate than the actual legislative deliberations. In Congress, advertising and network lobbyists far outgunned educational, nonprofit, and civic groups. In readers' columns, proponents of each side had an opportunity to articulate their position.

The radio magazines printed letters from readers who could see clearly the connection between the networks' financial power and the transformation of radio's political economy. Some letters complained that the powerful stations affiliated with the chains interfered with listening to independent stations. The chains thus curtailed radio hobbyists' ability to shape and extend radio receiver technology. A radio salesman from Gober, Texas argued, "We don't object to a chain but we do object to [chain stations] being scattered about two degrees apart all over the dial, and being forced to listen to them or go to bed." Most writers had no doubt that the Commission colluded with the corporations that owned radio networks. A laborer from Illinois warned, "The big companies with so much power within their grasp should consider well how they use it and not abuse it or they will lose it." A bookkeeper from Memphis, Tennessee commented that the familiar expression "freedom of the air," was often used loosely. He wrote, "Now, just what is meant by freedom of the air? Does it mean that the air belongs to a very few broadcasters? Or does it mean that the air belongs to the millions of receivers listening in every night?" Like boxing fans a few years earlier, he insisted, "In my opinion the receivers are in the majority, and therefore are entitled to some consideration." A claims clerk for a steam railroad in St. Louis, Missouri, reported, "I have been keeping tabs on the Federal Radio Commission since it began juggling wave lengths and clearing channels for the National Broadcasting Company," and quipped that chain stations "will keep out Havana or die trying." These readers objected to corporate monopoly and invoked the rights of independent radio producers against big business, much like the Progressive muckraking journalists who went after Standard Oil at the turn of the twentieth century.[26]

Listeners suspected the FRC of ulterior motives because corporate broadcasters' public relations campaigns obfuscated most of the issues in radio reform. In 1928 the FRC received enough letters from "Coast towns complaining about the chain broadcasting, particularly in Seattle where two stations have been broadcasting the same program" to order NBC to stop broadcasting over one of them.[27] But to listeners, the Commission defended its decision to allow several NBC affiliates in the same city:

> . . . you have, without doubt, a fairly good receiving set, evidenced by the fact that you are able to hear stations one-thousand or more miles away. You will, of course, appreciate the fact that thousands of people in your city and state are unable to hear distant stations, that many of them can only hear stations in their own immediate vicinity because of the inexpensive set they operate and which perhaps is all they can afford. Consequently, in the interests of these people, we feel the necessity of permitting a duplication of programs in each of the large cities on the coast.[28]

In fact, listeners who tuned in local stations had the same problem as DX listeners. All Philadelphians, for example, could hear the two chains at any time over eight stations. William Perry, a seed salesman and a *Radio Digest* reader and correspondent, pointed out to the FRC that "the National and Columbia broadcasts come into Philadelphia with just as much volume and if anything better quality direct from their key stations" as from local affiliates. As a result, he complained, "we hear more about what is going on in New York than we do Philadelphia." This FRC policy received more support from the business elite than from rank-and-file owners of cheap sets. The Radio Committee of the Omaha Chamber of Commerce, in a letter forwarded by NBC to the commission, argued that "thousands of receiving sets not capable of picking up the broadcasting stations in the East" would be able "through these [network] hook-ups to receive the best in the way of music, entertainment and instruction." Corporate broadcasters, national advertisers, and the FRC presented such a united party line in defense of the network system that Perry may not have been alone in believing that "the Columbia chain . . . is very likely another branch of the N.B.C."[29]

NBC President Mervin Aylesworth regularly used prominent listeners' letters to lobby for FRC approval for a particular station to join the NBC chain, or for a different time schedule for an NBC station. He sent Judge Ira Robinson "an interesting letter that you might show to the members of the Commission . . . from the father of Clarence Chamberlin and from Denison, Iowa." Aviator Clarence Chamberlain broke the world endurance record in his Bellanca monoplane in April 1927—ten hours longer than Charles Lindbergh's historic flight. His father's letter railed against "little bleating farmer stations condemning the chain broadcasting." Aylesworth's notes accompanying such letters told of a "great number," "several thousand," "eighty thousand nine hundred and ninety," "ninety thousand," and "more than a million" unsolicited laudatory missives—never actually produced by NBC—"pouring in" monthly to the network. Yet E. P. H. James, NBC's sales and promotions manager at the time, later cited "detailed audience-mail counts" showing only 352,064 letters received by the NBC Red Network in 1927—a far cry from the million a month claimed by Aylesworth.[30]

In 1928, the Commission ordered that station WHO of Des Moines, Iowa, had to divide its time with WOC, Davenport, and thus could no longer broadcast NBC programs. Aylesworth forwarded selected listeners' complaints to all FRC members to try to convince them to reconsider. Respectable Iowa citizens, including a Catholic school nun, had written every one of these letters. A "Club Woman" could no longer "appreciate good music, educational features," in Iowa only available from NBC. The proud owner of an expensive Atwater Kent radio set mourned "the ever-wondrous [NBC sponsored] Atwater Kent program." A Director of Music in the Des Moines Public Schools told of "over 713,000 schoolchildren of Iowa" deprived of the "Damrosch

Concerts sponsored by Radio Corporation of America." In the meantime, an M.D. complained, the Commission gave away clear channels to Iowa's independent direct-advertising "prune and harness selling stations." Aylesworth claimed to "have not requested any [letters] from the listeners," yet most of the letters cited the same statistics provided by NBC President in his WHO radio address—"a recent count for a week" showing 100 NBC hours for WHO as opposed to 50 for neighboring WOW.[31] Like the independent stations, the networks used listener mail to support their case with the federal government. But independent stations kept in close contact with their ordinary constituencies, whereas the NBC president rarely looked beyond his target upper-class audience that held the same views as his sponsors.

Most early radio surveys slanted their questions and conclusions to favor the chains. After a 1927 readers' poll, *Radio Broadcast* reported that listeners everywhere liked chain programs, when mostly radio professionals subscribed to the magazine. Such lapses stemmed from survey methods that were aimed at self-serving interpretation of results. National advertising and network advocates claimed that listeners preferred "professional" chain programs at a time when there were no defined radio genres to speak of, and the future radio blockbuster *Amos 'n' Andy* was only aired locally over WMAQ in Chicago. In 1928, half of the respondents to a Chicago survey still preferred local programs to chain broadcasts.[32]

The same year, NBC commissioned what it touted as "the first radio audience research study ever made" from Daniel Starch, the director of research for the American Association of Advertising Agencies. Starch, a psychologist, left academia to start his own market research consulting firm, Daniel Starch & Staff, in 1926, where he developed an advertising readership test, still used in print advertising today. He worked to disprove two popular notions about advertising, "that enormously large sums of money are expended for it, and that much of this expenditure is an economic waste." Frank Stanton, who worked with Starch in CBS research department in the 1930s, remembered him as "a businessman more than anything else."[33] His radio research was designed to promote, rather than inform, network broadcasting.

For the NBC study, Starch interviewed 17,099 families east of the Rocky Mountains across social strata and the urban-rural divide. Yet he claimed no difference in responses by class, residence, or region. He reported that three-fourths listened to local rather than distant stations with "no important differences . . . among the cities, towns, or farms, . . . occupations and income groups" at a time when observers maintained that 80 percent of the U.S.

geographic area still required distance listening to receive stations. According to Starch, urban, rural, wealthy, poor, Northern, and Southern respondents alike claimed to own mostly five- or six-tube sets, when the same year an FRC survey showed that 37 percent of radio owners still made their own sets, and crystal and single-tube models were still "in wide use on farms and rural sections."[34]

Starch organized and calculated his survey to make Americans of all classes seem equally ready and eager for network broadcasting. They were not. As late as 1933 the President's Committee on Social Trends found significant regional, urban-rural, economic, and racial differences in radio ownership, access to stations, and listening practices. Within a few years, George Gallup's study of newspaper comic strips would convince broadcasters that the majority of their audience was neither refined nor wealthy. But in the late 1920, Starch's survey found what network executives and national advertisers wanted to believe: that all Americans had the same tastes as their upper-class acquaintances, and all universally desired commercial network broadcasting.[35]

Starch's interviewers asked loaded questions such as, "Do you prefer programs like Eveready, Damrosch, General Motors, Collier's, Maxwell, Goodrich, and Ipana?" meaning, "You like NBC sponsored programs, don't you?" Four-fifths of the respondents agreed, most likely giving answers they thought interviewers wanted to hear. Later primers on audience research would use the survey as an example to caution against such "leading questions," where "the most natural reaction of a person is to say 'yes,' unless by doing so he runs counter to his prejudices." Advertising trade journals noted this bias almost as soon as the survey was published, yet Starch's reputation did not suffer. He continued to survey radio audiences for NBC and CBS into the 1930s.[36]

The Starch survey contributed to a larger campaign of reeducation that targeted advertisers and the public at large. Frank Arnold, NBC's director of development, convinced Aylesworth to commission the survey to help promote network radio to ad agencies, potential sponsors, and listeners. "Needless to say," he remembered, "this survey was quoted from liberally, sought after eagerly, and formed the first constructive basis on which our advertising department could solicit business." Officially, Arnold traveled the country as an educator on the "general subject of radio" so as not to alarm civic groups reluctant to invite advertisers as speakers. Arnold lectured to local listener groups, met privately with advertising men, and penned articles for general and trade magazines on the virtues of commercial broadcasting. "My work was very largely undercover," he described his promotional efforts. Arnold's covert educational activities continued those of Alfred Goldsmith, who in the early 1920s glorified RCA equipment and radio trust policies in the *Boston Globe*. Edgar H. Felix, then director of public relations at WEAF, assisted feature writers with "questions raised as to the advertising program;" he later became a contributing editor to *Radio Broadcast* and in 1927 penned one of the first radio advertising manuals. Corporate publicists culled and framed most radio survey results, which were reported as objective news in the general press.[37] All the more remarkable, then, that many listeners still disagreed with the networks.

That many listeners defined local, national, public, and commercial aspects of radio differently from the networks came out most clearly in the debates about advertising on Midwestern radio stations that catered to farmers. Even though not every farmer owned a radio in the 1920s, from the earliest days of radio farmers were an important audience. Stations broadcasting for farmers usually had powerful transmitters, because they needed to reach listeners across large geographic areas. But their subject matter consisted of specialized issues—weather and market reports, agricultural advice, old-time and country music, homemaking shows, and advertisements and promotions for local small businesses. Network programs still used indirect, "good will" advertising. Midwestern stations as a rule allowed local merchants to go on the air and hawk their products in a manner that recalled nineteenth-century street criers.[38] But because the stations had powerful transmitters, these local criers were heard all over the nation.

Networks and their allies used these homespun advertisements on Midwestern stations to justify national dissemination of their own, what they called more "high-class," metropolitan programming. NBC's own programs had a much more solid commercial basis than farmer programs because they were created by major advertising agencies. Network executives made decisions based on potential advertising profits. When Aylesworth forwarded to Caldwell a listener's request to add Buffalo station WKHW to NBC's Blue network, he added, "we have discouraged the move because I am not at all certain that we can sell our clients this station." The conflict arose not between direct and indirect advertising but between the affluent network clientele and the farm audience small commercial stations served. In 1928 in *Radio Broadcast* the president of the upper-middle-class Iowa Listeners' League complained that direct-advertising stations like the Henry Field Seed Company's station in Shenandoah broadcast "common music for common people." In the daily mail to the League, "letters from opponents of the principle of direct selling are on excellent paper and represent a highly educated class, while those from supporters of the direct seller are for the most part extremely hard to read, [and] are not noted for cleanliness."[39] Network broadcasters decried back-country selling strategies and used wealthy listeners' letters and trade radio journals' criticism to force farmer stations off the air.

Aylesworth forwarded to the Commission letters arguing that local unaffiliated stations hawked products while NBC stations provided educational programming. The Omaha Chamber of Commerce argued that a corporate national broadcasting system benefited "commercial interests" the most because the small stations pursued "methods which in our opinion were not for the best interests of the art, such as the direct sale of merchandise over radio, against which the Omaha Chamber of Commerce has gone on record, believing that as practiced at present, it constitutes monopoly." Letters argued that NBC "advertising is so worked into their programs that the interest in the program itself is never lost" while small stations such as WJR in Detroit "put on the worst sort of advertising programs from one day's end to another; they also run over their frequency." Farmer stations "fear that they will sell a few less shoe strings, or Prunes if people get in the habit of listening to your most wonderful programs." The only ones to object to the chains are "a few stations who have something to sell, or . . . a few DX fans who . . . cannot get a fifty watt station three thousand miles away with a two tube set." Summing up the mail he forwarded, Aylesworth concluded that any criticism of NBC would go away if not for "the attacks of some of the small broadcasting stations."[40]

Some letters printed in the fan magazines agreed with NBC. When wave-jumping became common, complaints intensified because small stations "jumped" the most, and according to one reader, "Iowa [was] the worst for wave jumpers." An Iowa resident argued, "it is most annoying to have to listen to old time fiddlers and farm talks when some very fine concert of real artists is being broadcast from New York."[41] Yet another reader complained to *Radio Digest*, "In another three months [radio] for Northern Iowa will be utterly ruined unless some action is taken to put such unethical advertising out of business. Some people may like to listen to some of their help sing, play and fiddle, but they shouldn't think that the people in general give a 'hoop' for such stuff."[42] But other listeners, from the Midwest and elsewhere, pointed out that farmer programs were more familiar and useful for them than the polished but bland NBC broadcasts. A Long Island listener wrote, "I wonder if these studio managers ever sit down in front of their sets and do a little DXing for the good of their own programs? If they would tune in on Al and Pat at WHT [Illinois] some midnight and listen to what those boys can do with an organ . . . they would probably run out and buy a good organ and get someone to play it who didn't wear a high hat." If the "chosen" network stations refused to "divide time with the better [small stations]," some listeners argued, "the latter were certainly justified in 'jumping their waves.'" Like Swedish Chicagoans, many Midwesterners insisted that they deserved stations "more suited to our needs." One listener from Monticello, Minnesota, noted, "I don't see why one station should be given unlimited power to reach across the continent and drown out some local station that has the needs and desires of the community at heart."[43] A group of farmers from South Dakota sent a letter to *Radio Digest* in favor of the Iowa stations and other Midwestern broadcasters:

> *Radio Digest* objects to direct advertising but we want to hear it. It is interesting and helps lower the prices on what we need. . . . The chain stations take up half the dial with fancy screaming. Why not let the farmers have a few stations that will give the programs of old time singing and talks about things we need. They are surely easier to tune out than a couple dozen powerful stations all broadcasting the same grand opera line of bunk.[44]

In other words, these farmers wanted the broadcasts they liked, and if the rest of the nation had to hear them too, that was just too bad for the nation. These listeners defended not so much direct advertising as their right to a radio station that would serve their interests.[45]

To local communities, farmer stations provided reciprocal services not reproducible on a national scale. In the early 1930s, as the Great Depression set in, radio advertisers' profits fell and new surveys showed that lower-income listeners predominated in the radio audience. Within a few years, network advertisers, too, had adopted the shrill and hyperbolic carnivalesque style, hawking soap and cereal and offering snake-oil remedies for mythical social and bodily diseases. "Never before the advent of radio did advertising have such a golden opportunity to make an ass out of itself," declared William Cameron, director of public relations for the Ford Motor Company, in 1938 about national radio. Far too "impertinent," "insistent," and "unmannerly," critics argued, network commercials served up nothing more than "sophisticated hokum." Networks and ad agencies remade the ad hoc farmer

advertising into a system. Occasionally surveys reported this strategy a success: irritating jingles appeared to promote brand recognition and some listeners who panned commercials then bought sponsored products. Other
surveys contradicted these findings.[46] The networks could not reproduce the
independent stations' practical knowledge of their audience.

Commercial farmer stations secured audience support because they
quickly responded to the needs of their rural listeners at the same time as they
sold prunes and seeds. In this, they mirrored the practices of many other independent stations. Not only small commercial stations, but also many non-
profits, such as labor station WCFL, could not survive without selling airtime.
In 1928 WCFL earned more than 30 percent of its monthly income by selling
time to grocers, department stores, jewelers, radio equipment manufacturers, and quack doctors.[47] Independent stations rented airtime to local groups
that broadcast ethnic and religious hours, and aired sales messages from local
businesses. Likewise, farmer stations devised commercial "neighboring" programs where local companies gave advice on farming and homemaking to
listeners who sent in questions. Music programming relied on listener requests as well. A secretary at WIBW in Topeka, Kansas later recalled sorting
the fan mail: "At night, I'd have to take a stack of letters and go through them
and write down the names of people who were requesting songs . . . I'd have
to have them written out the next day, because the announcers [on the air]
didn't have time to take those letters and read them. I had to make it as simple
as I could for the announcer."[48] Local musicians could be hired after audition-
ing at the station, perform to local studio audiences, be on a first-name basis
with their fans, and also double at the counter at the seed store. Stations like
Henry Field's KFNF and the Earl May Seed and Nursery Company's KMA,
also in Shenandoah, attracted listeners across the Midwest. Field reported
hundreds of thousands of followers and convinced many of them to lobby
Federal Radio Commission on behalf of the station.[49]

Unlike broadcast reformers who aimed to preserve educational and nonprofit broadcasting, the writers of letters submitted during FRC hearings
between 1927 and 1932 routinely defended nonprofit *and* commercial independent stations as necessary parts of a democratic radio system. Yet their
view of market relations differed from the unregulated free broadcast market
reformers feared. Listeners bartered patronage of local businesses for broadcast
content. When Harriett Stothard, a glove finisher at a mill in Brooklyn, asked
Herbert Jewelry Shop to have Rudy Vallée sing "Loretta" for her next Sunday
on their sponsored broadcast, she insisted, "Members of our family including

myself have visited your store many times and purchased various articles, all of which we have been very well pleased and satisfied with, so thought being a patron of your store, that perhaps the boys would favor me with this request."[50] The store, the orchestra, and the patron all belonged in the same neighborhood and mixed business and personal relationships. All understood broadcasting as a product of intimate reciprocal obligations. When the FRC began to legislate away listeners' favorite stations, the personal became political.

Defenders of the farmer stations advanced populist arguments congruent with the demands of ethnic station audiences, DX listeners, and even some representatives of the broadcast reform movement. All these groups would agree with WCFL manager and President of the Chicago Federation of Labor John Fitzpatrick, who argued, "Surely it is in the public interest, necessity and convenience that every reputable group shall have opportunity to sing its song, tell its story, or proclaim its message to those who desire to hear?" Populist listeners protested corporate power, not commercial radio in general. These views made for a less radical critique of the capitalist order than the demands advanced by certain representatives of the reform movement, who decried any form of commercial broadcasting, and attempted to secure a fixed percentage of airtime, as well as government subsidies, for educational and nonprofit stations.[51] Yet perhaps educators would have been more successful if the legislation they proposed had taken into account the practices and beliefs of these sundry radio fans.

Historians usually describe this period in radio history as listeners' failure to articulate alternatives to the network system. Robert McChesney has argued that because the network lobby blocked any "legitimate public debate" about the commercial basis of broadcasting, the reform movement "was unable to generate much popular momentum" which in turn "left Congress without incentive to force change" on a strong corporate radio industry. "People," Lizabeth Cohen concluded, "opposed [network broadcasting] without having any realistic alternative."[52] Yet parallels in listener views across the lines of class, occupation, ethnicity, and region suggest that many Americans did envision a specific, if not radical, alternative to the commercial network system. They demanded an equitable distribution of frequencies, power, and airtime among different social, political, ethnic, and cultural groups, and among network affiliates and independent commercial, nonprofit, and educational stations.

Most small stations that appealed FRC decisions did not get the higher wavelength they demanded. Although local and regional broadcasting did

not disappear during the Depression, the networks displaced the debates
about the moral economy of American broadcasting to the national arena.[53]
Yet the earlier fragmented mode of broadcasting had a lasting effect on popular perceptions of radio, as a communication network and as a system of
social relationships. In the 1920s stations were scattered across the dial without any predictable order or sense, inviting participation on both a local and
national scale. As a result of this uncodified experience, independent broadcasters and their fans came to perceive their loyalties as simultaneously local,
regional, and national. The earliest radio correspondence concerned the style
of broadcasting; the major controversies of the late 1920s shifted to its institutional structure. The earliest radio fans wrote to radio stations; by the end of
the decade listeners felt it necessary to appeal to the national government. To
shape the emergent network system, listeners needed to invent new criteria of
legitimacy and mutual obligation in radio. In doing so, they applied the ethic
of the local radio era to the corporate network system.

3

Voice of the Listener

Once the legislative dust had settled over licenses and wavelength, listeners faced an unwieldy network system. If in the 1920s fans addressed their letters to the artist care of their local station, now the growing network broadcasting system and its production process had become much more complex. In 1931, NBC broadcast its blockbuster *Amos 'n' Andy* over its Blue Network of affiliated stations. The Lord and Thomas ad agency produced it. Pepsodent sponsored it. Charles Correll and Freeman Gosden wrote and performed. This was only one of many possible combinations of agencies involved. Writers could work out of the ad agency, like soap writers Frank and Anne Hummert. Actors could be in charge of production, like comedian Jack Benny. Listeners now sent letters ending, "If I have addressed my communication to the wrong person, would you please forward it to the proper person," and got responses beginning, "Your very kind letter has been forwarded to me by the sponsor" (or network, or production company, or your local station).[1] In order to shape network broadcasting, listeners needed to make sense of this impersonal system.

During the Great Depression, fan magazines took the radio publishing field over from amateur periodicals and set out to reeducate listeners to accept and negotiate with the network system. Networks had to restore public trust, which had been damaged by the destruction of many local stations. Listeners wanted to know about the mechanics of broadcasting: "what happens before a radio show goes on," what goes on "behind the microphone," about engineers, screenwriters, and other cogs "in the spinning wheel of entertainment." Fan magazines investigated radio production for the listener and mediated between network broadcasters and audiences. In a kind of publishing doublespeak, they served as publicity outlets for the networks at the same time as they encouraged and published listeners' responses to the radio industry. Because of their roots in the populist pulp publishing industry, they encouraged less an impartial and reasoned public debate than personal and direct town-hall democracy. In many ways, they mirrored the strategies of the radio industry. Network programs, from President Franklin Delano Roosevelt's fireside chats to the man-on-the-street program *Vox Pop*, constructed a national public at the same time as they encouraged intimate relationships between broadcasters and listeners. Fan magazines at once made the commercial national system seem inevitable and created expectations of reciprocity in network radio.[2]

The shift from amateur to fan magazines in radio paralleled the shift from local to network radio. Both the amateur and the fan radio magazines shared modes of operation, styles, publishers, and audiences with the pulp magazines that flourished in the 1920s and 1930s. Mainstream "slick" magazines, such as the *Saturday Evening Post* or *Ladies' Home Journal*, commanded a middle-class readership nine times that of a given pulp magazine, were printed on glossy paper, targeted middle-class audiences, and received most of their revenue from advertising. Conversely, the pulps were printed on cheap paper, relied on newsstand sales for revenue, and inherited their less affluent audiences from the dime novels of the late nineteenth century. They covered such topics as romance, mystery, westerns, science fiction, movies, and radio.[3] The popularity of radio fan magazines coincided with the pulp era—during the war, they either switched their focus to movies or folded together with the fading pulp publishing industry.

Before the Great Depression, amateur magazines and independent publishers dominated the radio magazine market. In 1908 Hugo Gernsback founded the very first radio amateur magazine, *Modern Electrics*, renamed the *Electrical Experimenter* in 1913. It paved the way for the *Wireless Age* and *QST*, two magazines linked to amateur associations, and to the one "slick" magazine, *Radio Broadcast*. Born in Luxembourg and educated in Germany, Gernsback arrived to New York in 1904 at the age of nineteen. Shortly afterward, he opened the Electro-Importing Company on Fulton Street, a "great emporium of the amateur world," according to radio advertiser Edgar H. Felix, who purchased radio parts there as a teenager. *Modern Electrics* began as a catalog for the emporium. An independent publisher and strident defender of amateurs' rights and popular science in general, Hugo Gernsback pioneered pulp science fiction with *Amazing Stories* and

Scientific Detective, and in 1927–28 ran a regional fan rag, New York's *Radio Program Weekly*.[4]

For more than a decade, Gernsback's Experimenter Publishing Company shaped public and legislative debates on radio through *Electrical Experimenter* and especially through *Radio News*, which was founded in 1919 and commanded the highest circulation of all amateur publications: at its height, in 1925, the magazine reported monthly circulation of 266,243 copies. Then, in 1929, Experimenter Publishing Company went bankrupt and Gernsback lost all of his publications. By then, the *Wireless Age*, the amateur magazine that co-organized the Dempsey-Carpentier fight, had long ceased publication. Gernsback recovered with new radio and science-fiction titles, but the circulation of amateur magazines continued to fall: *Radio News* readership had fallen to under 50,000 by 1935. From then on, experimenter magazines no longer appealed to the general public and confined their fare to technical articles only.[5]

The pulp publishers who took over the radio fan market from independents like Gernsback and *Radio Digest*, another pioneering fan magazine that had provided the forum for debates about wave jumping, commanded large pulp magazine empires. Most radio fan magazine publishers also produced love, science fiction, and detective pulps, as well as movie fan magazines. Tower published *Tower Radio*, the *Illustrated Detective*, and the *Illustrated Love Magazine*. Fawcett published *Radioland*, *True Confessions*, and *Screen Secrets*. Modern Magazines published *Radio Stars*, *Modern Screen*, and *Modern Romances*.[6] The two most significant fan publications, *Radio Mirror* and *Radio Guide*, came out of pulp publishing houses that competed with major players such as William Randolph Hearst, a pioneer of yellow journalism, for national importance.

Radio fan magazines were part of the amateur literary production tradition started by confession magazines. Bernarr Macfadden, perhaps the most famous pulp publisher, produced *Radio Mirror*, the premiere fan magazine for women listeners. He also published *True Detective Mysteries* and the biggest movie fan rag, *Photoplay*. Born on a small Missouri farm, Macfadden overcame several ailments in his childhood, an experience that he made use of when he launched his first successful pulp, *Physical Culture*, in 1899. In 1919 he founded *True Story*, the first and most successful confessions pulp; ten years later its circulation was two million. Macfadden's populism changed over time: he flirted with fascism and a conservative political career in the 1920s but supported Franklin D. Roosevelt in the early 1930s. A ruthless business competitor, he was rumored to have orchestrated Gernsback's bank-ruptcy; in 1933, he entered the radio field with *Radio Mirror* as part of the so-called "Macfadden women's group," which also included two confession titles. Macfadden died from an attack of jaundice in 1955 but *Radio Mirror* lived on, in part because it had switched its focus to movies in the early 1940s.[7]

Radio fan rags were also part of a tradition of yellow journalism and the shady world of organized crime. Moses "Moe" Annenberg, a publishing and racetrack gambling magnate, published *Radio Guide*, dubbed by *Time* a "prof-itable pulp" and the "most alert of the radio fan magazines." He also pub-lished *Screen Guide*, *Stardom*, and *Official Detective Stories*. Annenberg, an immigrant from East Prussia, rose up from newsboy to become the circula-tion manager for William Randolph Hearst, then created his own publishing empire based on a racing-wire service linked to mob-controlled gambling. He founded *Radio Guide* in 1931 as a national weekly publication with seventeen regional editions, modeled on his *Daily Racing Form*, which had eight re-gional editions. Annenberg's publishing offices were ransacked several times by persons unknown. He was informally accused of racketeering, blackmail, and bribery, and formally jailed for tax evasion in 1940. He died of a brain tumor in 1942, a month after he was paroled. His son, Walter Annenberg, killed *Radio Guide* in 1943 because of the wartime paper shortage.[8]

If fan publishers endowed the genre with populism, sensationalism, and extralegal acumen, the magazine editors commanded authority in the indus-try because of their versatility. They launched new pulp titles, carried win-ning operating principles from one magazine to another, and rescued failing publications. Ernest Heyn founded and edited *Modern Screen* for Dell before moving on to *Radio Mirror*. He also edited *Photoplay* and *True Story*, founded *Sport* magazine for Macfadden, and revamped Hearst's *American Weekly* after the war. Curtis Mitchell came to *Radio Stars* after editing *Modern Screen*; he attributed *Radio Stars'* high initial "circulation of approximately 150,000 cop-ies" to his "experience in publishing the largest motion picture fan magazine in the world." Curtis later moved on to head *Radio Guide*, as well as another Annenberg pulp, *Screen Guide*. In 1941, he left *Radio Guide*, by then renamed *Movie-Radio Guide*, to direct radio publicity in the U.S. Army's press section.[9] Their versatility allowed editors to negotiate both pulp publishing and radio network bureaucracies.

The visual style and print content of the new radio periodicals extended the sensational and vivid styles of movie fan and pulp magazines of the period. Fan periodicals depended on the networks for access to information and promotional material. Glamour pictures were their main attraction, and fan magazines also often printed photographs on glossy paper, like many Macfadden titles and some confession magazines. While earlier radio periodicals had put young experimenters on their covers, a typical fan magazine cover depicted a glamorous actress. In fan publishing, dazzling celebrity photos accompanied gossip tales, serial stories, and beat reporting. As one woman explained in her letter, she liked radio magazines because they published "amusing articles, . . . stories about radio folk, their . . . photographs, menus, wardrobe and beauty hints, their private lives, work, romances, [and] hobbies." Listener magazines printed images galore: gag pictures, news pictures, candid shots, gallery portraits, glossy prints, "mats," and "informals."[10] Editors who came to radio magazines after running such successful pulp magazines as *True Story* or *Modern Screen* also introduced numerous popular interactive features that usually distinguished the pulps from the slicks: audience interviews, quizzes, contests, popularity polls, and expanded letters to the editor departments. Over a thousand letters published between 1933 and 1945 in issues of *Radioland*, *Radio Guide*, *Radio Mirror*, and *Tune In* have survived.

Depression-era fan magazines encouraged a more anonymous exchange than the earlier experimenter magazines. In the early 1930s, *Radioland* still included full address for some letter writers; by the end of the decade, *Radio Mirror* and *Radio Guide* listed only the city of origin, and published more letters signed with initials or not at all. The increasing anonymity contrasted with other entertainment magazines of the time such as science-fiction pulps and jazz periodicals. In *Amazing Stories* and *Down Beat*, the identities of letter writers still mattered because many fans were also aspiring engineers and musicians, respectively. In this respect, both these magazines mirrored the early experimenter periodicals that catered to radio amateurs. This practice encouraged correspondence between readers outside of the framework of the magazine.[11] Conversely, Depression-era radio magazines published letters of criticism by lay audiences, conjuring a more inclusive yet abstract public. In this new system, a magazine could more easily control and direct debates and contact among readers.

Depression-era fan magazines reached circulation heights unknown to the Jazz-Age amateur and fan publications. In 1934, *Radio Guide* had roughly the same circulation as the *Radio Digest* had at its height in 1928—around 150,000. By 1940, it reached 340,533—almost a hundred thousand more than the apex of *Radio News* readership in the mid-1920s. The slicks had much

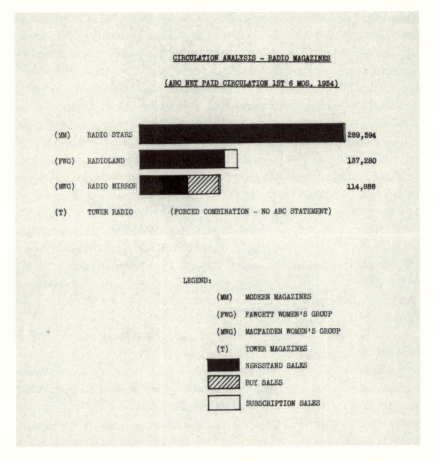

4. "Circulation Analysis—Radio Magazines," 1934. National Broadcasting Company Records, Wisconsin Historical Society.

higher circulation: in 1939, *Radio Guide* reported 324,242 average circulation, and *Radio Mirror*, 126,664, while *Ladies Home Journal* boasted 3,044,549. But the fan magazines' combined circulation matched: the top ten listener magazines combined were sold to three million Americans each month. Like all pulps, radio fan magazines relied on newsstand and newsboy rather than subscription sales. According to a circulation analysis of radio magazines for NBC, *Radio Stars*, *Radio Mirror*, and *Radioland* did not rely on subscriptions (fig. 4). In addition, more readers got hold of these publications without paying for them: from friends, barber shops, beauty parlors, waiting rooms, neighborhood clubs, cafes, amusement places, public libraries, and shelters for the unemployed. Housewives read *True Story* because it was "lying around in the beauty parlor while my hair was drying;" and dentists comforted their "pleased" patients with *Radio Guide*.[12]

Such free sources made magazines more easily available to poorer readers. According to Depression-era reading studies, the pulps, including radio and movie magazines, constituted the predominant reading matter in working-class neighborhoods. Radio and other pulps were read in large numbers by women laborers, housewives, stenographers, and female students, unemployed and unskilled workmen, and to a lesser degree by skilled workmen, shopkeepers, salesmen, clerks, and male students. By the mid-1930s, broadcasters discovered that radio was particularly popular among Americans on the lower end of the economic scale, and adjusted their programs and commercials accordingly. Fan periodicals linked broadcasters to the laboring classes—the core radio audience during the Great Depression.[13] The interactive and sensational content of radio pulps reflected the tastes of their largely lower-income audiences.

Because of fan magazines' association with the pulps, the populace, and populist ideas, network officials only grudgingly allowed listener periodicals to participate in the radio production process alongside ad agencies, sponsors, and production companies. In the 1930s, network executives and fan magazines established a love-hate relationship. The fan magazines attracted radio advertisers' attention in the late 1920s, just as the networks began to discover radio's lower-income audiences. At this time, corporate network broadcasting was taking shape and radio magazines were shifting to targeting fans exclusively, at the expense of trade and experimenter readers. The NBC corporate structure allotted a spot for magazines. "Press Relations" dealt with newspapers, general magazines, and fan periodicals, "Merchandising and Research" conducted audience surveys, and the "Mail Department" compiled fan letters (fig. 5). NBC charts included magazines and newspapers in a system that reinforced the sales pitch of a commercial radio program.[14]

Yet insofar as radio fan magazines were associated with pulp periodicals, they operated separately from the broadcasting system. Network executives refused to support what they called "the cheapest kind of dime novel magazine" on a regular basis. In 1934 NBC officials decided that that network would have "nothing to do" with *Radio Guide*'s national Radio Queen Contest because such contests were "usually crooked" and had "double-crossed" the

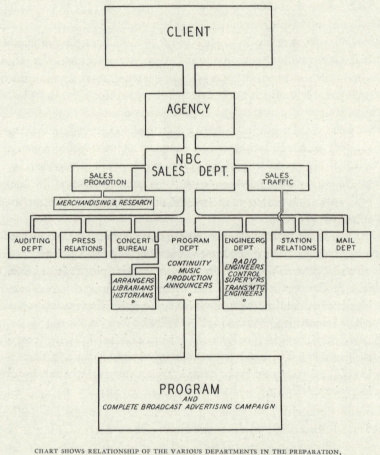

CHANNELS OF NBC SERVICE
TO BROADCAST ADVERTISING CLIENTS

CLIENT

AGENCY

NBC
SALES DEPT.

SALES
PROMOTION

SALES
TRAFFIC

MERCHANDISING & RESEARCH

AUDITING
DEPT

PRESS
RELATIONS

CONCERT
BUREAU

PROGRAM
DEPT

ENGINEER'G
DEPT

STATION
RELATIONS

MAIL
DEPT

CONTINUITY
MUSIC
PRODUCTION
ANNOUNCERS
o

ARRANGERS
LIBRARIANS
HISTORIANS
o

RADIO
ENGINEERS
CONTROL
SUPER'V'RS
TRANS'M'TG
ENGINEERS
o

PROGRAM
AND
COMPLETE BROADCAST ADVERTISING CAMPAIGN

CHART SHOWS RELATIONSHIP OF THE VARIOUS DEPARTMENTS IN THE PREPARATION,
CARRYING OUT, AND FOLLOWING UP OF A BROADCAST ADVERTISING CAMPAIGN

[92]

5. "Channels of NBC Service," 1932. E. P. H. James Papers, Wisconsin Historical Society.

network in previous years. When a *Radio Guide* editor requested that NBC consider his magazine for an advertising campaign, he was informed that NBC advertised in trade newspapers only. One network publicity executive suggested that fan magazines get their own "sales staff" because "we need our own people to sell [air] 'time.'" CBS did not send magazines regular updates of its programs even after NBC finally agreed to do so. Facing such indifference, a *Radio Stars* editor wrote an angry letter to NBC complaining that the network refused "all cooperation . . . except that which would directly procure publicity for your network," leaving *Radio Stars* and other fan magazines to "cut [their] own road without outside help" and to build their circulation, advertising revenue, and information sources "unaided by the radio industry."[15]

When program producers refused to cooperate, magazines retaliated. In 1936, Edward Bowes of a pioneering radio amateur contest program, *Major Bowes' Original Amateur Hour,* ignored a list of questions from *Radio Guide.* In response, the magazine sent its reporter Orville Edwards under cover as a contestant to check if the show was rigged. The resulting series of articles described how Edwards went through the audition process and appeared on the radio. He witnessed how Bowes made sure to correctly identify an opera aria from Giacomo Puccini's *Tosca* so that he would appear more cultured on the air. *Radio Guide* editors organized its staff to vote for Edwards over the phone and propelled its candidate to fourth place, proving that *Amateur Hour* could be rigged. The magazine also charged that vaudeville actors could sneak in as amateurs, and that some contestants were set up to fail and hence given only one minute to perform.[16] In this debacle, *Radio Guide* was able simultaneously to punish Bowes, demystify amateur radio for listeners, and uphold its reputation for impartial and critical investigative reporting.

Despite their disdain, network executives did carefully study the radio magazines. NBC president Merlin Aylesworth is a case in point. He once personally counted program highlights in *Radio Guide,* and upon discovering an equal number of highlights for NBC and the rival CBS, ordered his press department to provide details of NBC programs to the magazine. In the next issue, with fifty highlights for NBC and thirty-two for Columbia, he still found the ratio wanting, saying, "we should have two to one with two chains [NBC Red and NBC Blue] to their one." After examining five issues of *Radio Stars* page by page and finding "Columbia mikes predominating in almost every picture," he ordered so many publicity pictures with NBC mikes that a *Radio Stars* editor demanded pictures of "people rather than mechanical gadgets," complaining that on every NBC picture stars "wear a[n NBC] microphone under one ear or beneath their chins." Aylesworth found particularly compelling the magazine issues that glorified his own work and career. When he assured the editor that he was "delighted with the fine issue" of *Radio Stars* and found it "intensely interesting," he mentioned in particular "the fine article you wrote about me." He confessed to the *Radio Guide* editor, "I think you are showing a vast improvement in material and interest," then belatedly added, "I do not refer to the interview which was given me which I greatly appreciate."[17]

Insofar as fan magazines promoted the radio industry, its programs, and its policies, they formed a part of the radio production process. Although networks were often reluctant to endorse any fan magazine in public, their in-house publications recommended that sponsors advertise their radio programs in fan magazines to reach a captive audience of millions: networks calculated three radio listeners for every magazine sold because "a conservative estimate of families is at least three to the family" and "practically every reader is a person who owns or has access to a receiving set, and who listens in regularly."[18] Magazines printed publicity photos, puff pieces on artists, and stories based on radio serials. Both sides benefited. Networks got free publicity; editors got free publication materials, access to stars, and an inside scoop on production news and celebrity gossip.

Like Aylesworth, radio show producers and stars expected the fan magazines to satisfy their vanity. In 1935, Helen Sioussat was working with producer Phillips H. Lord as a liaison to J. Edgar Hoover for the *G-Men* program, which featured Depression-era bandits apprehended by the Federal Bureau of Investigation. While vacationing at Atlantic City, she overheard two women buying *Radio Stars* magazine because of an article about *Seth Parker*, another program produced by Lord. She picked up the issue as well. "There was one especially excellent picture of you—the one standing by the camera," she reported. "I would have sent you my book, but am sure you have this by now."[19]

Sioussat's attention to the pulp newsstand was not surprising, given that a few months earlier, Phillips H. Lord had used pulp editors as leverage in production. Lord was having trouble securing Hoover's official support for *G-Men*. Program supervisor John Ives asked Ernest Heyn of *Radio Mirror*, Curtis Mitchell of *Radio Stars*, and the editor of *Radio Tower* to wire "their frank opinion of the program" to Philips Lord. Heyn also wrote a "letter of criticism" to Joseph H. Neebe of Campbell-Ewald, *G-Men*'s ad agency. The editors' "extremely satisfactory . . . comment" helped Lord to appease Hoover in Washington. In negotiations between different radio industry agencies, fan editors' reviews held a prized place, alongside newspaper reports, telegrams from radio station managers, and endorsements from the Parent-Teacher Association.[20] Favorable reviews from fan magazine editors could sway official and commercial program sponsors.

The networks and magazines perfected the cross-marketing common among department stores, newspapers, movies, pulps, slicks, and comic strips in this period. Editors and program producers synchronized print and on-air tie-ins. In 1939, *Radio Mirror* editor Ernest Heyn wrote to George Tormey of the Blackett-Sample-Hummert ad agency. He asked to "work" into the script for an upcoming program a "knockout" portrait of Brenda Cummings, the star of the agency's soap *Second Husband*. That episode, he insisted, should air precisely one week after the magazine's release, because "by then we can be certain that complete distribution will have been made on that issue." At the time, *Radio Mirror* published a serialized story based on *Second Husband*. Heyn outlined his "grand plan." *Radio Mirror* prints Cummings' photo next to an installment of her story. A radio episode mentions this portrait, then the story refers to that episode, giving the listener no opportunity to miss either event.[21] Thanks to such precisely orchestrated campaigns, radio shows boosted their ratings while fan magazines jacked up their circulation.

When editors enthusiastically endorsed the radio industry, they procured network support. NBC dispatched eight hundred letters to its advertisers and sponsors endorsing *Radio Guide* because it could also include a *Radio Guide* editorial glorifying radio advertising. The *Radio Stars* editor got free network airtime to extol radio industry self-censorship and radio news services. Broadcasters rationalized, "of course he will get his magazine mentioned on the air but in doing so he will do a real institutional job for us." Eager to drum up network support, editors described their magazines to broadcasters as "good looking, husky periodicals devoted to the business of glorifying network broadcasting." Eager to raise circulation numbers, they solemnly promised listeners to "play no favorites" and "present the truth."[22]

Magazine layouts mirrored this promotional doublespeak. If editorials frequently spoke for the radio industry, listener sections conjured a democratic radio polity with a citizenry of listeners. Each year readers filled out "ballots" to choose their favorite performer, musical program, dramatic program, orchestra, team and announcer and sent them to *Radio Guide* or *Radio Mirror*. Magazine staff hand-counted the ballots and presented the results with great fanfare as if it were the outcome of a major political election. The magazine "acts merely as a clearing-house for your votes," *Radio Guide* editors assured their readers. "The sponsors who give you commercial radio programs and the network officials who pass on sustaining shows regard this poll as the infallible index of listener preferences. Stars who rate high in this election bear the stamp of the listener's approval—and they'll stay on the air." In fact, sponsors not only valued high standing in magazine polls but also these standings' effect on listeners. Mail summaries compiled by Kleenex for *The Story of Mary Marlin* recorded listeners' congratulations to stars who won magazine popularity polls. Likewise, networks not only followed these polls, but also used the results to advertise their stars and programs, reproducing the same democratic rhetoric. When NBC stars won in all six divisions of a *Radio Guide* poll, its publicity department announced the results of "this great nationwide election" in an ad in all the major trade magazines, including *Advertising and Selling, Printer's Ink, Broadcasting*, and *Tide*.[23] Magazine polls, and their claim that radio audiences directly controlled programming, validated all stages of radio production and distribution.

Together, editorials and listener sections tried to reconcile two conflicting ideals of listener participation. In the first, more congenial to advertisers, sponsors, and networks, consumers voted with their pocketbooks, buying the products of their favorite show's sponsor. When an editor railed, "Most pathetic of radio listeners, are those 'too proud' to make themselves and their wishes known. . . . Radio's 'box-office' cannot be checked as are theaters'; letters, votes, purchases reveal preferences," he equated shopping and voting. In the second, listeners were potentially both entitled and obligated to debate any and all topics pertaining to the industry. In several sets of close-ups in *Radio Guide*, a Polish window-cleaner, an all-American counter-girl, and a policeman appeared at work and in uniforms to declare their radio preferences. A German delicatessen proprietor posed with a butcher's knife, an Italian costume-finisher with a needle, and a secretary with a typewriter. These photo spreads at once portrayed fan magazines' imaginary audience—white laboring men and women across the lines of ethnicity—and declared listeners' right to voice their opinions to the radio industry directly. Such images promised to facilitate the direct face-to-face democracy of a town hall meeting when confronting a complex bureaucratic institution. This mode of democratic and egalitarian listener participation received its fullest expression in letters to the editor departments.[24]

If popularity polls conducted virtual elections of radio stars, letters to the

WHERE RADIO STARS AND FANS GET TOGETHER

Welcome to *Radioland's* open forum! Here's where radio stars, program executives, sponsors and fans have a chance to speak their minds on any topic involving radio. Join in the fun, don't pull your punches, and keep your letters brief! Address the Fan Mailbag, *Radioland Magazine*, 52 Vanderbilt Ave., New York, N. Y.

● "Mary Lou" Talks

Does this snapshot fit your idea of Showboat's *Mary Lou?* In real life, Rosaline Greene

Dear Sir:
It may sound bromidic—but it's true—your new letter department is most interesting. It is, indeed, flattering to know that you would like to receive a letter from me for inclusion in this column.
I hardly know what to write about (and then she went on for three or four pages!) unless it is to acquaint you with my plans for the coming season. I, naturally, hope to continue my work as "Mary Lou" on the Maxwell House Showboat Hour and on other programs, which are now in course of preparation.
My dad has a very delightful home in Bayshore, Long Island and the Clan Greene makes their annual hegira there about the first part of June. Commuting to New York, for the weekly stint at NBC, is a very simple matter and then, it's yoicks and away! for the return trek to Bayshore. And Bayshore, as you know, is right on Great South Bay and we are ardent boating fans!
At the present time I am readying a playlet—a sort of protean thing—for presentation in the vaudeville and de luxe picture houses. Don't expect to start this new work before late summer or early fall but will "double in brass"

6

and continue my broadcasting at the same time.
Thanks again for your interest. With kindest regards and salaams to RADIOLAND, I am,
Yours sincerely,
ROSALINE GREENE.

Congratulations on your theatrical engagement, Miss Greene. You might have explained, for the benefit of some of our readers who may not know it, that you are the "talking" *Mary Lou* of the *Showboat*, while Muriel Wilson takes the singing rôle.

● Children's Programs

RADIOLAND Magazine,
52 Vanderbilt Ave., New York.
Gentlemen:
Since certain publications have evidently given the impression that some children's programs have harmful effects on the young mind, I would like to take this opportunity of explaining the aims of the "Buck Rogers in the 25th Century" Program which is broadcast over a WABC-Columbia network. It is our purpose to provide constructive stimulation for the child imagination rather than anything which might inspire fear or suggest justification of even the least juvenile delinquency. Wholehearted approval, of both parents and Parent-Teacher Associations, leads us to believe that we have achieved our purpose. School boys who visit the studio know as a result of close attention to our programs describing the planes and other devices of the 25th Century.
I hope that this statement will clarify the opinion regarding at least one series designed to entertain boys and girls.
Yours very truly,
E. R. JOHNSTONE,
Author and director of the "Buck Rogers in the 25th Century" Program.

Unquestionably Mr. Johnstone has touched on a problem which concerns thousands of parents. The *Buck Rogers* program succeeds unusually well in giving a constructive slant to active young imaginations, but there are still too many "blood and thunder" children's hours whose hectic continuities follow the old bang-bang-heroine-on-the-buzz-saw formula. What do you parents have to say about it?

● Rooter For Rudy

Dear Sir:
A thousand cheers should be given Rudy Vallée for his unselfishness throughout his many broadcasts. He is always willing to step behind and give the other fellow the limelight on his programs. This seems such an unusual move in the entertainment world where everyone seems to try his darndest to keep to the fore.
He has "made" many of our present day favorites—thus opening the road to many in the movie world. He evidently maintains the policy "There is always someone better than myself."
P. E. VOYTEK,
52 Howe Street, New Haven, Ct.

Your sentiments about Rudy are shared by his fellow-workers in radioland, Mr. Voytek. Rudy is a superb showman whose philosophy is "the show's the thing."

● Tabloid Critique

Dear Sir:
I saw Lanny Ross in *Melody in Spring* and I was thrilled by his lovely voice and handsome appearance. I saw *Melody in Spring* five times, and Lanny is adorable. Who is the lady he is in love with and what does she look like? Has he a brother or sister and does he live with his father and mother?
I detest Bing Crosby and Rudy Vallée, and Frank Munn's voice is too old-fashioned and sounds like an old man. I like Conrad Thibault, at times, but I think Lanny is the best.
MARGARET,
Montreal, Canada.

Well, that's hitting straight from the shoulder! What do you have to say to that, you Vallée and Crosby fans? Lanny hints that he mourns a lost love in Sweden, but he hasn't described her for us. He lives alone in New York; no brothers or sisters.

RADIOLAND

6. "The Fan Mailbag," *Radioland*, August 1934. Library of American Broadcasting, University of Maryland, College Park.

editor columns served as radio's virtual public space. Democratic rhetoric buttressed both the magazines' circulation and their relations with the radio industry. Editors thus chose "The Open Circuit," "Voice of the Listener" and "The Reader's Voice" as titles for departments that invited listeners to "become ... contributing editors" and "speak their minds" to "radio stars, program executives, sponsors, and [other] fans" about "the sort of things you like to hear over the air, how you think broadcasting can be improved, just what is wrong and right about the programs you hear." A typical letters to the editor page included letters from readers and responses from broadcasters and magazine editors (fig. 6). Editors reported that these pages were popular, and listeners insisted that they be reinstated if editors let them lapse. Without the letter columns' "personal touch," one pulp publisher opined, "the editor and the reader would never enjoy that illusory companionship so vital to a magazine's success."[25] Editorial comments in readers' columns suggested that listeners governed radio. Readers' letters concurred.

Listener columns in fan magazines mimicked the collaborative production of pre-network radio, staging a primitive democracy of reader criticism. In the early 1920s, audiences shaped local station performances by mail. In the early 1930s, fan magazine readers shaped editorial commentary on network performances. The editors of listener columns would reverse their opinions about a performer's talents from one month to the next on the basis of readers' letters. In one typical review an editor confessed that in the previous issue he "stepped on a lot of toes when he found fault with Joe Penner, and the Penner fans rallied quickly to the defense. Fortunately," he continued, "[this month] Joe has improved." Immediately after listeners "jumped down his throat" for criticizing an actress, the editor declared that her "work has improved tremendously." In the very first fan magazines, editors sometimes published their own cranky letters under aliases to encourage spirited debate. Hugo Gernsback printed two incendiary letters in March and April 1927 under different names in the New York *Radio Program Weekly*. The first attacked, the second defended current programs. Both writers ended with identical appeals to "set me right" about all "things radiolly." Pulp editors prized this trick because veiled editorial taunts inspired many entertaining real letters. Both evaluation by popular vote and fake letters inciting a "public argument among the readers" constructed radio criticism as a town hall debate.[26]

Broadcasters' letters to the readers in these columns further reaffirmed listeners' power. In these letters, broadcasters usually explained themselves to the audience. With "the wrath of scores of listeners" hanging over his "defenseless head," writer Carton Morse hastened to explain that he did *not* "murder" Ann on *One Man's Family* because "by her death" her husband Clifford "gained an inner freedom." E. R. Johnstone, director of *Buck Rogers in the 25ᵗʰ Century*, averred that his children's adventure program did *not* follow "the old bang-bang-heroine-on-the-buzz-saw formula." Singer Maxine Sullivan did *not* think her "swing interpretation of a so-called classical song" could hurt the Scottish ballad "Loch Lomond." And bandleader Benny Goodman insisted that swing was *not* a "passing phase" or a "temporary fad." Putting broadcasters on the defensive, editors loved to publish angry listener diatribes like "You won't dare accept this letter," "I don't supposed you'll print this, but," or "Finally, see if you can't do something for the long-suffering listeners instead of playing-up indifferent so-called artists." Such staged battles proved editors' impartiality and made for exciting reading.[27]

Editors encouraged and organized the critical views advanced in published readers' letters. For pulp magazine editors, who sometimes published reader fiction in the main sections, "a good [letter] department balance[d] the issue" because it provided entertaining "story material" for free. Following the pulp tradition, fan magazine editors constructed muckraking controversies from a pool of reader letters. Editors' impartiality had its limits—they published a few letters against but none in favor of communism—but otherwise their interests meshed with listeners' desire to be published. Letter columns usually included from three to eleven letters per issue, or from forty to a hundred letters a year for a given monthly or weekly magazine. One-third of all letters were unsigned, or signed only with initials, pseudonyms, or common names. Of authors whose gender could be identified, two-thirds were women. Published controversies included the relative merits of swing and opera, or home and studio audiences. Also subject to debate were protracted serials, "blood-and-thunder" thrillers, and intrusive commercials. At times, readers generated topics that fell entirely outside the orbit of commercial radio's social prescriptions, in particular, those concerning alternatives to radio's corporate ownership and control.[28] Readers' letters, particularly those discussing advertising and larger social issues, point to listeners' perceptions of the radio industry and society that are not immediately obvious in fan mail to sponsors and networks.

The published letters unpack the abbreviated comments broadcasters recorded in fan mail summaries. In the 1930s, sponsors and ad agencies summarized fan mail coming to sponsors, networks, and radio stations, and forwarded it to radio writers to help them develop characters and storylines.

Over 800 letter summaries compiled by the sponsor Kleenex in 1935 for *The Story of Mary Marlin* writer Jane Crusinberry show that the assumption that listeners governed radio found its way into listeners' fan letters to broadcasters.[29] Private fan letters discussed some of the same subjects as published readers' letters. The parallels stand out even though Kleenex clerks briefly noted only statements and requests that they deemed directly relevant to the production process. But an opportunity to publish their opinions led fan magazine readers to elaborate more explicitly why they had decided to address the radio industry. Readers' letters articulated how Americans perceived the networks, the networks' responsibilities towards its audiences, and the audience's role in network radio production.

Like the editors of confession magazines who asked their women readers to contribute their own "true stories," radio magazine editors invited readers to "sit down and write your experiences," and to evaluate radio art in terms of their personal lives. Readers, particularly women readers, demanded that radio dramas adequately represent their personal experiences. One-fifth of the published letters dealt with radio drama; of those, 90 percent discussed the virtues of daytime serials from the point of view of a daughter, a housewife, or a mother. One woman listener loved *The Goldbergs* because its episodes "depict common, every day occurrences which might happen to any of us." Another thought that *Just Plain Bill* "could be an . . . appealing little sketch of real small-town life, if they'd eliminate the 'sob stuff.' . . . If I had a couple of long-faced boy friends like Dave and Cary," she concluded, "I'd give them both the air and go out looking for someone who knows how to laugh once in a while." Fan letters to broadcasters mirrored letters to magazines in that they also often related to drama characters as if they were real people. A summary of one letter to the *Mary Marlin* program stated: "Don't blame Eric for being in love with you. Would like to wring Elizabeth's neck." Another writer advised the serial writer Jane Crusinberry: "Michael should marry Mary – Henrietta could fall in love with Joe and Sally with Doe. Just for fun give Nora to Mac."[30] Encouraged to "vote" on stars and plots in magazines, these women felt entitled to express their wishes directly to writers and performers.

In letters to broadcasters the social and economic crises of the Depression and the War often came up indirectly, as in a letter from an unemployed woman who asked: "How long must I wait for Mary and Joe to go back to Main Street? Must go back to work next month." Printed letters also included offhand references to contemporaneous realities. During the Depression, too many raunchy radio jokes convinced one listener that "radio's censors must be on one of those sit-down strikes," while another argued that if a radio housewife "were really in need, she would be working for the WPA"—the Work Projects Administration. During wartime, one *Tune In* reader reported that her mother, "who works at a bomber plant, says that during rest period [the magazine] is her fellow employees' favorite," and another charged that, unlike the radio industry, "the movie industry seems to have passed an equal-rights amendment" because it had more women stars than radio.[31] Through such frequent asides, listeners perceived connections between radio, private affairs, and societal cataclysms.

Published letters explored exactly how listening spurred the physical and moral senses. Depression-era artists and critics insisted that radio always produced an active audience. Because auditors envisioned "more reality" than, say, movie viewers, actor Joseph Julian explained, the "creative expenditure of energy made the listeners collaborators in the truest sense." Many printed letters agreed. Radio "lets my imagination run riot," a typical letter blithely described, "I make my own scenes, faces, figures, and actions. . . . I make the radio voices bow to my mind and take the forms I wish them to."[32] Others offered a darker view of what an impressionable mind can perceive thanks to radio. A Kansas housewife related watching her son listening to a radio thriller:

> A boy and a girl, in terrible danger, were creeping up the stairs, hushing each other with very loud whispers. Suddenly some creature discovered them, and the screams and shouted warnings began, to end abruptly in a horrible silence. When this had lasted until one's nerves had nearly reached the breaking-point (it was wonderful timing), there were more screams and shrieks. At last there was a bone-crushing thud, a groan, and the program, mercifully, was over for that day. During all this, my son . . . sat, tense and actually pale, staring straight ahead and seemingly seeing the whole thing.[33]

Most immediately, this letter echoed contemporary debates about violent children's programs. But the writer also conveyed her frustration at being unable to control what her son felt and thought during the show. Potentially, letter authors worried, such a jacked-up mind could see connections and relationships between distinct social phenomena. Listeners who "live those stories" might imitate the hero and attempt to understand and control "the gigantic, mysterious forces known as The Law and Society."[34] Rarely explicit, the idea that radio inspired social imagination underpinned the social commentary in listener columns.

Letters to sponsors and advertisers, aiming to persuade rather than censure, rarely complained about commercials, and almost never attacked the commercial broadcasting system in general. A typical criticism in a letter to sponsor would begin: "Use both Kleenex and Quest. Could we hear less about them on the radio." In contrast, magazines printed a letter or two against protracted, "sneaked-in," and overwrought commercials in almost every issue. One-seventh of all printed letters concerned commercials. Out of those, less than six percent defended advertising, typically by insisting that "we must listen to commercials to get the stories." More often, listeners promised to go "on a sit-down strike against those sponsors who urge, 'Ask your mother to buy—.'" Commercial jingles were "just the thing to drive a defenseless listening audience to the movies." Sales talk took six minutes out of a fifteen-minute program, and ruined "the most thrilling part" of any radio story. "It seems that no sooner does the ghost start to walk or the hatchet to descend on the head of some shivering victim," one listener complained, "than I have to listen to a little drama within a drama about Mary Jane, who just learned a lovely new way to take spots out of dresses."[35] Such published listener opinions formed a counterpoint to magazine editorials glorifying radio advertising.

Listeners described radio's political economy as they perceived it. Announcers citing fan mail and product testimonials on the air should know that no one in the audience "is deceived by the spurious letters so obviously fabricated to their own purposes." Bill Hays has no right to announce, "The Pepsodent Company gives you your Amos 'n' Andy," because "all programs belong to the public. If it wasn't for the public there wouldn't be any Amos 'n' Andy, nor would Bill Hay have a job as an announcer." These listeners looked beyond advertisers' immediate claims to see the entire commercial structure behind a given radio broadcast. "I know that the cost of every program I listen to—and lots of those I don't hear—are added on to my grocery bill each week," one listener assured, "That money comes out of the consumer's pocketbook and nobody else's." These statements echoed a familiar and potent rhetoric of consumer activism, resurgent amid anticorporate sentiments inspired by the Great Depression and New Deal policies.[36] These letters undermined broadcasters assertions, based on fan mail to sponsors, that most listeners considered the commercial broadcasting system natural and inevitable.

Magazine editors printed letters proposing both risible and reasoned economic solutions. Studio audiences "are essentially part of the show, and . . . should demand remuneration as members of the cast, and eventually apply for membership in Actors' Equity." Philanthropists should endow radio programs like colleges, for the purpose of "informing" and "inspiring" listeners. Several readers suggested a radio tax.[37] One listener proposed a wholesale reform for "the development of American music" and radio: "Why not have the government impose a small tax of not more than one dollar a year on all radio receivers? With the proceeds, a national department of music, under federal control could be established, which would have the following objectives: The development of promising singers and musicians; and the sponsoring of local symphonic and opera companies."[38] These published letters described alternative forms of broadcasting where the public would have more control over radio production than advertisers.

Some letters to radio magazines discussed the distribution of power not only in the radio industry, but also in society at large. "My years of observation and personal experience," began one *Radio Guide* reader, "have convinced me that most of our hard times and consequent suffering are caused by narrow-mindedness and short-sightedness on the part of those few eminent bankers, high financiers and masters of industry who insist on having 'whole hog or none.' They build such huge reserves and take such great profits that the worker and consumer have no show." The writer further argued that "the worker is the greatest consumer" and suggested that "A carefully arranged radio program, permanent and frequent, depicting the suffering, deaths, broken homes and lives, with the underlying cause thereof, would in time build public sentiment to force a change, slow but sure!"[39] This letter is unique in the way it asserted the authority of working-class consumer culture over network corporate culture. Yet this reader only took to its logical conclusion the way listeners appropriated and redefined promotional populist rhetoric of radio fan magazines, and the invitation to rely on the authority of their own experience, to assert their right to shape broadcasting as an art form and as an economic system.

Because letters to magazines belonged in a published discourse, readers' public statements extended the limits of the norms governing the listeners' role in radio production. The public debate between magazine editors and readers set the terms of the relationship between listeners and the corporate broadcasting industry. Magazines built informal bonds of accountability and entitlement between broadcasters and listeners. Listeners debated how the radio industry and society should be structured. This debate started out from an assumption that listeners have the power to control broadcasting, and led readers to expect that network broadcasters are accountable to their audiences. Listeners then enacted these expectations when they confronted broadcasters directly.

4

Listeners Write the Scripts

In the Jazz Age, vaudeville actors moving into radio frequently put on minstrel skits—humorous, often derogatory, imitations of Southern black speech and singing. Among all of them, Wendell Hall stood out as the first national radio star. Originally a small-time Chicago vaudeville performer, Hall started in radio in 1921. His popular tours of radio stations, organized by the Ayer ad agency for his sponsor, the National Carbon Company and its Eveready Batteries, made him a national attraction before the network era.[1] By the 1930s, Wendell Hall was no longer popular, his old-fashioned style having been eclipsed by crooners like Rudy Vallée, big-time vaudeville comedians like Jack Benny and Fred Allen, and especially radio serials. Audiences ignored his performances and instead tuned in daytime "soap operas," "strip" adventure shows, "continuity" evening dramas, and "situation" comedies like *Amos 'n' Andy*.

Network audience departments, advertising agencies, and sponsors compiled summaries of fan mail and forwarded them to serial writers to assist them in preparing radio scripts—sonic "comic strips," each with an open-ended storyline, a set of recurring characters beset by everyday problems, and an intimate setting, a small town or an urban ethnic neighborhood. Statistical surveys showed that by 1930, 40 percent, or 12 million, of all American homes had radios; by 1935, 70 percent did; and by 1940, 86 percent, or 40 million homes, listened on average four hours daily, not counting 6.5 million radios in cars. The first ratings services emerged in 1930s. Yet four years later a study found that the mail response was "the most available and universally used indicator of audience reaction." Women and poor listeners, surveys showed, wrote most of these personal letters, expressing "attitudes" in common with other listeners, but unique "in their ability to transgress the barrier between themselves and the impersonal broadcasting company."[2]

In 1938 Gertrude Berg, producer, writer, and performer on a popular radio serial, *The Goldbergs*, published a thank you note to her listeners in the fan weekly *Radio Guide*: "It has ever been my contention that listeners write the scripts for radio serials. I do not mean by this that radio authors like myself are the recipients of ready-written scripts, all set for production. But I do mean that listeners writing to tell me of themselves, their problems and the real lives they live, which I try to portray in my scripts, give me invaluable assistance in my work."[3] To flatter her listeners, Berg described a new, relatively open production process, where radio writers relied on the informal knowledge of the audience derived from fan letters rather than scientific ratings data.

Radio writers invented serial radio genres in collaboration with listeners. In early radio, engineers had shaped sound technology with amateurs' help; during the network era, writers created storylines relying on fan letters. The serial production process was less open than Berg would have had her listeners believe. Network bureaucracies were more likely to thwart listeners' demand for reciprocity. Occasionally, fans wanted something to happen to the character, and writers made it happen. More often, letters set the boundaries and parameters of what radio characters could do and say. Most of the time, they produced no direct effect at all. New serial formats inspired moral economies rooted in solidarities of gender and class but also in racial exclusion. Nevertheless, listener correspondence put limits on the power of corporate bureaucracies, allowing scriptwriters and stars to gain some autonomy from network executives.

The minstrel tradition provided the initial ground for the invention of radio serials. The transformation from vaudeville performances to the success of the first national serial hit, *Amos 'n' Andy*, is a case in point. Of the over 200 letters Wendell Hall received between March 1923 and March 1926 and preserved in his archive, nearly one-third concerned the minstrel performances he gave on the radio. These came mostly from his white listeners, many of them recent migrants from the South to the North, or from rural to urban areas. New radio styles may have emerged in response to such letters from white listeners across the United States, who were eager to participate in the "love and theft" of black Southern culture.[4] Listeners' migration experiences transformed the old-time minstrel vaudeville skits into blackface serial stories of migration like *Amos 'n' Andy*.

Hall's minstrel dialect stories were often directly lifted from popular vaudeville skits. Other blackface radio performers presented no stories, just humor and songs lifted directly from vaudeville. Such skits used jokes that were published in collections such as *Darktown Jokes* from 1913, along with collections of jokes about the Jews, the Irish, the Dutch, and the Chinese. These blackface jokes in turn borrowed from popular nineteenth-century minstrel theater performances. A retired vaudevillian from Iowa wrote that Hall's song "Thirty-first Blues" reminded him of playing Chicago's high-priced vaudeville house on Thirty-first Street. "Lord," he added, "how I would like to put on the grease paint once more."[5]

Like many nineteenth-century minstrel performers, Hall created an ambiguous racial identity on the air. It is possible that some listeners, like one four-year-old from Indiana who demanded to hear the "Red-Headed Niger," for a brief moment assumed he was black. "Good thing you told us you were a white man and had red hair," a New Jersey woman wrote, "for your singing makes one think of the old darkies in Virginia, as we just came back from there." A listener from Kansas called him a "white boy," recognizing his gall in venturing into another's cultural territory. A Baltimore listener mocked Hall's fake Southern origins: "[I'd] wager that when your Mammy crooned to you, down south in Chicago, her lullabies were praises and adoration."[6] If nineteenth-century theater audiences had focused on visual racial imitation, these letter writers enjoyed decoding the racial sonic clues Hall used to build his radio persona.

Many migrants from the South to the North used Hall's blackface skits to convince themselves and others of their own expertise in the black vernacular. Such interpretations were more common among migrants to the North than among residents of the South—Tennessee, Washington, D.C., or Oklahoma. A bookkeeper who had moved from South Carolina to Detroit felt "competent" to congratulate Hall: "There are a great many who attempt the negro dialect but few come anywhere near the perfection that you give it." An insurance investigator who had migrated from Georgia to Brooklyn, New York, testified that Hall had "the negro dialect down to perfection." Another savant of what he called "the genuine darkie as seen south of the line" claimed he alone could "appreciate the true and capable impersonation of the darkie vernacular and crooning singing."[7] These listeners flaunted their Southern identity as a measure of Hall's ability to provide them with a nostalgic trip to the slaveholding plantation South. This is not to say that all migrants from the South thought this way, but that those who responded to Hall's performances tended to like them due to such interpretations.

Conversely, some urban workers infused Hall's minstrel skits with egalitarian meanings. Once, Hall read a letter on the air asking him whether he was white or black. In response, the wife of a weaver from Rhode Island wrote: "The very idea of that lady wanting to know if you were white or colored. What's the difference as long as she was being entertained and enjoyed it? We all have paid good money to hear and see colored entertainers while she was getting her concert free. I suppose your southern drawl threw her completely off the track, and she could only picture you with a dark face when she heard you speak." Her family came from Ireland and her neighbors, like her husband, were mill workers, with families from Ireland, Belgium, France, and Canada. Yet she requested, "won't you please send me a photo of yourself, regardless of color?" Such interpretations may have stemmed from a different urban context of interaction between black and white neighbors, and are particularly remarkable because of the segregation common in Northern cities in this period. A Connecticut resident of a similar neighborhood of mill workers reported having black neighbors with red hair—a wood worker's family that lived a few blocks away—and made fun of other listeners' "inference . . . that a red headed fellow must necessarily be white."[8] Northern laborers enjoyed Hall's vocal versatility because his racial ventriloquism reminded them both about boundaries between acceptable white and black performance on the air and about the racial divisions in their own lives.

Black listeners took pains to distinguish between Hall's commendable performance style and distasteful traditional minstrel content. A Washington, D.C. black listener informed him: "Your numbers were enjoyed until you gave your jokes on the 'negro.'" The wife of a Baltimore hardware store clerk reported her friends' dismay upon hearing "Mr. Hall refer to our race (Colored) as Darkey after I had just told them of his exceptional ability as a broadcasting artist." Hall replied to her: "Sorry I was offensive. I will see that it won't happen again. I appreciate your thoughtfulness in writing about the matter."[9] These listeners made distinctions between the old-time material and the new, radio-inspired, style of Hall's performances.

Hall's listeners, across class and region, argued that modern experiences required new interpretations on the radio. While some listeners approved of Hall's traditional minstrel jokes, others asked for new material. Many sent Hall minstrel jokes of their own, hoping that he would perform them on the air. One young woman offered Hall a story "from true life" that put old blackface themes in a new urban environment. She wrote: "A friend of mine, an employee of a music shop, was waiting on a negro girl she said she wanted to buy a record, it was 'By Request.' The girl look for the record and found she dident have one by that name and turning to the negro ask where she heard it, and she said, 'You know the orchestra at the Colonial Theater played it and when they finished the man said, "That was by request," and I just wanted to see if I could get it.'"[10] This story asserted white superiority, yet it described a situation likely to happen to many migrants from rural areas into the city, regardless of race.

Such stories of migration in the long run may have inspired the narrative format of *Amos 'n' Andy*, which told of two poor black Southerners who moved to New York City and started a taxicab company. The main difference between *Amos 'n' Andy* and Wendell Hall's performances was the personal relationship listeners formed with the fictional characters. Developing the initial "sonic comic strip" format, Charles Correll and Freeman Gosden, the white creators and performers of *Amos 'n' Andy*, modeled their radio stories on intimate local experiences. Whereas Hall impersonated anonymous stock characters from minstrel shows, Correll and Gosden created two recurring characters with biographies and aspirations.

Twenty-nine letters from 1929 have survived in archives. *Amos 'n' Andy* still inspired smug letters from Southerners congratulating the authors on their accurate rendition of black dialect. The show, however, also elicited a completely new type of letter. A timekeeper at a plant in St. Joseph, Michigan, wrote a long letter reporting that workers talked of Amos and Andy "as if they were realy some neighbor they knew." Comments included: "I hope the widow Parker sues Andy again he's such an old fool," and "you know that big stiff Andy you just watch & see if Amos gets the Co. on its feet, the piker will try & get all the credit."[11] Such comments were typical in letters and articles about the show.

Amos 'n' Andy's serial narratives seemed universal at the same time as they encouraged racial ventriloquism. Charles Correll argued that their "comedy is human . . . The Negro characterization and dialect merely point it more." At the same time, performers' voices, "colored" according to region, class, ethnicity, race, and even species, marked radio localities. Given that production manuals required radio voices to convey "the character's age, social status, nationality, character, eccentricities, and mood," the ability to sound off in a particular dialect implicated performers in the class, gender, and racial hierarchies linked to a particular way of speaking. To match radio's varied sound effects technologies, performers in this period developed a set of recognizable voice imitations including "Negro," Brooklynese, Cockney, French,

German, Irish, Italian, New England, Southern, Spanish, and Western.[12] These artificial voices aspired to represent audiences across the boundaries of class, ethnicity, gender, and region.

The radio serials' intimacy depended on local listening to the national program. In the 1920s, people congregated to listen to news broadcasts, prizefights, and baseball games. A decade later, neighbors also got together regularly to catch up on their favorite serial shows—comedies, dramas, and thrillers—a popular format that *Fortune* magazine in 1932 declared "the closest approach to a generic radio art." Fan magazines lauded *Amos 'n' Andy* as "the first daily 'comic strip' on the air." Every day at seven, this program drew together crowds of people across class, racial, and ethnic lines, around radio stores, barber shops, friends' porches and living rooms. These diverse audiences—60 percent of all listeners, sometimes more than 40 million people—usually experienced the show without leaving their familiar environments. According to Waldo Freeman, son of black composer J. Lawrence Freeman, early in 1930 people gathered around Harlem's radio stores and barber shops, even in the rain, "until the entire sidewalk was blocked." These black listeners sometimes thought they heard a black team, Flournoy Miller and Aubrey Lyles, instead of white performers Correll and Gosden. At the same time, Correll and Gosden kept in contact with their black listeners, particularly in the early 1930s. They collected clippings of responses to their show in the black press, and participated in parades in black neighborhoods such as Chicago's South Side.[13]

The audible boundaries of such local listening communities extended to home radio sets heard on the street. Ralph Latta, a cotton mill worker in Piedmont Heights, North Carolina, chose to walk from his brother's to his girlfriend's house when *Amos 'n' Andy* was on, because "if it was summertime, or a lot of times in wintertime, . . . people played their radios pretty loud, [and] I could listen to that all the way." This way of listening spanned popular shows everywhere: by 1940 one could catch "practically the whole *Grand Ole Opry*" walking down the block of a small town like Honea Path, South Carolina.[14] These sounds elicited a powerful sense of a common experience with listeners within one's earshot, a sense of a "national pastime" as a routine neighborhood activity, and, by extension, of the modern industrial society as a set of immediate local relationships.

In the admen and writers, this sense of intimacy created expectations of profits. William Benton, an assistant general manager of the advertising agency Lord and Thomas, remembered walking in 1929 from his office in the Palmolive Building, a new Art Deco skyscraper in the business district in Chicago, to his apartment on "a hot muggy night" and listening to "colored voices leaping out into the street, from all the apartments." The very next day, he claimed, he convinced his boss, Albert Lasker, "to buy 'Amos and Andy' for Pepsodent." Carlton Morse, creator of the long-running evening serial *One Man's Family*, recalled "walking down the streets of a small town listening to the theme music for the old *Amos 'n' Andy* program clicking on in first one house and then another. Neighbor after neighbor would hear the theme music coming from next door and run to turn on his own radio." This experience convinced Morse that a strong opening musical or sound-effect "signature" is essential for a radio serial. Morse set out to build a national audience by appealing to listeners' local loyalties: "The characters of a serial must have the same fascination, the same interest-appeal to a radio listener that friends and acquaintances in a neighborhood have for an old resident. The radio public has the same likes and dislikes for radio personalities that it has for the people next door, the grocer down the corner, the friends across the street."[15] In the 1930s, a sociological study *Middletown in Transition* reported that when "one walked down Middletown's residential streets in 1935 everywhere the blare of radios was more pervasive than in 1925." Like a modern newspaper reader, who upon seeing others peruse the same morning edition in barbershops and subways imagined a synchronous national community, advertisers and writers took such reports of local simultaneous listening as evidence of an American national radio market. The tension between fan letters and program ratings as tools in the radio production process mirrored the tension between intimate local listening and national broadcasting.[16]

Soap operas epitomized the tension between reciprocity and scientific management of audiences. "The soaps" advertised cheap household brands like Ivory Soap specifically to female audiences. Soap producers set up "writing factories," where several writers under the supervision of ad agency producers like Frank and Anne Hummert, or just one prolific author like Irna Phillips, churned out five fifteen-minute scripts a week per show for several programs at once. Radio writers required listener response to knock off a daily dose of "commercial appeal." Rudolf Arnheim, a German émigré scholar at Columbia University's Office of Radio Research, concluded in his 1941 study of soap opera making: "Letters in which the listeners express approbation or protest are carefully studied. Telephone surveys determine the approximate size of the audience of each serial. On the basis of such data, . . . the plots, the characters, the settings of the serial are made to order."[17] In this the soaps

perfected and streamlined a mode of production common to the entire industry.

Ratings and fan letters competed for importance in this process. Networks, ad agencies, and production companies had subscribed to ratings
services since the early 1930s. Like the Starch survey of 1928–29, the first
systematic ratings service, which emerged in 1930, was designed to buttress
sponsored radio and the networks. Pioneer radio researchers conducted telephone interviews. The earliest agency, Crossley, Inc. performed and tabulated
the Cooperative Analysis of Broadcasting "telephone recall" surveys, jointly
sponsored by the Association of National Advertisers and the American Association of Advertising Agencies. Interviewers made calls four times a day,
asking about the preceding three to five hours of listening. Crossley generated
biweekly reports from 1500 calls to families chosen by rental classifications in
thirty-three major cities.[18] The more successful ratings service, Hooper, Inc.,
began in 1934 and continued into the late 1940s. Hooper employees called
people up and asked about the shows they were listening to at the time of the
call. Results were then calculated statistically. Both Crossley and Hooper sold
their reports to networks, agencies, and sponsors.

For all their scientific rigor, these ratings services neglected to ask the
most pertinent questions. Let us suppose, for example, that a Hooper interviewer caught a male "head of household" one evening with his radio on. She
then asked a series of questions. "Were you listening to the radio just now?"
"To what program were you listening, please?" "Over what stations is that
program coming?" She did not ask whether he liked a program or not; or
whether he listened to it often. Maybe he liked only part of it. Maybe his wife
or children were listening, and he just happened to be in the room. And what
about people who had no radio and went to a friend's house to listen? What
about those who had no telephone, or simply refused to pick it up? Telephone
ownership actually declined during the Great Depression—by the end of the
1930s over 80 percent of Americans owned a radio but only 40 percent had a
telephone. Such details were impossible to take into account, but they could
ruin final survey results. In 1946, a study concluded that the Cooperative
Analysis of Broadcasting ratings agency had folded because its interviewers
waited for only four rings before classifying a home as "not occupied" and
"not listening," while the more successful Hooper interviewers waited for six
rings. With such a wide margin of error, the exact audience value of a given
show remained a mystery.[19]

Network managers and radio researchers shared skepticism about scientific measurement. When Frank Stanton, the future CBS director of research, wrote to the networks in 1932 to offer his services as audience researcher, NBC was not interested. CBS did offer him a job setting up their research division, yet when he arrived his boss told him not to unpack his furniture "because we might not go ahead with this idea." In 1934 a survey by Frederick F. Lumley, a researcher at Ohio State University, found 732 studies of radio audiences, by local advertisers, commercial stations, nonprofit stations, and universities. Many of them were based on small-scale interviews or fan mail analysis. Nonprofit researchers focused on education rather than selling products; they "asked different questions," as Stanton put it. "I always thought they felt there was something dirty about money," he remembered about academics like Princeton professor Hadley Cantril, the co-author of an influential 1935 study, *The Psychology of Radio*, that had critiqued commercial broadcasting. As late as 1935, Herman Hettinger, marketing professor at Wharton and author of several radio advertising manuals, lamented "the lack of standardized information regarding . . . listener data."[20]

Agencies, networks, and writers perceived and used the audience differently as fan mail and survey data circulated within the radio industry. When networks sold time slots and ad agencies shopped programs around they marketed aggregated commodity audiences—time slots, and the programs in them, cost more or less depending on the rating. Commercial broadcasters' practice of selling quantified listeners like cattle was known beyond the industry and the trade press. In 1939 a cartoon by Carl Rose, who drew for the *New Yorker*, *Saturday Evening Post*, and the leftist magazine *PM*, pictured an NBC representative barging through the door of an advertising office leading a lassoed-in crowd of "radio families" (fig. 7). Ratings services sold their reports primarily to networks and agencies and sometimes denied writers full access to the numbers. In 1938, Emmons Carlson, an NBC promotion manager, informed writer Irna Phillips that Cooperative Analysis of Broadcasting prohibited NBC from passing on CAB program ratings to their clients, including Phillips and her advertiser, Proctor & Gamble. The penalty would be the loss of their subscription.[21] Because ratings provided a convenient way to make program policies without closely monitoring shows, network executives, most of them men, leaned towards the ratings and scientific analysis.

Once a show passed into production, however, the audience, no longer a commodity, comprised individual letter writers—writers and program managers continued to use direct communication from individual listeners as an

"Mr. Jones of NBC to see Mr. Wilmott, with 3,500,000 MORE radio families!"

7. Carl Rose, "Mr. Jones of NBC to See Mr. Wilmott, with 3,500,000 MORE Radio Families," August 1939. George H. Clark Radioana Collection, Archives Center, National Museum of American History, Smithsonian Institution.

everyday corrective to ratings. As late as 1938, H. A. Batten, head of radio activities at the Ayer advertising agency, confidentially informed his employees, "A precise method of gauging the quantity and quality of the audience . . . of radio programs, has not yet been devised. We subscribe to [ratings] surveys and watch them carefully, but we do not consider them useful as indications of commercial effectiveness." The production system instead rested on letters and what Batten vaguely called "our experience and knowledge of all forms of advertising." In 1937, Sidney Strotz, a manager in the NBC program department, sent writer Irna Phillips several complaints about *Today's Children*: "Evidently your dear listeners are not entirely pleased with the development of the story and I am simply passing the criticisms on for your information." He added, "kindly return the letters to me after they have served your purpose."[22]

At the time, the famous and prolific Phillips wrote and produced *The General Mills Hour*, made up of a quarter-hour of music and three interrelated soap operas—*The Guiding Light, Today's Children,* and *The Woman in White*. When writers like Phillips where subjected to network or agency pressure, it was most likely accompanied by a pile of mail. When H. King Painter of Knox Reeves ad agency passed on to Phillips what he called "a rather remarkable collection . . . the sort of thing you want to have"—thirty-eight copies of letters referring to a speech, a Memorial Day talk, and conversation from *The Guiding Light,* he added: ". . . from the mail, I suspect that listeners to *The Guiding Light* prefer the Tim and Clare Lawrence story to the Reverend Richard Gaylord–Jake Kransky–child delinquency story. Possibly the use of these two story lines, which really have very little to do with each other, may account for our falling off in Hooper; although, as you know, the CAB shows exactly the reverse picture, and the ratings, as usual, are not a clear indication of anything."[23] Because letters provided a familiar and convenient way to interpret the dubious and contradictory ratings numbers, soap writers, most of them women, preferred the epistolary trial-and-error process to rigid rules and regulations.[24]

Such uses of letters proliferated during the early network era. Before the 1930s, local station managers and artists, often working without a sponsor, used letters informally. The new commercial network system incorporated analysis of letters into its bureaucracy. Radio production agencies—networks, ad agencies, sponsors, production companies, and affiliated stations—maintained audience mail departments and routinely forwarded fan letters to one another. To encourage listeners to write, program managers organized contests, provided free offers of sponsored products, and aired special appeals to the audience. Broadcasters used fan letters, an early study discovered, "to locate the audience, judge popularity of programs and stations, and find out about audience habits and activities." Comedians like Jack Benny asked listeners to "keep writing those letters telling us what you like, what you don't like, and what you want. You're the boss and I'll get it for you—even if I have

Q-62
DOC
10/10/38

Seth Parker Fan Mail Analysis - Week 10-2-38

	No. Received	No. Product Mention
1. General Fan Mail	157	56
2. Fan Mail Kicks	22	2
3. Requests for Tickets	9	0
4. Requests for Photos	2	0
5. Requests for songs or poems	12	0
6. Requests for words to songs or poems	6	0
7. Requests for Sunday Plan	99	2
8. Program Suggestions	4	0
9. Requests for jobs	3	1
10. Requests for autographs	2	0
Total	296	61

Copy to:

Patterson
Mabry
Lord
Slate

8. "Seth Parker Fan Mail Analysis," October 10, 1938, Phillips H. Lord Collection, American Heritage Center, University of Wyoming.

to keep my writers up all night to do it." Production companies like that of Phillips H. Lord, which produced the religious music program *Seth Parker*, had clerks copy selected "fan mail complaints" and classify letters as "General Fan Mail," "Fan Mail Kicks," "Program Suggestions," and requests for songs, poems, photos, autographs, tickets, and jobs (fig. 8).[25] This sense of a face-to-face relationship, shared by writers and listeners, created bonds of reciprocity between writers and audiences. It conveyed to writers the authority to contest network and agency decisions, and to listeners the authority to direct writers' narrative choices.

Occasionally, program producers fulfilled listeners' demands at the expense of sponsors' preferences. In 1934, when Penn Tobacco Company picked up *One Man's Family* to promote its new product, Kentucky Winner cigarettes, NBC program producer Don Gilman assured a disgruntled Michigan listener that "the viewpoint of Henry Barbour and his family will be unchanged, and no doubt will more or less present, without modification, the same principles which would have been presented without a sponsor." NBC managers agreed to meet about this matter, but in the meantime, a month later, the program left Kentucky Winners' sponsorship and continued as a sustaining program until the next season, when it was picked up by Standard Brands. NBC permitted "no cigarette or medecine sponsorship" of the program in the future. A station in Cleveland received 153 calls when the papers announced that the program would be discontinued, and in Asheville, North Carolina, a station manager reported that "the switchboard at WWNC had been swamped all day as a result of the cancellation."[26]

A few months later, when *One Man's Family*, now promoting Royal Gelatin for Standard Brands, was about to be moved to an earlier time, Gilman wired to insist on later rebroadcast for the Pacific Coast. He urged that "something has to be done" to respond to "the million" men and women who "are already writing letters protesting early hour both to us and to newspapers," and that "client feels that he is being harmed already by the antagonism expressed toward the early hour six weeks before it takes the air." To network executives who argued that the earlier time would do fine for the sponsor's "house hold brand," Gilman retorted: "while we can consider sponsors we have also to consider audience and programs."[27] NBC executives opted to air the program twice, and made sure that the J. Walter Thompson agency did not interfere with the production of the show.

Sponsors used letters to advise radio writers. In 1935, when *The Story of Mary Marlin* was just beginning national broadcasts, George Isaac, Director of Radio at the Lord and Thomas advertising agency, forwarded to Jane Crusinberry "a log of the voluntary mail" to the program compiled by the sponsor, Kleenex. Kleenex managers had ordered that these logs should "incorporate the idea which seems to dominate the letter." Isaac added: "the mail has been picking up recently, which indicates an increasing interest in the current plot."[28] With fifteen-minute *Mary Marlin* episodes broadcast every weekday, it was easy to trace audience reaction to even minute changes in the storyline, and modify the narrative to mollify or entice the show's constituency. The Kleenex staff listed the name, address, and date received for each letter, and noted every mention of the sponsor (fig. 9). Between July and December 1935, Crusinberry received summaries of over 800 letters. Of these, a third requested a copy of a poem or a song heard on the radio, a quarter requested a change in broadcast time or station, and the remainder suggested changes to the plot, characters, and sometimes the whole style of the show. Most authors addressed their letters directly

9/26	Toby B. Sunshine 1918 S. Sawyer Ave., Chicago, Ill.	To Mrs. Crusinberry - Mary should marry Peter.
9/26	Helen Handgis 1152 Maplewood Ave., Ambridge, Pa.	New listener - wants synopsis of first part of story.
9/26	Rose Nehill 506 Grand St., Troy, New York	"Please call the ladies' antion to the fack of speaking loweard" (Evidently they should speak a (little louder)
9/27	Mrs. Walter Kelly 40 Arnold Ave., Amsterdam, N. Y.	Any way to get story? Heard first part is working now.
9/27	Anonymous Brooklyn, N. Y.	"We were in hopes Mary Marlin would have gone over a cliff".
9/27	Emily Hill Main Street, Dallas, Pa.	Most human and fascinating skits on the air. Each of the cast to be praised - Swears by Kleenex and Quest.
9/30	Mrs. Neele Moore 1037 Alvarado Los Angeles, Calif.	Please broadcast story 8:00 or 8:15 A.M. So we can hear it before going to work.
9/30	Elizabeth Everett 17 W. Central Blvd., Palisade Park, N. J.	So glad you are going to review story - lost out during school last year.
9/30	Mr. & Mrs. Tony D. Clark 3063 Santa Ana St., South Gate, Calif.	Welcome to Vinton Haworth - doubly interesting to Myrt and Marge fans.
9/30	Mrs. Constance Johnson Bayhead, N. J.	Story is floundering. Mary be- coming affected - laughs too much. Dont know whether Sally or Mary heroine. Hope Joe and Mary are united.
9/30	Hattie A. Waltman 2226 13th Street, Boulder, Colo.	Glad story is to be reviewed. Leave music out - blots out some words.
9/30	Mrs. B. Olbeter Chicago, Ill.	How many more times are you going to review the story. Every time story becomes interesting start all over again.

9. *The Story of Mary Marlin* fan mail summary, September-October 1935. Jane Crusinberry Papers, Wisconsin Historical Society.

to Mary Marlin or other characters on the show, rather than writing to the sponsor or writer, thus betraying a strong personal connection to these fictional people.

Because listeners advised the characters directly how to act, the writer could create and resolve situations on the basis of this advice. Mary Marlin separated from her unfaithful husband Joe in the early episodes and vacillated between going back to Joe or divorcing him and marrying one of her many suitors. Kleenex employees summed up in one or two sentences advice from Boston: "Divorce Joe, or if you must go back, make him wait and suffer;" from Philadelphia, "Don't go back to Joe. Choose between David and Peter Fortune;" and from Los Angeles, "In spite of David's fineness, don't marry him—the home should be unviolated." Most listeners enjoyed the sexual tensions arising from Mary's and Joe's separation, but also wanted to hear about traditional small-town family life. They particularly liked the initial small-town Midwestern setting of Cedar Springs, Iowa. When Crusinberry moved Mary Marlin to "Paradise Pent House" in New York to make her a reporter, listeners declared "Cedar Springs episodes most interesting," asked for "More Cedar Springs," and not to "spoil story with Paradise Pent house."[29] By keeping Mary and Joe alternately close to or further from reconciliation, and by shuttling the action between Iowa, New York, and later Washington, D.C., Crusinberry held the audience's attention until 1945, when the serial ended.

Between 1935 and 1944, Crusinberry successfully used her fan mail to take control over daily production decisions. In addition to the letter summaries, Crusinberry preserved over 300 complete fan letters spanning the years between 1935 and 1947, with many of her own responses. Women wrote at least four-fifths of both the summarized and the full fan letters. In 1945, when agency-imposed changes failed to improve *Mary Marlin*'s dismal ratings standing, Lord and Thomas would cancel the program.[30] But in 1935 Crusinberry preserved control over her work despite disappointing numbers, because the agency and the sponsor preferred to wait while *Mary Marlin* slowly climbed the ratings. The show remained among the top ten for the following six years. When the Lord and Thomas agency suggested in 1935 that *Mary Marlin*'s numbers had declined, Crusinberry listed "the following points in the letters from listeners to our program":

> Letters from New England States, by the dozens, complaining that they can no longer hear the program because of interference of a new station.
>
> Letters signed by many names, saying they can no longer listen to the program in California because of the change of time. The program is now too late.
>
> Letters by the dozens from Iowa and the middle west, saying they cannot listen because the broadcast comes at noon when they must be getting dinner on the table for husbands and children.
>
> Dozens of letters—constantly—from the East, complaining of the reception. These are listed *every* week.[31]

Statistically, fifty-eight letters complaining of poor reception provided a sample far inferior to phone rating surveys of major American cities. Yet Crusinberry successfully argued that low ratings demonstrated nothing about listeners' assessment of the program.

Even letters specifically sent to inform the networks about technical reception problems provided a vivid contrast to the bare numbers in the ratings. Kleenex typists reported that at Frewsburg, New York "host of admirers cannot hear you on W.H.K.," whereas a listener from Gridley, California, "never misses broadcast - characters speaking after program talk too low." A typical letter declared *Mary Marlin* the "best program on air" despite the fact that "WABC programs cannot be heard during day." A simple aside could convey a sense of listeners' education ("Please call the ladies' antion to fack of speakin loweard"), daily routines ("Postpones shopping until 12:45 WELI crowding out WABC"), cultural milieu ("Ardent listener of program. Polish Station insists on crowding out story"), favorite scenes ("Static was so bad did not hear 'confession!' Can't wait from day to day"), and even peculiar listening habits ("Wish you were back on NBC WGY not at all clear. Take my lunch and almost sit in radio").[32] Detailed and open to interpretation, letters contextualized the listening process and gave writers the means to defend their stories against unfavorable statistics.

A "gift economy" of sorts accompanied the daily interaction between broadcasters and listeners. Audience gifts predated sponsored radio. As early as 1920 Westinghouse engineer Frank Conrad reportedly received over 500 records from listeners after an offhand on-air appeal for phonograph records to use for programming on his amateur station. By the 1930s, grandiose gifts from listeners were a staple of network publicity. Mail contests, less scientific but far more dramatic indicators of program popularity than ratings, so impressed sponsors that they often refused to make contest results public "because they did not want their competitors to know just how good it was. . . . most everybody on the air," one agency executive explained in 1930, "does his best to keep the facts from getting to anybody in tangible form." Contests organized to measure the appeal of early serial shows *Amos 'n' Andy* and *The Goldbergs* brought in floods of mail, which provided vivid anecdotal evidence of radio's popularity. A 1932 report by the NBC Statistical Department on "the appeal and popularity of *The Goldbergs*" spent three and a half pages analyzing fan mail in response to an on-air offer of Beetleware tumblers, and one paragraph on the Cooperative Analysis of Broadcasting ratings reports. Harlow P. Roberts, advertising manager for Pepsodent, the program's sponsor, wrote in *Broadcast Advertising* for April, 1932: "The offer was last broadcast nearly two months ago and we are just now mailing out the last of the premiums, because the manufacturer couldn't keep up with our demand."[33] Such reports narrated rather than quantified audience enthusiasm. In 1935 the Pepsodent Company ran a contest for *Amos 'n' Andy* and received an unprecedented two million pieces of mail, which the Pepsodent staff was hardly equipped to handle. NBC statistician T. J. Sabin described to E. P. H. James, the network's sales and promotions manager:

> They have a staff of 240 employees, working in two shifts, opening and sorting, addressing and mailing maps. They have . . . University graduates from 31 Universities in the United States, Canada and Europe reading every contestant's letter and classifying them.

A separate room contained "unusual" contest entries, including "a double bed spread quilt, . . . pillows, and embroidered banners." Another correspondent reported: "The volume of mail has required the Pepsodent Company to take over temporarily the entire eleventh floor of the Palmolive Building and to employ 600 girls in three shifts of 200 each continuously for the past eight days."[34] Despite the commercial nature of network broadcasting, listeners treated radio as a sphere appropriate for personal economic relationships.

For their part, sponsors and agencies used every opportunity to provide listeners with any program-related materials they requested, including song lyrics, poems, and photos of the cast. As late as in 1943 William Ramsey, the company's promotion executive, vividly described to Crusinberry how listeners would surely resent copyright restrictions set by a major company like

Procter & Gamble. Their thoughts, according to Ramsey, would run something like this:

"Procter & Gamble must own the copyright and like all big business they don't think enough about people like me to go to the trouble of filling my requests." When this happens these same eight women who asked for "The Last Frontier" tell their friends how thoughtless and unpleasant Procter & Gamble is—then one of the friends who has some other little grievance works up the story and passes it along to her circle of friends. Before very long Procter & Gamble has lost considerable good will among quite a group of people.[35]

Thus Crusinberry's objections notwithstanding, the eight *Mary Marlin* listeners received copies of "The Last Frontier," Joe's love letter to Mary. When NBC could not send a poem or speech or a song due to copyright restrictions (for example Irna Phillips's "The Lonely Heart") they looked to the author "for some ways to answer these letters—preferably to tell them that it is published and that copies can be bought."[36] In such small ways, broadcasters bent their copyright rules to meet listener expectations.

Crusinberry consistently encouraged interpretations and advice in her replies to letter writers. A schoolgirl wrote, "Some of the girls in our club . . . call his friendship with Mrs. Underwood, an affair, and say he isn't good enough for Mary, but I think he is very human." Crusinberry replied, "You are quite right—Joe's friendship with Eve is not an AFFAIR—and I should know if anyone does—don't you think so?" Listeners wrote, "please don't write Joe Marlin out of the script" and "if [Joe] goes to Russia, I'm afraid the fine story will be lost." Crusinberry replied, "you need not worry," and "he is not leaving the cast as you will see as the story progresses." She was not alone in following advice from listeners. In 1943, even a traditional exponent of ad agencies' assembly-line production, Anne Hummert of the Blackett-Sample-Hummert ad agency, upon receiving "a lot of very bad letters" about the characters on *Second Husband*, ordered her writers to "use the Monday script to effect a reconciliation between Grant and Brenda."[37] In their correspondence with listeners, the sponsors and writers, like Berg in her letter to *Radio Guide*, claimed to share the authorship of radio stories with their fans.

Advertisers and sponsors insisted that during contests the show should evolve in a dialogue with listeners. In 1935, when Lord and Thomas had just picked up *Mary Marlin*, the agency, in order to "gauge the feature commercially," decided to run a contest "to continue for two weeks on the subject of whether or not Mary shall return to Joe." The launch of the contest was scheduled for February 9. In mid-December, George Isaac sent specific instructions to Crusinberry: "In order that the audience may be sufficiently acquainted with the pros and cons and that the interest may be at a peak, both characters should, of course, be back in Cedar Springs the first weeks in February and should be debating the situation themselves." Isaac instructed Crusinberry "to deal actively and intimately with the subject in as many interesting ways as your ingenuity can devise." The agency was "enormously interested in getting maximum returns" because they needed to estimate the size and composition of the initial *Mary Marlin* audience. This endeavor required the storyline to anticipate, encourage, and incorporate listener response.[38]

In June 1944, *Today's Children* character Bertha Schultz, the daughter in a German family living on Hester Street in New York, stood trial for murdering her lover Tom. Announcer Charles Lyon had asked listeners to send in their verdicts. H. King Painter of the Knox Reeves ad agency forwarded about a hundred fan letters to Irna Phillips. Fans unanimously believed Bertha innocent, but variously pegged every other character as the culprit, including her sister, the butler, the park policeman, and the elevator man. Some suspected a woman who had screamed when she touched the poker, the murder weapon. Most got the broadcasters' clue, pointing to the stranger who had called several times on the day of the attack.[39]

In the end, Phillips and Painter incorporated listeners' views. During the trial on *Today's Children*, producers called studio audience members to the mike to suggest possible solutions to the crime puzzle over the air. Painter called the trial letters "a remarkable flood of mail" and "just the reaction we want." Delighted to have reached listeners "smart enough" to notice the persistent caller, he asked Phillips to "pay off those telephone calls in some way." Just two weeks earlier, Painter had lamented, "radio fans just do not write the way they used to." Now, he delighted at fans' enthusiasm and finely argued opinions, and praised the many script elements that elicited and incorporated plot suggestions from listeners.[40] Phillips responded to listeners' wishes. Bertha Schultz was acquitted. A few months later she married a stranger who had been posing as her long-lost brother. *Today's Children* fans shared responsibility for her fate.

Women prefaced their letters to Bertha's lawyer John Murray—a fictional character—with disclaimers like "I am not a lawyer but I am wondering" or "While I cannot attend court in the Bertha Schultz trial, it occurred to me

I might write a letter" and then proceeded to dissect the details of the case. Willie Mae Jackson, a black woman working as a waitress in a hospital in Little Rock, Arkansas, insisted that the woman the elevator man took up before Bertha arrived looked much guiltier. She knew because for over a year she had required the story as much "as a noon day meal." "Hope this letter will be consiter as a dayly listener," she emphasized her credentials again in the end.[41] Listeners laid out their ideas for plot development as a gift to their favorite show. In return, they expected broadcasters to take their views into account.

Soap writers' reciprocal relationship with listeners hardly revolutionized the view of the social order presented in the serials. In Latin America in the 1990s, activist television writers would use the popularity of soap operas to disseminate information about social equality, abortion, AIDS, and women's rights. Nothing comparable happened in depression-era America. Yet perhaps because writers promoted reciprocity in their correspondence with listeners, the form of daytime serials had political possibilities and promoted social justice. *Rita Quill, Union Member,* produced by an International Ladies' Garment Workers' Union local, was a success, while serials produced to tout corporations were mocked by *Variety.* To women, soaps showed the value of the practical knowledge of knowing *how* to perform a given task, something that could not be conveyed in writting but had to be learned by trial and error—an approach shared by midwives, skilled laborers, and early radio engineers. Fans reported to sociologists that serials taught them how to deal with everyday problems, saying, "When my lawsuit was on, it helped me to listen to Dr. Brent and how calm he was," or "When Clifford's wife dies in childbirth the advice Paul gave him I used for my nephew when his wife died." At the same time, when serials emphasized the authority of women's experience, they also gave them an opportunity to stay complacent about the social inequities in their own lives.[42]

Because, unlike Correll and Gosden, most serial producers implicitly invited response from white audiences only, white Southern listeners could claim cultural authority based on their presumed knowledge of black vernacular. As late as 1935, a former Southern belle, Mary Blakeslee, wrote to Jane Crusinbery, asking for a job on *Mary Marlin*, impersonating a "negro mammy." Blakeslee had married an engineer and radio salesman from San Francisco and moved with him to Hollywood from Georgia in the early 1930s. Her grandfather Willis A. Hawkins, a slaveholder, had voted for secession as a delegate from Georgia and fought on the side of the Confederacy during the Civil War. Yet in her letter she claimed that Hawkins, as "a former

Georgia Supreme Court Judge," could "naturally help with some real negro sayings." In the era of the slave market, slaveholders' identity had stemmed from their slaves' abilities and value.[43] Now white Southern migrants' identity as Northern radio listeners often depended on the skills and culture of their former black neighbors.

Such stories help to explain why some listeners took fictional racialized spaces literally. In 1940 Jane Crusinberry made Mary Marlin a senator and moved her to the Washington, D.C., area. Crusinberry picked an actual house in Alexandria for her character and gave it a fictional address on Princess Street. Soon after, Lynne Hofstetter, a stenographer from Alexandria, wrote to demand that Crusinberry move Mary Marlin to "a nicer neighborhood," because "the darkies have virtually usurped" that part of town.[44] This demand seems incongruous to us, but it is symptomatic of the ways many American listeners perceived, and helped construct, racialized radio soundscapes. Born to immigrant parents, Hofstetter had changed her name from Lenchen to Lynne to sound more American. By refusing to distinguish between her own racially segregated world and the women's world of soap operas, she further reinforced her sense of belonging in a national community of white listeners.

Although Mary Marlin's lifestyle clearly upset the racial boundaries Hofstetter was accustomed to, Crusinberry used other, favorable, fan letters as an excuse not honor her request. Mrs. Grace Squires, wife of an electrician at a farming implements factory in Batavia, New York, had written to Mary Marlin a month earlier, describing how she asked her daughter, a United States Housing Authority worker, to take her to see the house: "do take me to Alexandria, so I can see where Mary Marlin lives, for I would know the little grey house with the green shutters! and daughter said, but mother, that is a radio story. Well, of course I know it, but you are so real to me for I have wept with you Mary Marlin."[45] Eager to shore up the continuity between the show and this listener's personal experience, Crusinberry replied, "I am so sorry you didn't go to Alexandria when you were in Washington, for even though Mary Marlin is only a story, there are many things in it that are true, and one of them is the little grey house with the green shutters. . . . I don't know who lives there but to me it was Mary Marlin's home. So, if you ever go to Washington again, go to Alexandria and you will find it."[46] One can only imagine a farmer mother and her social worker daughter looking for a Senator's grey house in a depression-era black neighborhood. Given such enthusiastic response, Crusinberry refused to move Mary Marlin out of the house. "There will be very few of our audience who know it," she argued, and her heroine is "so well established" on Princess Street that "it wouldn't do to make a change."[47] Recurring voices, sound effects, running gags, and landmarks such as Mary's house established intimacy, continuity, and recognition in depression-era radio. As broadcasters negotiated these sound, narrative, and moral aspects of serial localities with listeners, the same intimacy that defined the racialized radio soundscapes reinforced the reciprocity between broadcasters and listeners.

Radio serials addressed women primarily as consumers, housewives, and mothers. When the J. Walter Thompson agency hired writer Irna Phillips to "pump up the CAB" ratings on their daytime shows, she wrote: "Let's get back to plain Mary Marlin, the plain, average, everyday woman in a small town who loved her husband—a story that in many ways served as a mirror for a daytime audience in which their own lives were reflected." Phillips was wrong in that family life was not the sole occupation of women listeners. In 1938 soaps *Mary Marlin*, *Ma Perkins*, and *Betty and Bob* were most popular among listeners earning under $2999 a year. Working women remained fans even though these programs aired in the middle of the working day. "Arrange lunch hour as often as possible to hear program," one *Mary Marlin* listener reported in 1935, "Shame it does not have an hour when working people can hear it." Others managed to listen even during working hours—a sign painter reported remembered seeing a Lithuanian bar owner's wife turn on a little radio to listen to *Dan's Other Wife* and *Road of Life* every day before mopping the floor.[48]

But Phillips was right in that many of these working women expected Mary to end up in a marriage where the wife kept the house for her breadwinner husband—a popular depression-era ideal according to social surveys like the 1937 *Middletown in Transition*. Some women claimed to have average lives even when they had professional experience and ambitions. The wife of a custodial officer at Leavenworth Federal Prison wrote to Crusinberry, "We are average people," then continued, "I write a Women's Page column for a labor paper, (A.F. of L.) in St. Joseph, Mo. . . . I want to write fiction and be successful." At Niagra Falls, a housewife, "like millions of others," offered her services as a stay-at-home scriptwriter: "its impossible for me to go to Chicago, Illinois now with the children in school, and my husband and home to take care of." A grocer's wife wanted Mary reunited with Joe, who at the time was lost in Siberia: "is he going to be found & when, could you tell me? because that is one day I don't want to miss it, I don't want to be taking Care of the store while the owner goes fishing." Letter summaries made the contrast even more obvious. "How long must I wait for Mary and Joe to go back to Main Street?" a clerk at Kleenex rendered "Betty" from Buffalo, New York. "Must go back to work next month."[49] These responses made for conventional plot resolutions but allowed women to negotiate authority with broadcasters based on their daily lives.

By the 1940s, even these limited relations of reciprocity became the exception rather than the rule. Radio genres had standardized, and networks and ad agencies came to evaluate programs primarily by ratings averages and market segments. Armed with established genre formulas, producers no longer invited audiences to participate in the creation process, but only allowed them to express taste preferences. Writers lost their relative autonomy and listeners were reduced to voting on a limited number of existing programs, whereas earlier they had been able to shape radio shows' conception and meanings.

5

Measuring Culture

In 1938, philosopher Theodor Wiesengrund Adorno arrived from Germany to assume a half-time position at the Princeton Radio Research Project, funded by a grant from Rockefeller Foundation. The project's director, Paul Lazarsfeld, invited him to study listener mail to classical music programs, conduct interviews with music industry executives, and in general supervise the music division of the project. "When I was confronted with the demand to 'measure culture,'" Adorno later remembered, "I reflected that culture might be precisely that condition that excludes a mentality capable of measuring it. In general, I resisted the indiscriminate application of the principle 'science is measurement' [and t]he prescriptive right-of-way given to quantitative methods of research, to which both theory and individual qualitative studies should be at best supplementary." Adorno despised the industrial methods of cultural measurement such as ratings and music popularity charts. His contempt cost him his job. Three years later, the Rockefeller Foundation refused to renew his grant. In 1941 he left the project and joined his friend and colleague Max Horkheimer in Los Angeles to resume work at the Frankfurt Institute for Cultural Research, relocated from Germany. In 1944, Adorno and Horkheimer wrote a book that has since become a classical critique of American commercial cultural industries.[1] Yet Adorno had more in common with commercial broadcasters than either his critics or his followers have recognized. Because Adorno believed that cultural industries deprived their audiences of their ability to think independently, his work at the Radio Project showed how this same belief underpinned scientific audience research.

Adorno's work at the Radio Project, from 1938 to 1941, marked the time when the "closed" radio production process based on ratings and marketing surveys took over. By the 1940s the Princeton Radio Research Project, more than any other academic radio project, had transformed communication research methods in both universities and the industry. The short-lived notable exceptions, such as Adorno's critical theory, or cultural analysis based on in-depth interviews practiced by another project scientist, Herta Herzog, prove all the more the common trend in the academy and the industry toward scientific measurement of culture. At the project, Adorno advanced a critique of empirical methods that got him fired, but he also described key ways of thinking about radio listeners that sustained market researchers attempts to pacify the audience. Market research shaped broadcasters' sniffish conceptions of their audience, their standardization policies, and their ratings-based production process. Social scientists, and their audience research techniques and theories of audience behavior, justified the new "closed" radio system based on ratings and marketing surveys.[2]

Adorno's elite European cultural upbringing prepared him well for the tradition of cultural hierarchy in American radio. He grew up happy in Germany, in a family of an affluent wine merchant; both his aunt and his mother were accomplished musicians. He began to study philosophy at fifteen and music at twenty one, and considered becoming a composer. His future colleague at the Frankfurt Institute, Leo Lowenthal, noted young Adorno's "admirable material existence and a wonderfully self-confident character." In America, his self-esteem attracted several elite critics, notably the composer and music critic Virgil Thomson, who shared with Adorno a disdain for radio music education, found his articles on music "of absorbing interest," and excerpted them in his Sunday column in the *New York Herald Tribune*. Radio managers', advertisers', and marketers' self-confidence derived from less illustrious but still considerable education and income that made them conscious of the gap that divided them from their typical listener.[3]

At least since one advertiser opined in 1901 that his public was "woman, pure and simple," the whole profession believed that women spent between 80 and 85 percent of all U.S. consumer dollars. During World War I, U.S. Army intelligence tests and other well-publicized psychological studies defined the "average mental age" of Americans as between nine and sixteen years old. As a result, most executives agreed with S. H. Bliss, manager of WCLO, Janesville, Wisconsin, that "fourteen-and-a-half-year-olds . . . not only represent 90 per cent of today's radio audience but 90 per cent of the purchasing power of these United States." By 1940, in an in-house questionnaire, most interviewers for the authoritative *Fortune* opinion survey first declared all poor respondents culturally and intellectually inferior, then ranked all lower-income men "superior in intelligence" to upper-income women. Poor women, argued radio writer Max Wylie in 1942, listen because they cannot reason: "being unanalytical, they cannot figure out what is really the matter with them; and being inarticulate, they cannot explain their problem even if they know what it is."[4] Scientific, rational, and instrumental professionals faced an irrational and emotional lay public.

Black listeners were accorded network executives' disdain as well. Managers considered black listeners' complaints excessive and fulfilled them reluctantly. In 1935, John Royal directed the NBC Music Department to "eliminate the word 'nigger' wherever possible" with an aside: "Of course, these darkies put a lot of pressure on us and they are sometimes too exacting, and there are certain songs where the word 'nigger' must be used." A few years later, NBC reminded its sponsors and program producers that all songs using words "darky," "nigger," and "coon" were barred from the air because these "always bring complaining letters from negro listeners." The NBC Music Department employees shared the opinion that some numbers, such as nineteenth-century minstrel Stephen Foster's songs or Oscar Hammerstein's "Old Man River," had to be regarded as "well-known" and "well-loved" classics that should be exempt from the ban, that the complainers were "one or two small negro societies" and "an isolated group," and that "all intelligent negroes do not resent these words which are used affectionately in such songs." Nevertheless the Music Department put these songs on the list of restricted numbers and asked its production people and announcers to eliminate such words "to save us the embarrassment of further complaints."[5] Ratings reports and research studies used by networks mirrored such disdain in that they excluded black populations in their studies.

This snobbish view of listeners was matched by the critics' contempt for populist radio genres. *Current History* argued that advertisers and sponsors prefer radio serials because "the comic strip" appeals to listeners' "15-year-old intelligence." *Commonweal* thought that the desire to reach the "creature with the fourteen-year-old mentality" inspired the "vaudeville formula" in radio. And *Harper's* insisted that a sponsor's "wife, the maid, the chauffeur, the stenographer, or the office boy" inspired radio to take direction from "the movies, newsstand thrillers, and popular fiction."[6]

These preconceptions shaped an expressive and direct style appropriate for a modern non-visual broadcasting medium. To compose scripts "on the level of 13-year-olds," the Federal Bureau of Education commanded, "Write out your exact wording. Begin with one or more striking statements. . . . Anecdotes, short and clearly to the point are good." The Philips H. Lord Productions company instructed writers on the sensational true crime program *Gang Busters* to "make all explanations clear and concise" because "age mentality of average radio audience is eight years," Radio manuals advised: "delete unnecessary words . . . The use of any but simple words and phrases has a tendency to disturb the listener, who may be wondering what is meant instead of listening to what follows." Such a concrete, terse, and vivid style conformed to the contemporaneous efficient modernist style in architecture, fashion, and design.[7]

In the 1930s, while writers corresponded with listeners, program producers felt trapped by popular tastes. In a typical statement, advertiser Chester Bowles in *Printers' Ink* defended radio jazz and serials: "We can't give the farmer's wife and the grocer's daughter a taste for Beethoven and Brahms; we can't make them like Shakespeare or Greek tragedy. . . . If people don't listen, they don't buy. They'll listen only to what they like." While serving on the NBC Program Planning Board in 1934, Willis Cooper fumed to Sidney Strotz, head of NBC's Chicago Bureau, about a proposed serial likely to appeal "to the crude emotions of the shopgirl type of listener." Because such shows "have attained such popularity," he continued, agency executives purchase these programs, all the while insisting "that the public is composed exclusively of high-grade morons." This show "that pretends to be a section of life," he predicted, "will sell cheap products to vulgar people" who "sit entranced before the radio," read "sensational pulp magazines," and "shed tears over the excapades of John Dillinger and his long-suffering molls."[8] So Adorno's low opinion of radio listeners mirrored long-standing prejudices shared by marketing researchers and network executives.

Adorno came to participate in radio research at a time when American social scientists were romancing the radio industry. Since the early 1930s, the industry had made use of academic studies like Herman Hettinger's marketing research on Philadelphia audiences and George Gallup's survey for Young and Rubicam on listening to commercials. Network executives even "kept in touch" with the nonprofit Institute for Education by Radio at Ohio State University. Most scholars favored "administrative research," which aimed to preserve, rather than transform, the existing broadcasting system. The Princeton Radio Research Project brought radio industry professionals and social scientists together to study "the value of radio to listeners," and to make educational and commercial American broadcasting more effective. Funded by the Rockefeller Foundation, it was organized in 1937 by Princeton psychologist Hadley Cantril and the director of research at CBS, Frank Stanton. Cantril and Stanton invited Austrian sociologist Paul Lazarsfeld to direct the project. The Radio Project later moved to Columbia University, became the Office of Radio Research, and eventually evolved into the influential Bureau of Applied Social Research.[9] Looking for raw data, funding, and legitimacy, the project's founders quickly made themselves useful to the radio industry. The project established radio production as a scientific endeavor.

The founders planned the project's research hoping that the industry would eventually adopt their scientific methods. When the Rockefeller Foundation considered the project in 1936, its administrator John Marshall charted the broadcasting industry's knowledge of its audiences against the project's research program and found the industry wanting. "On the question of program *preferences*, no systematic analysis has been attempted by the broadcasters," Cantril concurred, "Program rating services are available by subscription, but they are, for the most part, inadequate because the information is not available by important breakdowns such as sex, age, income, and interest groups." The industry "guards" what little data is available "and is inclined not to seek out other findings." Pollster George Gallup agreed: "Since the results have no immediate commercial value, it is extremely unlikely that such a project would be undertaken by industrial concerns." And Stanton reported that when he "urged on CBS . . . the desirability of making a study of listener interest which would indicate on what their liking for programs rested . . . the proposal was turned down on the grounds that it would have no immediate commercial value." A scientific radio research project, founders hoped, would "set a style which the broadcasters cannot afford to disregard."[10]

From the outset the Radio Project established close ties to the industry. Although NBC, CBS, the Mutual network, and the National Association of Broadcasters had no plans to expand their own audience research, they "agreed to underwrite administrative expenses and projects to a total cost of not less than $120,000 during the first two years of activity." After research began, the industry cooperated closely with social scientists and took advantage of audience studies conducted by the project. NBC opened its files to researchers for work on the *Town Meeting of the Air* show, musical programs, and news broadcasts. After NBC Chief Statistician Hugh Beville analyzed the Cooperative Analysis of Broadcasting ratings data to determine the "social stratification of the radio audience," NBC ordered one hundred copies of this Radio Project study, and CAB sent out "many thousands of copies . . . in pamphlet form . . . for their own promotion." Research assistants on the project went on to work for networks and ad agencies, such as CBS, Mutual, Dun and Bradstreet, McCann Erickson, and Market Research Company of America. Industry professionals Beville and Stanton penned articles and edited books for the project, while Lazarsfeld gave speeches at NAB conventions. To get additional funding, Lazarsfeld conducted surveys for organizations such as CBS and the NAB.[11] From 1937 through the late 1940s, academics and broadcasters shared data, funds, workplaces, and approaches to audiences.

As the project adapted its research to the industry's demands, it perfected its quantitative methods. In 1936, the project's founders had imagined their research as an alternative to slanted and abbreviated commercial studies. The project should be "highly centralized," and "coordinated"; the data "closely knit" and "well-integrated"; the researchers "technically trained" and "not bound by any rigid commercial or educational sponsorship." Researchers used all available sources—an inventory of materials used up to 1939 listed fan mail, interviews, questionnaires, panel experiments, case studies, program analysis, rating scales, and even telephone traffic records. Yet from the outset project leaders believed that fan mail provided a "poor sample of total audience" and personal interviews could at best provide "leads for further statistical studies." By 1946, the project's predominantly statistical methods served the needs of the industry. Lazarsfeld and NAB President Justin Miller sent out to broadcasters the published results of a statistical survey conducted jointly by the NAB and the National Opinion Research Center of the University of Denver and ana- lyzed by Lazarsfeld at the Bureau of Applied Social Research. Lazarsfeld offered the industry "good figures" and "serious looking tables" to show that "people like[d] radio" and "only a small proportion of listeners resented commercials." He suggested that broadcasters use his work to "gain a lot of prestige in your community" as "a cultivated industry."[12] The Radio Project had morphed from an independent critical agency to a branch of the broadcasting industry.

Adorno's career at the project shows that the more broadcasters used statistics, the less they trusted theoretical and qualitative studies. Adorno refused to study how listeners' "reactions" can "be measured and expressed statistically" because in this case "the radio industry's conception of its mis- sion may become transformed into the fundamental presuppositions of the social researcher." Instead, he explained how listeners' attitudes and behavior were "conditioned by the structure of society as a whole." Initially, the indus- try supported his "social critique" of radio music as an "unorthodox" experi- ment. In May 1938 Adorno set out to examine NBC music programs to flesh out "certain concepts of the social critique, such as 'deterioration,' musical trademarking, [and] raised entertainment." Beville and Ernest La Prade of NBC's *Music Appreciation Hour* considered Adorno's conceptual classification "rather elaborate" but his approach "a reasonable although an extremely technical one." They recommended that the network "cooperate with this study as far as possible" and provide "a list of all musical compositions during the weeks he plans to study." The station WOI of Ames, Iowa, forwarded Adorno a set of fan letters to its classical music program, *The Music Shop*, and Stanton arranged for him to interview several radio music professionals. In 1938 and 1939, Adorno trained students, supervised research tasks, printed articles in the project's publications, composed a book-length manuscript, and circulated papers among broadcasters and social scientists.[13] While the production process was still in flux, broadcasters entertained alternatives to their emerging scientific methods.

As scientific management technologies became more common, Adorno's theoretical analysis seemed superfluous. Lazarsfeld refused to circulate Adorno's manuscript for fear that broadcasters would object to the author's "disregard of evidence and systematic empirical research." Radio professionals requested Adorno's interview questions in writing to prevent him from misrepresenting their ideas, and complained to Stanton, "Why do you waste my time talking to this mad man?" In December 1939 an NBC music expert informed Walter Preston, Jr., assistant to the vice president in charge of programs at the network, that Adorno's paper "On a Social Critique of Radio Music" was "so full of factual errors and colored opinions, and its pretense at scientific procedure is so absurd in view of its numerous arbitrary assertions, that it is hardly worthy of serious consideration." In 1940 and 1941, despite Lazarsfeld's repeated requests, the Rockefeller Foundation did not renew Adorno's fellowship because his social critique had no "remedial utility" for the broadcasting industry, and thus did not serve the Foundation's goal of bringing educators and broadcasters closer.[14] When Adorno started to work at the project, audience measurement technologies still coexisted with more intuitive and personal methods of radio production; when he left, audience ratings had become more and more commonplace in the industry. Empirical science justified the primacy of ratings.

The Radio Project redefined "listener response" for the radio industry—from open-ended interpretations to knee-jerk preferences. When early broadcasters had announced contests for the best letter "telling the truth" about the station and its programs, they took care to ask no specific questions to make sure that "the listener expressed entirely his own opinion." Initially, project scientists adopted the same catholic approach. Scholars working on the *War of the Worlds* panic in 1938 lamented every lost resource, including 900 free-form letters sent to the *Newark Ledger* "essay contest for experiences attendant to hearing the broadcast" but thrown out two weeks before the study began.[15] But the project's best-known research tool, the Program Analyzer, a "clinical" electronic instrument that Frank Stanton and Paul Lazarsfeld invented in 1940 and nicknamed "Little Annie," measured "likes" instead of open interpretations: listeners pressed a green button when they liked bits of a prerecorded broadcast, and red when they disliked something. In two years, the Radio Project slipped from extended personal interaction with listeners to electronic measurement. Its codified interview techniques such as the analyzer, expeditiously adopted by the industry, ensured that listeners could no longer participate in the creation process.

As researchers deciphered minute-by-minute reactions to shows, they learned to ignore listeners' expressed opinions. When Herta Herzog, Lazarsfeld's wife, began to work at the Radio Project, she insisted that to find out "what the program really means" to listeners scholars need to follow up "statistical hunches with searching interviews determining the personalistic meaning of an appeal to a given listener." Between 1937 and 1940, she closely analyzed interviews and quoted listeners at length, relating their reactions to their beliefs and experiences. She speculated on why listeners identified with soap characters or quiz contestants, and she used empathy so successfully as an interview technique that some respondents called her "dearie" during sessions. Taking advantage of her Austrian accent, she feigned a foreigner's ignorance of the American broadcasting system to elicit listener analyses of the industry. In the early 1930s, hundreds of local studies by small stations, university researchers, and their students followed a similar approach, interviewing listeners a hundred or less at a time and focusing on particular communities: housewives, Midwestern farmers, textile workers, or Asians in San Francisco. Authors apologized that their tentative results had to await a more systematic analysis. Yet Adorno later articulated their method when he explained his own way of writing. A man forced to learn a language in a foreign country derives nuanced meanings from particular contexts; this serves him better than memorizing a dictionary. "Just as such learning remains exposed to error," Adorno argued, "so does the essay as form; it must pay for its affinity with open intellectual experience by the lack of security." Thus an essayist deliberately "abrogates" certainty and proceeds "methodically unmethodically"—a style that makes Adorno's writing about radio music valuable even when he misses some of its context. Herzog, in a different way, also looked for such practical knowledge, always specific and aware of its own fallibility.[16]

Herzog got little support for her methods from senior researchers, who valued only standard questions and answers that could be translated into statistics. She conducted and interpreted several interviews for the study of the *War of the Worlds* scare, but got little credit for her analysis and did not get paid for some of her work. In 1941, she proposed a study based on in-depth interviews of child listeners, but it never happened. By 1942, Herzog was directing the Program Analyzer Department at the McCann-Erickson ad agency. Whereas in her early work she had listeners analyze their encounters with commercial radio, at the agency she plied her empathic skills to discern why subjects pressed green or red buttons twenty minutes into the program.[17]

As scientists mastered new investigative techniques, they expanded their interpretive authority over listeners. Theodor Adorno's classification of listening "types," used in project interviews, shored up this new hierarchy. He described eleven verifiable musical types, from "the musical-expert" to "anti-musical," and placed himself in the expert category. Several decades later, Adorno would affirm "the utter obscurity of what we call 'musical experience.'" But in 1939 he still believed it was a fallacy to separate "esthetic judgment and tastes from scientific research." It was an "emp[i]rical fact that . . . the teacher is able to convey to his disciple a very definite and clear-cut idea about right and wrong in the construction, say of music." Having had the privilege of that kind of education, Adorno could prove the superiority of even frivolous "early 19th century waltzes" to "present-day jazz . . . in very definite technical terms." The less fortunate philistines resided not just on the wrong side of education and class, but also of ethnicity and gender. A particularly pernicious "emotional" listening type represented "bad individuality in its isolation, impotence and social unconsciousness" and could be found "particularly often among people of Slavic origin, also among younger female persons." Armed with this typology, researchers set out to interview lay listeners.[18]

Radio, they discovered, allowed listeners to transform existing works and genres with no regard for established norms. The dial and the volume knob granted listeners too much control over radio music. The listener could "turn off the music whenever he pleases. He can arbitrarily supersede it—in contrast to the concert hall performance where he is forced, as it were, to obey its laws." Listeners could override composers and conductors to emphasize different parts of symphonies. "When I sit in the front seat of the car and listen to music," an enthusiastic listener described, "I can turn it loudly or softly to suit the passages. You know you can sit there and just tune it in at the proper places when you know it should be." Listeners could mix and match radio music based on personal experience rather than systematic musical training. A piano teacher preferred classical music because she applied it "to conditions in life," but also "liked swing if it were smooth and if the attack and release was good." A real estate salesman preferred "old-time tunes" on the radio but liked a classical concert because "the lightning effects were very impressive and I liked to watch the execution of the violinists in unison." "I like to dance and therefore like swing music," a housewife reported, then added, "also like cowboy songs." These informants' eclectic definitions of good radio music included "Blue Danube Waltz," John Philip Sousa's "Stars and Stripes Forever," and boy sopranos in the Cathedral in Washington, D.C.[19]

Analyses based on Adorno's taxonomy declared such unruly listeners passive and incompetent. According to Adorno, the "emotional" type was "passive" and "introverted" because "when listening to music he does not bother so much about music as an objective entity, but is always ready to translate it in terms of his own psychical life." Based on this analysis, one interviewer, Hazel Gaudet, declared a twenty-seven-year-old clerk from Minneapolis "an emotional listener of the passive type" and "an introvert" because when listening to wedding music she thought "of possibility of my own wedding" and "of the bride coming down the aisle." A piano teacher reacted to music "in a passive introverted emotional way" because she claimed classical music "leaves me in peace and brings my problems to satisfactory solution." Adorno considered himself immune from such labels and later remembered with disdain how "a young lady" at the project—perhaps Gaudet herself—had inquired whether he was "an extrovert or introvert," trying to fit him into "rigid and preconceived categories."[20] Adorno forgot that the categories were his own.

Afflicted with passive "commodity listening," lay Americans, Adorno believed, could not affect production because they could not perceive the larger social structures that affected a radio program. He argued that each musical performance interpreted, expressed, and constructed a social order. A live performance of Beethoven's Fifth Symphony, for example, inspired "the feeling and the awareness of the possibilities of a community where at the same time the drives and desires of the individual are fulfilled and brought into a perfect equilibrium with the needs and necessities of society." But only a properly trained professional could understand how radio transmission

destroyed this "equilibrium which dispenses with all the antagonisms between individual and society." One could not properly perceive the meaning
and effect of the work without seeing its place in the social structure. Lay
listeners by definition could not see social structures, and therefore failed to
understand the work. At roughly the same time as *Gang Busters* producers
dismissed listeners who pointed out "the weakness and fallacies in the structure of society," Adorno theorized them out of existence.[21]

Historians usually cite this argument to place Adorno in opposition to
empirical methods and commercial broadcasting. Adorno believed this himself. "Empirical sociology," he later recalled, "stood . . . threateningly before
my eyes in the form of that machine, the program analyzer." In fact, by the
1940s both commercial broadcasters and empirical social scientists at the
project shared Adorno's beliefs in expert authority and passive emotional listening. When Adorno charged that broadcasters aired "low-grade programs"
because they shared "bad taste" with their audiences, Lazarsfeld pointed out
that few "radio officials listen to their own programs in private life." If Adorno
confessed that "exuberant" fan letters "were so enthusiastic as to make me
feel uncomfortable," social scientists in the late 1930s began to speculate that
fan-letter writers were "the neurotics, the deviates, the abnormal among the
listeners."[22] Scientific qualitative research, epitomized by the program analyzer, reserved all interpretive authority for the experts.

In the 1940s, neither quantitative nor qualitative social scientists allowed
listeners to participate in production. While earlier broadcasters had invited
listeners to "write the scripts," the program analyzer specialists from CBS and
the War Department advised producers: "It has been found unprofitable to
ask subjects how a program should be changed in order to improve it. The
very idea of arranging a broadcast," they claimed, was "foreign to the listener's
experience." Their article left it to "the writers and the producers, with suggestions from the researchers, to improve the broadcast." When networks and ad
agencies adopted the analyzer in the 1940s, they tabulated, charted, and interpreted analyzer results the same way they did ratings. "The level of approval
built up to a 90 per cent climax in the program's closing episode," a 1945 CBS
analyzer report on *Easy Aces* concluded, "This indicates a successful development of comedy suspense" (fig. 10).[23] As the former personal relationship
with listeners gave way to occasional analyzer tests, ratings became the only
way to guide the everyday production process.

Like the social scientists, in the 1940s the network executives, advertisers,
and sponsors thought of radio and its audiences in terms of figures, tables, and

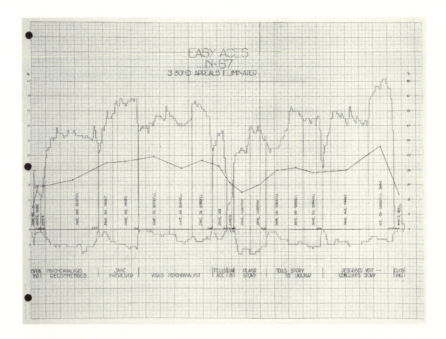

10. "'Easy Aces' (Broadcast October 12, 1945) Summary of Listener
Reactions," June 1947. Recorded Sound Reference Center, Library of
Congress.

charts. Broadcasters competed for audience share rather than individual listeners. Networks used ratings to attract agencies and their clients; advertisers, to
lure sponsors; and sponsors, to chose networks, broadcast times, and genres of
shows. Here broadcasters yearned to match Adorno's description of the American "society of commodities," where monopolies mass-produced standardized
goods. Many industry executives agreed with the president of the National Association of Broadcasters. Harold Ryan, who declared radio as much "a product as the vacuum cleaner," and George Washington Hill, the president of the
American Tobacco Company, who assigned 90 percent of "total radio value" to
commercials and only 10 percent to programs. When the Radio Music Project
promised to show that "the freedom of production and the alteration" of genres
had been "eliminated," and these genres had become "frozen" and "institution-
alized" by "the central agencies," it anticipated the radio network policy of the
1940s. Initially, this strategy succeeded—the size of the radio audience, the
number of affiliated stations, and sales of network time to advertisers climbed

higher every year until 1947–48.[24] This self-contained "closed" rational and profitable system required no input from individual listeners.

According to this system, a program was successful only when it overcame the competition in ratings standings. In 1940, upon examining C. E. Hooper's ratings chart showing "the relative value of acts or shows to other acts and shows," Niles Trammel of NBC Program Department found a definite cause for concern. "I feel we are arriving at a definite cross-roads in the matter of radio entertainment," Trammel reported to John Royal, "There is a decided lull and lack of excitement among the agencies in show production." NBC needs to "protect" its current "first six or eight in the CAB rating" and the next thirty programs in the rankings. "If there should be a falling-off in interest on the part of clients and agencies in shows" CBS would immediately seize the top spots. To get rid of "a series of weak links among our shows," Trammel concluded, NBC had to choose all programs "based on the importance of them from an audience standpoint." Five years later, when companies flocked to the networks to take advantage of wartime tax breaks for radio sponsorship, the Ayer ad agency perceived a crisis once again: "we can be certain that it is much more difficult now to increase the program's audience than it was five years ago because of the growth in the total number of network programs, all of which compete with each other throughout the week. For the first time in history, all four networks—NBC, CBS, the Blue and Mutual—are completely sold out all evenings, except for a few undesirable periods on the minor networks."[25] The agency calculated the relative popularity of its program, *The Telephone Hour*, from its Hooper and CAB ratings as compared with those of the competition, *Lux Radio Theater* on CBS and news commentator Gabriel Heatter on the Mutual network. "A big rating increase," the agency concluded, would be impossible without "getting away from the Lux competition."[26] As executives voted laggard shows out of the broadcast grid and juggled time spots to evade higher-rated competitors, particular listeners' opinions seemed irrelevant.

The networks put the development of old and new genres on hold as they streamlined program categories for long-term ratings analysis. Fifteen major program classifications existed in 1936. In 1940, to simplify its program analysis, NBC outlawed "purely arbitrary terms" such as "special events" and "international" and abolished "educational" as a major classification category. A comparative analysis of NBC Red and CBS programs prepared in March 1941 classified all programs into six groups—"dramatic, variety, audience participation, popular music, semi-classical music and news programs"—and churned out charts and tables showing the relative popularity of NBC Red

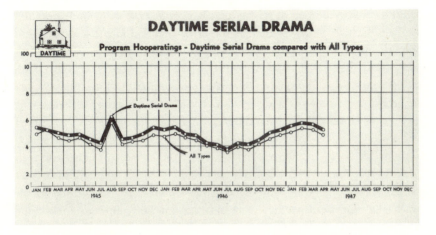

11. Daytime serial drama ratings, "Radio Handbook (Reference Data on Radio, Television, Films). Prepared for the confidential use of Thomas J. McDermott, property of Radio Department, N. W. Ayer & Son, Inc.," 1947. Thomas J. McDermott Collection, American Heritage Center, University of Wyoming, Laramie.

and CBS genres by ratings. "Of the 7 Red dramatic programs," ran a typical comment, "4 of them outstripped the competition at their respective hours while 13 out of 18 CBS shows did better than their competition." By 1947 it was no longer necessary to describe genre content in detail—it was self-evident. In its "Radio Handbook" for executives, the Ayer ad agency defined existing programs into nine types and charted them by ratings averages and market segments (fig. 11). Ratings for variety and comedy ran "higher than the nighttime average." Popular music was "excellent for some products with specialized market" of "younger age groups." Concert music was a "good institutional vehicle" with "low average audience." And daytime serial drama attracted the "highest daytime audience . . . limited chiefly to women."[27] This system depended on shows of the same genre being interchangeable and predictable in their appeal.

In this new formulaic system, writers lost creative autonomy and ratings-minded executives controlled the day-to-day production process. Scientific audience research had less to do with accuracy than with control over production, as its failure in the film industry shows. In 1940, at the same time as empirical radio audience studies were coming into prominence, George Gallup convinced studio executives to commission his Audience Research

Institute studies instead of relying on such biased and, in Gallup's opinion, unscientific sources as personal exhibitor reports and movie fan mail from impressionable teenage girls. Yet within a few years writers, actors, and exhibitors would charge that Gallup surveys had merely enforced studio executives' power and turned filmmaking into "a sterile, glutted and intractable thing." Scientific polls, they insisted, failed to reveal complex individual reactions to films as works of art, social differences among viewers, and the regional specificity evident in exhibitors' personal letters. Critics particularly despised Gallup's Televoting machine, which was based on the radio program analyzer. Screenwriter Ranald McDougall remembered his work with the CBS analyzer with disdain when he argued that audiences would forget to push the button especially when absorbed by the narrative, and usually showed a slight delay in reaction. As a result, "a moving scene will register nothing and slightly afterwards a dissolve from a door opening to a door closing will appear on the graph as one of the finest pieces of acting yet this year." By the end of the 1940s, film studios had dropped Gallup surveys as inaccurate and ineffective, in part due to protests by movie stars, the Screen Writers' Guild, and the Allied Association of Motion Picture Exhibitors. Conversely, the more centralized broadcasting industry embraced surveys, ratings, and the analyzer. CBS even built a bigger analyzer, the Big Annie, to probe more than fifty listeners at once. The "closed" definition of radio production persisted in the broadcasting industry, as broadcasters and advertisers continued to use the analyzer in television through the 1970s.[28]

Cultural critics and radio writers fumed that the "curse of ratings" and "hooperism" destroyed radio's creativity—by 1950, they pointed out, 108 network series had been on the air for at least a decade, twelve of them for two decades. Comedian Fred Allen, considered by John Steinbeck "unquestionably the best humorist of our time," called ratings the "great statistical figment" and once inquired if ratings services counted Siamese twins as one or two listeners. Then Allen went from a 28.7 rating in January 1948 to 11.2 in January 1949 on NBC because of a competing giveaway show on ABC, *Stop the Music*. By 1950, he had lost his sponsor, Ford Motor Company, and had to leave radio. Modernist writers Arch Oboler and Norman Corwin, credited with creating pioneering "plays fundamentally for the ear" during wartime, by the late 1940s had lost their jobs. "Radio, for the dramatist," Oboler concluded in 1948, "is a huge, insatiable sausage grinder into which he feeds his creative life to be converted into neatly packaged detergents." Artists like Oboler, Corwin, and Allen associated ratings with audience tyranny. Because "the audience of twenty million women has taken over control of the daytime serial," humorist James Thurber concluded in 1948, "the formula has been fixed.... The few serious writers who have tried to improve on it are gradually giving up the unequal struggle."[29] These authors defined creativity as freedom from listener response.

In fact, the ratings also curtailed a form of radio creativity based on listener response. By 1947, fan letters, telegrams, and phone calls no longer served to demonstrate a program's popularity to advertisers. When Procter and Gamble refused to sponsor one of her new serials even after twenty to twenty-five phone calls to NBC and 300 calls to station WMAQ in Chicago in defense of the program, soap writer Irna Phillips complained, "you begin to wonder about agencies when the radio head tells you that regardless of calls or mail these would not be in any way of interest to P&G in the purchase of program." Frustrated with growing agency interference with her work, Phillips quipped that a writer should "never be permitted to know the ratings," that even Mr. Hooper "himself can't explain them or believe in them," and that soap sponsors Procter and Gamble, General Mills, and Standard Brands "undoubtedly" should have at their "command surveys other than the Hooper-Dooper and Nielson to determine the commercial value of a program."[30] The new, codified definition of listener response eliminated the creative impulse that individual listeners had given to writers.

The end of the New Deal and the rise of anticommunism contributed to the demise of both artistic autonomy and reciprocity in radio, as the history of news reporting suggests. During the war, correspondents broadcast from London streets and bomb shelters during air raids, solicited ordinary people's opinions for their news broadcasts, and read listeners' letters over the air. As a result, listeners related to each correspondent as a friend. In November 1940 in New York on his way to the studio Eric Sevareid, a CBS correspondent famous for reporting every hour form Bordeaux as France fell, asked his Jewish cabbie, Harry Romer, whom he would vote for in presidential elections. Afraid to lose a customer, Romer hedged his answer, but after hearing Sevareid's broadcast that mentioned the conversation he wrote confessing that Franklin D. Roosevelt was always his choice. "I'm anxious that you know the truth," he insisted. In August 1941 Sevareid read on the air a letter from Nora Adams, the railroad conductor's wife, who had just sent her son off to war. Five years later, Adams still remembered the broadcast. Her son had survived the war, she wrote; she was going to visit him in Boston from South Carolina, and would Sevareid like to come meet with her at the train station on her stopover in Washington, D.C.? (He demurred, with apologies, writing that he was going to be in New Mexico that day inspecting a nuclear research facility.) Then in 1947 the network fired its other leftist war correspondent, William L. Shirer, and demoted Sevareid "from his independent position as commentator and put him to reciting news items," as Oscar Hammerstein's ex-wife Myra Finn wrote in her letter to CBS. Less privileged listeners agreed. "Are we arriving at the final stage of the throttling of all ideas not put forth by the American Association of Manufacturers?" inquired Esther Schreurs, a schoolteacher and a member of the League of Women Voters from Tucson, Arizona. Fans voiced their objections in vain. By the late 1940s formerly passionate and egalitarian radio war correspondents were announcing news without expressing either their listeners' opinions or their own.[31]

At the same time as broadcasters turned to scientific research, the American public grew disaffected with national commercial radio. Between the Munich crisis and V-E Day, Americans consistently praised the role of the networks in covering the war. As soon as the war ended, however, listeners abandoned their loyalty to the networks, just as they left behind rationing and other wartime obligations. The share of respondents who thought that radio was doing an "excellent" job dropped from 28 percent in 1945 to 14 percent in 1947, while the share thinking that radio was doing only a "fair" or "poor" job rose from 11 to 22 percent. This rapid disillusion with radio in the postwar period becomes less surprising if one notes that listeners were beginning to tune out network radio before the war's end. Between 1943 and 1947, independent stations boosted their winter daytime and summer audiences by nearly 100 percent. Already by wartime listeners were writing fewer fan letters. "The tendency to write letters concerning radio programs is waning sharply," the Ayer ad agency reported in 1940. According to NBC press releases, in 1936 the network's mail department handled "an average of 39,000 letters daily" but NBC's daily mail in 1942 only added up to "more than 1500." The letters that did come were more critical and less welcome. By 1941 CBS Chairman William Paley warned that people were most "likely to write and mail a letter because of violent disagreement."[32] Postwar polls reflected an earlier trend—commercial radio had become less interactive and personal. Pollsters, however, did not allow listeners to articulate their moral judgments of radio's economy. But the producers of shows such as true crime drama *Gang Busters* did.

6

Gang Busters

In Depression-era Oklahoma, at a remote farmhouse in Comanche County, local sheriffs caught up with two small-time armed robbers, George Sands and Leon Siler. A gunfight ensued, and the owner of the farm died in the crossfire. Three years later, in February of 1939, a popular "true crime" radio program, *Gang Busters*, reenacted these events over the national CBS network.[1] After the broadcast, producers received a letter from the farmer's widow, Berniece Medrano, who declared *Gang Busters*' rendition of the gunfight a fraud. Medrano insisted that the lawmen deliberately shot her husband: "In the first place, the Bandits did not order us to cook dinner, there was much more shooting than you had in the play—and my husband *was not* killed in cross fire—one of those honorable, and noble, Gang Bustin' laws did it—*deliberately*—and I can prove it if given a chance. . . . I don't know that you have any right using my name without permission concerning a bunch of *lies*."[2] The broadcast failed to depict the social order as Medrano saw it—rigged against farmers, with lawmen cast as villains and bandits as victims. Eyewitnesses interviewed for the broadcast also objected to the script. They insisted that one of the deputies killed Adrian Medrano, a farmer of Mexican descent, solely because of the dark color of his skin, mistaking him for a Choctaw criminal on the loose. The widow's letter thus at once indicted cops' casual racism, the legal order that condoned it, and the radio system that elided it. Medrano's arguments hinged at once upon her sense of racial justice and her way of listening to radio.

Gang Busters' conflicts with its publics between 1939 and 1942 marked the point when radio's moral economy broke down. To be sure, as a true crime program, *Gang Busters* spurred a unique set of conflicts between broadcasters and their publics. Between 1935 and 1957, the program dramatized the lives, crimes, and capture of famous and small-time bandits. The show's correspondents split four ways: broadcasters—advertisers, scriptwriters, investigators, and local station managers; law enforcement officials—state troopers, beat cops, and police chiefs; lay "informants" or "witnesses"—bandits' relatives, friends, neighbors, and bystanders like Berniece Medrano; and listeners in no way connected to the crimes.[3] Ordinary people's lives literally became part of the story but broadcasters often interpreted and edited these lives contrary to their subjects' opinions. Informants' objections to inaccurate reporting and the interpretation of particular cases set the show apart from entirely fictional comedies, soap operas, and radio music.

Yet these informants' worldviews may have been characteristic of the show's audience, which in turn represented the majority of the American radio public. Many gangsters grew up and operated in urban immigrant or down-and-out rural neighborhoods. Consequently, broadcasters were appropriating stories of poor bandits, witnesses, and victims. The show's audiences came from the same humble background. *Gang Busters* appealed most to working-class and nonwhite men and children. Among 10,000 Minnesota men questioned in December 1936 and January 1937, only 20 percent of professionals, but 45 percent of "slightly skilled" workers, listened to *Gang Busters*. A California survey found that while wealthy kids preferred historical plays and middle-class kids soap operas, low-income "Oriental" and Mexican children favored crime and mystery stories like *Gang Busters*. And a Chicago sociologist observed his black working-class informants listening to "'Gang Busters' on the radio at nine o'clock." These fans belonged in the majority of the radio audience. A 1935–37 ratings analysis showed that listeners earning less than $3,000 a year predominated in the *Gang Busters* audience, while those earning more than $5,000 usually tuned out the program. It also showed that four-fifths of the total radio audience earned less than $3,000 a year.[4] As a top-rated program with an important radio constituency, *Gang Busters* spurred heated legislative, academic, and public debates. Because the program reenacted actual confrontations between poor people and state authorities, it inspired its working-class and nonwhite listeners and informants to articulate popular dissatisfaction with the emerging impersonal corporate power in the broadcasting industry.

Gang Busters' formula opened the show up to conflicting interpretations. For advertisers and officials, *Gang Busters* producers rattled off anticrime rhetoric; for listeners, sounds of gunfights and stories of rebels and outlaws. At the outset, the narrator reminded the audience that crime does not pay.

After the bandit had gotten his comeuppance, *Gang Busters* aired "clues"—national alerts for actual criminals wanted by the Federal Bureau of Investigation or the police. In between, robberies, gunfights, and getaways served up as much action and suspense as possible. During the half-hour of the "Sands-Siler" case, bandits George "Choc" Sands and Leon Siler kidnapped a taxi-driver, killed one policeman, kidnapped another, robbed a bank together with Sands's girlfriend, "gun moll" Grace Turner, and when traced by a police plane to a remote farmhouse, surrendered to lawmen only after a vicious gunfight.[5] Reviews and listener interviews showed that the details of gangsters' lives and sensational sound effects at the core of the story undermined the official authority affirmed at the beginning and the end.

An earlier stint with FBI Director J. Edgar Hoover had taught *Gang Busters'* creators that bombastic sound attracted audiences and sponsors. Between 1933 and 1936, Hoover waged a "war on crime" media campaign to promote federal agents and counter public admiration for urban mobsters and Midwestern bandits. In 1935, he collaborated with the independent Phillips Lord, Inc. production company on *G-Men*, a radio program based on actual FBI cases. Hoover insisted that his own writer, Rex Collier, draft the outline of each case. Then Lord would write the dialogue, complete a production script, check again with Collier, and clear it with Hoover. Only then the script was ready to go. Convinced that Collier's outlines "left out all the color," Lord packed his opening with sirens, woman's shrieks, slamming doors, police calls, and newsboys' cries. Hoover dismissed Lord's scripts as "too sensational." By the last *G-Men* episode, Hoover's effects-free opening praised "the giant eraser" of the FBI that "rubbed the outlaw and his henchmen out of the headlines." Hoover deep-sixed the gunfights and instead had an agent look for a moll's marriage license for six weeks to demonstrate that "this methodological research is part of our job." After one thirteen-episode season, the collaboration collapsed, the sponsor, Chevrolet, dropped the show, and Hoover disassociated himself from the program. The new incarnation, *Gang Busters*, began broadcasting the following fall and ran as a sponsored program for over twenty years, its basic style and content unchanged through the war and its aftermath. It started off with unused *G-Men* scripts but focused on gangsters at the lawmen's expense. It reenacted less-known cases not from FBI memoranda but from police files, detective pulps, original interviews, and special investigators' reports. Lord acted as a narrator on *Gang Busters* until 1938, reviewed all rehearsal recordings, and wrote revision suggestions for many episodes. In comparison with Hoover's flat-footed directing, Lord's style left much more room for interpretation by the audience.[6]

Gang Busters' producers let their penchant for style eclipse their avowed political loyalties. To be sure, the opening din trumpeted the producers' allegiance to state crime fighting:

(POLICE WHISTLE)

ANNOUNCER: Palmolive Shave Cream and Palmolive Brushless Shave Cream—the shave creams made with olive oil, Nature's first skin conditioner, present:

(MACHINE GUN)

GANG BUSTERS!

(SIREN)

(MARCHING FEET)

(MACHINE GUN)

JOHNSON: Calling the police . . . Calling the G-men . . . Calling all Americans to war on the underworld.[7]

But most often, the writers composed—and the actors delivered—lines to amuse rather than instruct the audience. "Don't forget that the opening speech of the script must be the hook on which the script is hung," an internal memo for writers advised. "Do not moralize here—our purpose here is to interest the listener in the case to follow." Producers espoused effects for effects' sake. "The whining of brakes was good, but there should be a final big crash of glass and debris," Lord typically requested. "The revolver shots throughout the entire scene should be intermittent," Lord wrote about the shootout in the Medrano farmhouse. "This, after all, is a gun fight." This approach grabbed listeners' attention but left them to fend for themselves in constructing the meaning. It worked. "I like a radio program to be exciting," New York children praised *Gang Busters* to interviewers. The show's opening inspired the colloquial expression "to come on like gangbusters"—"to enter, arrive, begin, participate, or perform in a sensational, loud, active, or striking manner." In presenting "life with the dull bits left out," *Gang Busters* announced its own artifice. Fans listened for sensational sound effects and plot twists rather than for an authoritative narrative defined by its conclusion.[8]

The public's admiration for robbers held the show's meanings hostage. Bandits and gun molls like Clyde Barrow and Bonnie Parker became heroes for many Americans who were coping with the hardships of the Depression. Millions consumed true detective pulps, gangster movies, and sensational newspaper coverage of gang shootouts and bank robberies. *Gang Busters* benefited from the popular appeal of the gory details, the first-person eyewitness accounts, and the tough masculine style of crime writing. It also absorbed the populist politics of printed and performed bandit lore. Gun molls' autobiographies in pulp magazines described bandits as former farmers or laborers driven to crime by unjust laws, and gangs as informal family units governed by a strict code of honor and personal obligation in opposition to state authority. Radio episodes about the notorious Oklahoma bandit Pretty Boy Floyd (and lesser Southern and Midwestern gangs) recalled Woody Guthrie's song "The Ballad of Pretty Boy Floyd," popular in California migrant camps in the late 1930s, which described Floyd as a friend and benefactor of farmer families on relief. The penultimate stanza summed up the relationship between bandits, farmers, corporate bureaucrats, and the law, as many laborers and tenants saw it: there were two types of crooks—"Some will rob you with a six gun / And some with a fountain pen." *Gang Busters* never justified banditry as resistance to farm foreclosures as explicitly as Guthrie's ballad did. But interviews and criticism showed that the program could not escape associations with such populist beliefs.[9]

Using writing rules common across radio genres, *Gang Busters* placed the bandits at the center of every broadcast. Guidelines to "make all explanations clear and concise" required pithy, vivid, easily recognizable stories. The robbers could hardly appear weak or daft when producers required writers to bring out "a tough quality" appropriate for outlaw characters and lifestyles. Hair-raising sketches of rugged and clever outlaws inspired curiosity rather than fear. Asked to describe *Gang Busters*, young New Yorkers stressed the bandits' lives and personalities as much as, if not more than, the police work. *Gang Busters* "shows you all the facts about a person—a criminal, how he had scars in his face and all," a teenage daughter of working parents from the Lower West Side reported, then remembered, "and then they tell you how they found him." A twelve-year-old boy opined, "[the program] shows how they catch bandits after they escaped from the pen," then added, "I want to know what bandits are like." Pithy jargon seeped into everyday speech. Producers instructed writers to "give leading criminal several minor characteristics or pronunciations or expressions which will occasionally designate him." Critics reported that young offenders used *Gang Busters* dialog "as a sort of lexicon," greeting officers with, "Listen, flatfoot, I ain't talkin' to you coppers."[10]

As a result, legislators, listeners, and reviewers charged that producers were advertising gangsters' methods to the audience. In a letter to New York City Mayor Fiorello LaGuardia, a concerned Long Island citizen complained that the program taught young men how to break locks, pick pockets, hide corpses, and evade the police "by changing the criminal's clothes or if riding in a car to throw away and change license plates." Phillips Lord hastened to assure LaGuardia's office that these details were "simply a statement of fact; not a statement of method as to how to go about it." Reviewers disagreed. Magazines described the show as a how-to manual for would-be gangsters rather than a "crime does not pay sermon." A probation officer reported to *Time* magazine that in 1939, among the juvenile delinquents caught on his watch, "forty-six young law busters admittedly took their cues straight from *Gang Busters*." Broadcasters aired a "solid moral lesson;" listeners heard a "noisy, blood-and-thunder" gangster tale.[11]

While aware of such criticism, the broadcasters nevertheless refused to change their formula. They tabled advertisers' requests to tone down the details of crimes, and hired writers who cited pulp journalism among their credentials. One self-proclaimed "expert in libel" and "drama," offering his services, claimed to have written "20 accounts of crime and criminals for the detective magazines." He went on to compose case summaries for *Gang Busters*. The show's writers scoured true detective pulps and crime news reports for broadcasting material. Phillips Lord saw fit to publish illustrated *Gang Busters* stories in sensational newspapers owned by William Randolph Hearst (fig. 12). To charges of too much gore, the producers retorted, "in no instance do we ever treat a case where the criminal comes out ahead of the police." Far from being fooled by such an excuse, many listeners used the lawful ending to justify the outlaw barrage and banter at the core of the story. Among Wilmette, Illinois grammar school children interviewed about *Gang Busters*, grade one students liked "the shooting in it," grades three and four thought it "exciting," and grade five appreciated "the true story of criminals." Older students, however, reeled off the expected reasons such as "It teaches that crime

By **PHILLIPS H. LORD**
Creator of "The Gang Busters".
Illustrations by Austin Briggs.

The machine gunner barked the signal for the 2nd raid. . . .

The Clue of the
WHISPERING
WIRES

Terror reigned in California as the will-o'-the-whisp bank bandits remained a mystery — to all but little Jimmy

"THIS is Jimmy," a thin voice whispered through the telephone. The sergeant at the San Diego police station reached for a pencil automatically. "I saw the Black and White Gang enter a house on Clay Street. The address is . . ." The sergeant in fury choked off the child's voice by slamming the receiver . . . but the address was on his mind.

"Even the youngsters are kidding us about the 'Black and White Gang'," he snorted to the assembled policemen.

As the sergeant's anger cooled, his mind wandered back to the phone message. His pencil traced a circle around the address on Clay Street given by the youngster.

The sergeant refused to believe that the cleverest gang of bank robbers in America could be spotted so easily—and by a child. But it was possible, he reflected. He had followed so many bad hunches and leads, he might as well follow this one.

The gang was a complete mystery to the police of Southern California. In two years, the bandits robbed 29 banks, with a loss to the banks of more than $200,000.

The Black and White Gang, so called because it was composed of two white men and one negro, operated so smoothly that until the day it was captured the identity of its members was unknown.

During the rush of an ordinary business day, the gang would slip into a bank, hold it up and escape before the customers gained the full import of the daring venture. The members of the gang never shouted or bullied the bank employees or patrons, but their work has found little equal in the annals of crime.

The holdup of the Bank of Italy, in Los Angeles, was pointed out by witnesses as one of the best planned and executed jobs of bank robbing ever performed. It was done in the best tradition of the movies.

Three men walked into the bank. A man of about 28 years, apparently the leader, jumped on the desk in the center of the bank, a sawed-off shotgun in his hands.

"Ladies and gentlemen," he announced quietly. "This is an ordinary holdup. If everyone keeps calm there will be no shooting and no trouble."

The calm of the gang leader seemed to transfer the patrons and employees of the bank into a hypnotic state, according to eye witnesses. One member of the trio walked from window to window, scooped up bank notes. The third member of the gang was at the door, his gun trained on the people coming into the bank. Once they got in he warned them to keep calm.

Out of the bank with their loot, the gang sped by auto toward the outskirts of the town. Police blockades proved ineffectual at every turn and the bandits escaped.

After each getaway, the gang's car was always found in midtown of the city in which the bank robbery occurred. It seemed that they used two cars, starting towards the outskirts in one to throw police off the trail, and then cutting back to the heart of the town, where they could change cars and then lose themselves in the flood of traffic.

Although none of the gang wore gloves, no fingerprints were ever found that could be traced through police files. Although the getaway cars were always found, they proved to have been rented from rental garages, where the attendants never recognized or identified the men who had hired the car.

It wasn't until months later that a break came for the police when the First National Trust and Savings Bank of San Diego was robbed by the gang. This was the same bank that the gang had robbed two years before. In fact, it had marked the beginning of their career. It was to

serve also as the end of the crime trail for them.

In their usual cool manner, the trio entered the bank. The leader jumped on the manager's desk and ordered everyone to be calm. But something was wrong this time. Manager H. M. Royle, dropping to the floor with a pistol in his hand, began blazing away at the bandits. For the first time in their history the bandits began firing. Bullets crashed around Royle's head as he ducked behind his own desk, but none hit him. In turn, he emptied his gun without hitting any of the bandits who were now fleeing the bank—but not before scooping up a lot of cash.

Again the holdup car whisked them away, with the manager and two policemen who had been drawn to the scene, blazing away. When the getaway car was found later, it had 29 bullet holes.

At once, a police blockade was formed, but again there was no sign of the Black and White gang along the roads leading out-of-town. Police knew then that the gang was hidden somewhere in the city. Fingerprints were useless; there were no means of identification from the getaway car. The men had disappeared into thin air.

And then in desperation the police sergeant decided to follow the telephone tip furnished by

. . . but something went wrong this time. The manager began to shoot.

the youngster, Jimmy. Six men, led by Patrolman Mike Shea, were detailed to the Clay Street address. In police prowl cars they coasted up and down the street within a block of the house they wanted. Finally three officers went to the back door of the house; three went to the front. Policeman Shea slid cautiously through the rear door and found the house in pitch darkness.

"Nobody even lives here," he whispered to himself as he groped in the darkness.

"Drop your gun," a husky voice answered, and Policeman Shea felt a pistol in his side.

Shea whirled about and stabbed his gun into the dark outline.

"Put 'em up yourself," he snapped back. Shea heard a gun drop to the floor. A moment later two men slipped into the darkened room.

Shea covered the new arrivals and walked out with three men in front of him, their arms high.

"Here's the Black and White Gang," he announced to the other policemen.

The Black and White Gang was sentenced to five years to life in San Quentin.

Before going to prison, Keith, the leader, explained how the gang ran its streak of robberies.

"We just went in and took the money without scaring anybody. Two of us never handled anything but the guns because our fingerprints are on file. The third member of the gang had never been arrested before so that no matter how many fingerprints they got on him, they couldn't find them in the files."

And little Jimmy—the kid who had called the police . . . San Diego officials tried to find him to reward him. But he was never found.

"This is Jimmy," a thin, frightened voice whispered.

Copyright, 1935, King Features Syndicate, Inc.

12. Phillips H. Lord, "The Clue of the Whispering Wires," *New York American*, 1942. Phillips H. Lord Papers, American Heritage Center, University of Wyoming, Laramie.

does not pay."[12] These kids tuned in to hear the "blood and thunder" yet gave the standard answer to the uninitiated sociologist.

Listeners, critics, and broadcasters agreed that in New Deal America populist sentiments constituted the dominant meaning of *Gang Busters*. When old *Gang Busters* episodes went into syndication in the 1960s, the show flopped, perceived as police propaganda. In the 1930s and early 1940s, a listener would not have to stray far from *Gang Busters'* social prescriptions to adopt a critical view of the Depression-era social order. Fans made their critical sentiments explicit when they applied the program to their own lives. After five months of "seeking a position with no avail," Samuel Zucker, an unemployed college graduate from Brooklyn, confessed in 1940 that he had come to the point where he had "planned the robbery of almost every large store in the neighborhood. If something doesn't break soon for me," he warned, "perhaps some time in the distant future, you will be presenting my story on your program." Not content to make their own meanings in private, letter writers like Zucker assumed that it was radio's responsibility to broadcast listeners' analyses of their own lives.[13]

At the outset, *Gang Busters'* producers had used listener criticism to define the up-and-coming true-crime show's signature sound—the very feature that made the program popular and open-ended—but by the time Zucker sent his letter they were less likely to live up to listeners' expectations. In 1935, their first year on the air, the broadcasters collected personal responses from listeners, newspaper and fan magazine radio editors, and station managers who reported both their own and their local listeners' reactions. After the first *G-Man* program, Lord's assistant John Ives forwarded a set of telegrams from station managers to Joseph Neebe, an executive at Campbell-Ewald ad agency, including both compliments and "genuine critical angles." Lord, Ives, and Neebe studied listener responses concerning transition music, dead air, sounds of cars, guns, and dialogue color. "Criticism of the use of chords as made by station managers in telegrams you received, as well as by radio editors in their printed comments check with most comments by listeners," Neebe reported to Lord about the second episode of *G-Men*. In this broadcasters were continuing common practice—Lord had used fan mail summaries for his earlier popular program, *Seth Parker*. Once *Gang Busters* became the highest-rated detective show, however, the correspondence between program producers and the agency more often included lists of stations that aired the program, with data on Crossley rating service coverage, network affiliation, and station transmitter range.[14] By the 1940s, producers rarely used personal responses in negotiations with ad agencies and networks, and consequently paid less attention to listeners' requests.

In constructing each episode, *Gang Busters* creators had to placate ad agencies, sponsors, and networks, and to negotiate their true-crime storylines with government law enforcement agencies, from the FBI to a small-town sheriff's office. In 1939, the *Gang Busters* show was produced by Phillips Lord, Inc. for the Columbia Broadcasting System, and sponsored by the Colgate-Palmolive-Peet Company, which was represented by the Benton and Bowles advertising agency. To produce the "Sands-Siler" episode, Lord employed Program Supervisor Leonard Bass, who supervised the scriptwriter, Stanley Niss, and the "local representative," George Norris, who researched the case. The crew also included nine actors, one announcer, two sound technicians, and a specially invited police narrator, Colonel Norman Schwarzkopf. Lord, his staff, the agency, the sponsor, state officials, witnesses, and listeners all wanted to author a piece of the final script. By the time producers got around to listeners' concerns, few aspects of a given episode remained open for negotiation.

Lord worked hard to make the *G-Men* and the *Gang Busters* production crews more independent and credible. He reported writing his *G-Men* scripts in a Department of Justice office; he launched *Gang Busters* from "a special office, turned over . . . by [New York] Commissioner Lewis J. Valentine." He hired eminent law enforcement officials to serve as speakers and narrators. Valentine had delivered short talks on the opening *G-Men* broadcast and several subsequent episodes. "We have had over two hundred telephone calls in our office alone during the last two days, expressing approval of the address you made," Lord informed Valentine after one "fine speech." As thanks for the "courtesy," he enclosed "our check in the amount of $100, which I should like to have you use in any way that you see fit." As a superintendent of the New Jersey State Police, Colonel Schwarzkopf had vied with Hoover for jurisdiction over the investigation of the 1932 Lindbergh kidnapping. In 1938, Lord hired him as the *Gang Busters* narrator—the man Hoover believed epitomized "the obstacles" the FBI "confronted in conducting this investigation."[15] (Schwarzkopf's son, General H. Norman Schwarzkopf, would become famous during the first Persian Gulf War.) Paid to enhance the show's authority, Schwarzkopf and Valentine had no intention of controlling production. Unfortunately, everyone else did.

Sponsors and advertisers routinely took over directing episodes, as they often did in commercial radio. When Tom Revere of the Benton and Bowles agency expected the sponsor, Colgate-Palmolive, to attend a *Gang Busters* dress rehearsal, he commanded Lord, who acted as a narrator at the time, to also read the commercials. "Give it in your best and most sincere voice," Revere directed, "so they can have a good impression of the entire show, with you in the commercial," and "be sure to get at least two mentions in the script of 'our Palmolive Shave Cream audience.'" Bass complained to Lord that the agency's "integrated" commercials extended from their allocated time and took over the main narrative. The agency's announcer interviewed the case officer, while "the narrating chief [was] indirectly plugging the product." Instead "the announcer should stick to his commercials and the Colonel to his interviewing," Bass proposed. For their part, the producers bucked the agency's attempts to change the direction of the show. When Benton and Bowles asked them to place more stress "on police work and less emphasis on horror and crime," Lord outlined thirteen possible ways to do it.[16] Once he had placated the agency, he used none of them.

Local officials assumed final authority on plot details—an impediment to production that was unique to true crime radio. For every deputy who praised the way broadcasters "brought out the fact that the small town sherriff is as good a servant of the public and just as smart as any other officers," there were several who railed against "grossly misrepresented" cases. "I was already in the furniture store and had Underhill handcuffed," one slighted deputy objected, "when Sheriff Rogers and other officers entered the place." Because Bass could not always control the many people who researched, told, and rewrote the case, he demanded a lot of paperwork to verify ordinary people's stories. "Sign the usual warranty and also have your resume okayed on official stationery by a competent police official," demanded Bass of his investigators. "There are always repercussions about the facts," he complained to one of them, "I want to protect myself by knowing in advance the source of your information."[17] Listeners and witnesses had to contend with the demands of these officials and other competing authorities.

In addressing the program, then, ordinary Americans encountered a complex bureaucratic structure. In 1940 a farmer family from Vale, North Carolina asked *Gang Busters* to broadcast an appeal to their missing son in place of the customary criminal alert "clue." Their son, James Houser, had left his small town in June and was last seen in September heading from Baltimore to Washington, D.C., in search of work. His missing person's card listed his "aptitudes" as "Public works such as Automobile mechanics or filling station work, grocery or drygood store work." His trade made him a typical *Gang Busters* listener. "The boy always listened to Gangbusters," his father wrote, "and where ever he is he might hear the information wanted and will write home." *Gang Busters* "regulations" did not make this easy. Bass agreed to broadcast the appeal, but requested duplicate copies of release forms for the husband, the wife, and their son, and "a letter from your local Chief of Police or Sheriff, as well as a letter from your local minister. Both these letters are to be on official stationery." The Housers' home town ordinarily bypassed such formalities. "I am sorry I do not have official stationery," The Housers' pastor apologized in his letter, "I hardly have need for it in my Rural work here."[18] Like the Housers, many witnesses and listeners did not get a satisfactory reply on the first try and had to exchange several rounds of letters, telegrams, and forms with broadcasters. The program greeted citizens with the same red tape as Depression-era government welfare agencies, national banks, and industrial corporations.

To be sure, the producers as a rule did answer listeners' letters. But they refused to let listeners' views of the social order dictate radio storylines. When Italian jeweler Donato Cugino heard that *Gang Busters* planned to reenact his little brother's crime career, he wrote to explain his brother's violent temper. A drunken neighbor in their poor Italian district in Philadelphia, he insisted, had fractured his kid brother's skull. Instead of sending eleven-year-old Tony Cugino to a hospital, the authorities had shipped him off to reform school, where he became a criminal. The jeweler invited producers to use his letter to test the official version of the story—"to make notes of any information you think neccessary to question the police." The producers carefully read the letter and underlined every relevant point. But they incorporated the information into the script in a way that portrayed his brother as a remorseless killer. Cugino argued that his brother killed a man in prison *"purely [in] self-defense he was duly acquitted of the charge."* On the air, his brother stabbed the inmate on purpose—"I hate him," he declared, "I made me a knife out of this spoon, and I'm gonna stick it thru his heart." Cugino believed in vain that the true-crime show entailed fairness to bandits. "I'm convinced," he concluded his letter, "that *Tony is just another victim of environment slum living conditions, reform schools, [and] curropt public officials.*" The broadcast instead blamed his brother's incorrigible temper.[19] The producers made sure to include such popular features as the tough immigrant milieu and criminal lingo, but retold the case following their own class and ethnic notions, against this listener's advice.

In case after case, the broadcasters fell short of their correspondents' expectations. Listeners asked for assistance in finding relatives, and offered corrections, social criticism, and life histories, because the show's raucous sound and outlaw characters—elements created in part with listeners' input— appealed to their social imagination. Yet when it came to the social analysis of particular cases, the radio industry was no more likely than other national business and political institutions to fulfill its obligations to the public.

In 1939, the radio industry failed to meet its obligations to the Medrano family. The farmers' story, as reported by *Gang Busters* investigator George Norris, provided ample raw material for a thrilling radio skit. Adrian Medrano lived with his wife and children on a small farm near Elgin, Oklahoma. After robbing a bank, two bandits hid in the Medrano farmhouse, taking the family hostage. The Ambrose family walked over from a neighboring farm with their children and also became hostages. A group of deputies descended on the house and, after the bandits shot one of them, opened fire. Adrian Medrano was hit and died the following day. A farm family with soon-to-be-fatherless children made the perfect innocent victims of radio banditry. This same quaint rural background led *Gang Busters* producers to ignore the farmers' interpretation of these events. Having seen officers mistake Adrian Medrano for an Indian bandit, shoot him, and cover up the murder, farmers now discovered parallels between lawmen and radio men in their indifference to farmers' lives and opinions.

As they shaped the episode for public transmission, *Gang Busters'* creators enacted their own fantasies about their informants and, by extension, their audiences. The scene in the Medrano house took up over three minutes of a half-hour broadcast. The show depicted the farmers as piteous, helpless victims: a mother of three cooking dinner at gunpoint, and a hard-working father coming home from the fields only to meet his untimely death. In fact, Berniece Medrano received no orders to cook that night and had only one child at the time of the gunfight—her second child was born five months later. Anxious to cull data to fit their preconceptions, the producers showered Norris with requests for more research. "Is it OK to say Medrano had been plowing referring to Medrano's coming into the house just prior to the bandits' entry," Leonard Bass worried. "Please check very carefully and rush your answers." The public broadcast did not mention Medrano's skin color, but production correspondence dwelled upon his racial identity. "Medrano was rushed to the Indian Hospital at Lawton, he being part Indian," Norris stressed in his case summary. He chronicled "a rather romantic" family history: "Bonney Medrano, Adrian's father was a Mexican stolen as a child by the Comanche Indians. He was raised by the Indians and made a member of the tribe." This tale called up stories of nineteenth-century Comanche raids into lands on both sides of the Mexican border. In the 1930s, many adopted captives still lived in Oklahoma and the Southwest, as field workers discovered when they interviewed former Comanche raiders, their New Mexico trading partners the Comancheros, and former Mexican captives. As mixed-race agrarian innocents—both Bonney Medrano's parents were born in Mexico—the Medranos appealed to the producers' perceptions of Indians as noble savages untouched by technology, a common view at the time, from Wild West shows to ethnography and modern art. The producers' ethnic notions tinged their relations with the Oklahoma farmers.[20]

In molding the episode according to popular views of Indians, the producers betrayed their own fascination with native cultures. A scene depicting an encounter between a primitive Indian tribe and a modern police plane had nothing to do with the main plot, but it launched the "Sands-Siler" episode. Norris claimed that Sands was a Choctaw nicknamed "Choc," but local authorities insisted he was an Arapaho. Bass asked Norris to "check very carefully and let us know immediately" because "we play up this 'Choc' business." An Oklahoma radio station and the ad agency pointed out that the Choctaw, like the other so-called Five Civilized Tribes, had established their own modern American-style literacy, law, and polity in the nineteenth century, only to lose their institutions and lands to the U.S. government and white speculators by the early twentieth. "It must be realized that there are few illiterate Indians in this state," argued Waymond Ramsey of KOMA, Oklahoma City, "and as the Choctaw Tribe was on the Five Civilized Tribes the beating of tomtoms and the broken English which your script writers have given to the Indians does not adhere to the actual conditions." Chester MacCracken of the Benton and Bowles agency balked at the contrast between the modern airplane and backward Indians. "Oklahoma Indians see a lot of planes," he pointed out, "and I sincerely doubt that in 1935 even an old Indian Chief would call a police plane a 'big red bird,' as on page four." Despite these objections, the script changed very little. The tom-toms stayed. Choctaw Chief Lone Bear "played the part in person," enunciating lines like "Good man in sky—bad men down here." A police radio bulletin warned residents to "watch for cunning Indian known as Choc . . . full-blooded Indian—extremely dark." But the revised script mentioned no birds and the Chief asked, "You take big red plane into the sky now?"[21] The producers admitted that they owed some fairness to the Oklahoma Indians, if only when their interests were represented by station managers and admen.

The broadcasters recognized no such obligation to Oklahoma farmers. Eyewitnesses insisted in vain that the deputies had deliberately killed Adrian Medrano. "Ambrose says," Norris reported, "that Medrano was killed by the officers by mistake because they thought he was an Indian and a member of the gang, rather than being shot by accident. Old man Medrano is very bitter about this." During the trial, deputy sheriff Everett Agee—the man Berniece Medrano believed shot her husband—and another officer involved in the gunfight swore that neither of them shot Adrian Medrano. Newspapers reported their testimony without comment. "The Ambroses seemed bothered by the fact that the newspapers at the time did not blame the officers for Medrano's untimely death," Norris noted. "As I informed you, they thought it deliberate rather than accidental, because Medrano looked like the Indian that the banker had described." The Ambroses offered a logical explanation, given that since the mid-nineteenth century, white officials and settlers had often mixed up dark-skinned captives and Comanches and called all swarthy captives "Mexicans," applying the term to Mexican and American citizens alike. In Oklahoma's Comanche County, "Mexican" meant "dark like an Indian." Yet in the final version of the script Berniece Medrano accused one of the robbers, Leon Siler: "You shot *my husband!*"[22] Like the government officials, deputies, and reporters before them, the broadcasters refused to consider the farmers' view of social relations.

Every stage of production chipped away at the farmers' authority. When researching the case, Norris believed news reporters and deputies before farmers. Newspapers placed "the Ambrose girl . . . at the Medrano home during the battle," but Mrs. Ambrose insisted that her daughter had gone to see her grandmother. "I did not know which to believe," Norris confessed, "therefore I did not change the newspaper account." Norris reported, at length, that both Bonney Medrano and the Ambroses thought a deputy killed Adrian Medrano, then concluded, "I am inclined to believe [deputy sheriffs'] statement that Medrano was fatally wounded accidentally." After the broadcast, Bass declared to Berniece Medrano that *Gang Busters* would not have aired her version of the story even if it was true: "If we had known that the facts in the case were such as you say, we probably would not have done the case."[23] *Gang Busters'* creators made it plain to their ordinary informants that their radio stories were no longer open to negotiation.

For their part, witnesses sided with the bandits against the lawmen. During the gunfight, officers riddled the house with bullets, targeting not only Medrano and Sands, both dark-skinned men in their early twenties, but also the other bandits, farmers, and children huddled inside. "I personally made an examination of the Medrano house," Norris proudly reported later, "and counted 32 visible bullet holes." After such an experience, it is not surprising that both Berniece Medrano and the Ambroses emphatically denied that the outlaws had coerced them in any way, the widow adamant that robbers "didn't ask us to cook dinner," and the Ambroses describing the robbers' failed efforts to secure a bloodless outcome, "when the officers could not hear Siler's cries that they surrendered Sands pulled off his shirt and waved it out the window." The officers, the widow concluded, "could have taken the bandits without firing a shot." Instead, they "took an innocent man's life, and left two fatherless children," forcing them into an itinerant life—after the gunfight, the widow moved between her farm, the elder Medrano's in Apachee, and her mother's in New Mexico. By the time of the broadcast, she lived in El Paso, Texas.[24] These witnesses empathized with bandits and resented people in power and officers of the law, in a way similar to the *Gang Busters* listeners interviewed by academics and reporters.

The broadcasters' indifference then led farmers to draw parallels between injustices in the media and in society. Norris "spent several hours" interviewing the Ambrose family, and Bass showered the Ambroses and Berniece Medrano with consent forms to sign and requests to "send us in your own words exactly what took place in the Medrano farm." The Ambroses signed the forms but asked that Norris "submit a copy story to us to read before broadcasting." Once they realized that the broadcasters had accepted the officers' version of events, the Ambroses withdrew their consent to broadcast their names. "We learned [the investigator] & others had cooked this story up," they explained. "We don't want our names used unless facts are stated." The broadcast did not mention them at all. Berniece Medrano also objected, "I don't know that you have any right using my name without permission concerning a bunch of *lies*." Broadcasters, she concluded, get things "crooked."[25] These farmers made it plain that they no longer expected fairness from the radio industry. *Gang Busters* established moral outrage at broadcasters as an appropriate response to its own social prescriptions.

Within four years of the Medrano case, in 1943, *Gang Busters*' ratings had slipped and other shows superseded it in the popular imagination. By this time, *Gang Busters*' creators were dealing with listeners and witnesses in ways that matched the changing attitudes and practices in the entire radio industry. Convinced, like audience researchers, that radio-making was "foreign to the listener's experience," they dismissed their correspondents' demands for reciprocity and justice. When in 1940 Samuel Zucker related to a *Gang Busters* broadcast about "the Ape Bandit," who like Zucker was a college graduate out of work, he argued that any man was justified in becoming a robber if he could not find work: "The fault, I assure you, did not lie with him but with the weakness and fallacies in the structure of society." Bass calmly retorted: "I . . . can assure you from past experience that it is not weaknesses and fallacies in social structure that can be blamed. Many times it is more personal." When in 1939 Elsie Detrich, a stenographer from St. Louis, protested an episode featuring her brother as a member of a gang, Bass sent her his regrets but no apologies, citing the authority of "an eminent criminologist" and official police files. He left unanswered Detrich's economic point about true crime radio's propensity to "commercialize" people's lives.[26] In every exchange, listeners attempted to tease out the underlying logic of the show; broadcasters, to foreclose debate.

As the *Gang Busters* correspondents saw it, this indifference violated a long-standing arrangement between broadcasters and listeners. Like the Ambroses, many listeners who initially trusted the strident populist program may have felt betrayed when broadcasters discarded their opinions. This sense of entitlement extended beyond just this one true-crime show. In the 1930s, the radio industry had encouraged expectations of reciprocity by explicitly courting women consumers. Accordingly, *Gang Busters'* women correspondents—sisters, mothers, and widows like Berniece Medrano—most adamantly demanded attention and objected to broadcasters' brush-offs. At the same time, only one author, Elsie Detrich, directly threatened the sponsor—vowing to have "no more Palmolive Soap, Shampoo or Palmolive Beads in my home."[27] Most letter writers transcended the terms of consumer entitlement set by admen and sponsors. Like Medrano, who applied her sense of racial justice to the media economy, they held the radio industry complicit in the larger system of power relations.

Working-class letters to *Gang Busters* provide an unorthodox view of radio's transformation in the 1940s. Listener alienation from national radio occurred in the midst of a government investigation of the radio industry. The Federal Communications Commission, an independent agency that had been overseeing radio since 1927, began investigating the networks in 1938, forced NBC to sell its second, "Blue," network in 1943, and attacked the radio advertising system in a controversial 1946 report. Intellectuals and regulators contended that the public needed less commercially sponsored entertainment and more educational and public affairs programs. In contrast, *Gang Busters*

listeners did not see how curbing sponsored radio would redress their griev-
ances. Instead, they believed that the commercial broadcasters of a "blood-
and-thunder" show like *Gang Busters* could and should be accountable to
their core lower-class audiences. Their reasoning helps explain the rise of
local commercial radio in the 1940s, before television, and the popularity of
disc jockeys who were more accountable to their local constituencies and less
to national corporations. As television and niche marketing made national
radio less viable, the popular perception of radio as a system of reciprocal social relationships framed new local formats.[28] When the networks abandoned
their constituencies, their publics in turn helped reshape the radio industry.

7

Vox Jox

Radio station WANN announced its presence to Annapolis, Maryland, on New Year's Day of 1947 with the white big band sound of Glenn Miller, Tommy Dorsey, and Perry Como. But this is not how Morris Blum later remembered the birth of his station. For months, his engineer insisted on playing Bing Crosby records and stuck the blues and gospel records in the closet. "He'd say 'you don't want to play that, that's race music.' Then one day when he was on vacation, the deejay, Joe, and I went in there and got some of those albums," Blum later recalled. "We went off the air at 5:45 p.m. and I told Joe 'play these from 5 until we go off.' We had a post office box and we'd normally get so few letters you could count them on one hand. Two days after we played those, I went down there, put in my key, and the letters blew out of the box onto the floor. I knew we had tapped into something."

The show, *Savoy Swingtime*, established an identity for the new station. By the early 1950s, WANN represented black personalities and publics. Several black disc jockeys and preachers broadcast from the station, and a new engineer, a graduate of Howard University, ran WANN's Baltimore studio. WANN's format may or may not have been due to a DJ's ingenuity—in another interview Blum remembered changing the format in response to a black minister's advice.[1] But the unexpected pile of letters conveys the sense of a reinvented medium—a sense of how in the 1940s a reciprocal radio production process reemerged in local radio.

Scholars usually describe the decline of the networks and the rise of local DJs after World War II in terms of niche markets and business institutions, to which payola—payments to DJs for playing particular records— and other informal economies provided an unfortunate criminal backdrop.

Historian Adam Green calls the rise of rhythm and blues radio in Chicago a "marriage of market and cultural values." Media scholars Eric Rothenbuhler and Tom McCourt describe a process of institutional growth whereby early experimental disc jockey programs evolved into "Top 40" radio format, a "well-oiled sales machine."[2] Certainly many jockeys, record promoters, and even some members of the audience aimed to—and did—make money in the process. Yet as disc jockeys invented new radio formats in collaboration with local audiences, they blurred the lines of ownership and control in music radio. The listeners who phoned, wrote to, and appeared on local music shows provided free labor and program content in exchange for a say in what music would go on the air. These transitional practices undermined established ideas about who owned and controlled the airwaves, the music recordings, and the sound itself.

In the 1940s, radio was transformed from a primarily national to a local medium. The U.S. radio and music industries confronted resurgent institutions unaffiliated with the national networks. In radio, the number of independent stations soared from 45 (5 percent) in 1945 to 916 (44 percent) in 1950. In the music industry, the "big three" music labels and the original performance rights organization, the American Society of Composers, Authors, and Publishers (ASCAP) were losing ground to independent labels like Savoy, National, and Chess, specialty music markets like hillbilly, bebop, and jump blues, and a new specialty artists' performance rights group, Broadcast Music Incorporated (BMI).[3] The key cultural institution of the period—the disc jockey—both demonstrated the existence of new local audiences for radio music and served as an instrument of these audiences' formation.

By the late 1940s, the independent stations had developed new audience-friendly formats, including talk radio, regular local weather reports, and numerous disc jockey programs. Between 1943 and 1947 indies boosted their winter daytime audiences by almost 100 per cent, and their summer audiences by a few points more than 100 per cent. In fact, the indie constituency probably grew faster than these numbers showed, because national telephone rating surveys such as Hooper routinely underrated the audience for unaffiliated stations. Surveys showed that audiences for independent stations increased as income level declined, and that popular music and disc jockey shows were particularly popular among the lower middle class and poor economic groups.[4]

WANN was a typical small independent station. Its Jewish owner, Morris Blum, had served as a Navy officer during the war, retired at the rank of

Lieutenant in 1946, and set up his radio business with little personnel apart from his brother Charles. Blum later recalled that he became interested in extending services to black audiences because of his experience with black servicemen in the Navy. WANN attracted an African American presence within its first week of broadcasting. The very first Sunday lineup featured a black preacher, Reverend LeRoy Brown, and a few weeks later a local black mortician gave Blum the station's first advertisement check. An alternative origin story credited another preacher, Theodore C. Jackson of Gillis Memorial Community Church in Baltimore, with the idea for the rhythm and blues format for the station. When WANN went back on the air after its transmitter burned down in 1948, Blum and his station manager, Tom Carner, set up at the control board and the microphone, respectively, fielding requests from "listeners from far and near telephoning and writing in."[5] By then, the station had begun to broadcast rhythm and blues music.

Once it began serving black audiences, the station received thousands of letters a month, mostly from black working-class listeners. Only a few dozen fan letters to music and religious programs have survived from this correspondence. In 1953, a sponsor analyzed the first thousand letters sent to its program in the first twenty days of its existence, and found correspondents from nine states, including Pennsylvania and North Carolina. A 1953 promotional booklet for the station touted WANN's audiences as "Negro fishing boat hands in Milford, Delaware; Negro clerical workers in Baltimore, Md.; Negro government employees in Washington, D.C.; Negro tobacco farmers in St. Leonards, Maryland." An ad in *Printer's Ink* offered the booklet free to advertisers and agencies. Whereas local broadcasters in the Jazz Age had tended to overstate the wealth and consumer sophistication of their listeners, Blum recognized his black working-class audience and represented it without compunction to potential advertisers.[6]

The station's relationship with listeners exemplified a kind of radio intimacy similar to pre-network radio. Not only did listeners expect their letters to be quoted on the air, they also expected live answers to their questions, "I am 15 years old and I am going to high school in the 10th grade," one girl wrote. "I was to be a hair dresser when I finish school do you think I will be successful? Answer on radio. I listen to your program every day in school. I will be listening for my answer." "I injoy your program very much," an unemployed listener wrote to a religious program, "an as soon as I get work I will be sending you a little donation." This unprecedented cross-racial intimacy between independent broadcasters and listeners stemmed from postwar prosperity and black purchasing power—radio, *Sponsor* magazine proclaimed in 1949, needed to reach "the forgotten" fifteen million black consumers.[7]

Taking advantage of the emergent specialized ethnic markets, disc jockeys spearheaded the production of new music radio formats in collaboration with sundry local audiences. Al Jarvis began what is considered the first disc jockey show in 1933, but DJs did not become a national phenomenon until the 1940s. Propelled by the ASCAP recording ban of 1942 and by the reinstatement of transcription as a valid form of radio music, three thousand disc jockeys were on the air by 1947. Of these, sixteen black DJs operated in twelve cities, attracting interracial audiences and "flocks of fan mail." By the early 1950s, Latin disc jockeys were operating in California, New Mexico, Michigan, Massachusetts, New York, New Jersey, and Philadelphia.[8]

In the mid-1940s DJs were still a novelty. Bebop jockey Symphony Sid was an "emcee" for the first few years of his career, black entertainment columnists referred to "so-called disc jockeys," and the *New Yorker* defined the term as "the name radio people unfortunately have for an announcer who plays phonograph records, interspersed with frequent commercials, on the air." The networks did not lift their ban on record shows until 1947. Yet already in 1944, a survey found that teenagers and soldiers knew small independent "hot jazz" labels only because of their exposure via disc jockey programs. Teenagers encountered new records primarily on disc jockey programs; for GIs, DJs were second only to juke boxes.[9]

Soon, the trade periodicals *Sponsor*, *Broadcast*, *Cash Box*, and *Variety* were closely following disc jockey developments. Starting in 1947, the foremost U.S. trade music publication *Billboard* tabulated weekly polls of 1200 DJs across the country to determine what tunes were "played over the greatest number of record shows."[10] The magazine also conducted extensive annual disc jockey surveys, printing hundreds of pages on their programming strategies and marketing suggestions, and ran a weekly column called "Vox Jox," where big- and small-time DJs published their news and opinions.

From March 1948 until the 1970s, "Vox Jox" provided a national picture of the fragmented disc jockey culture and a primer for a new art. DJs mailed short notes reporting their news and opinions for publication in the column, and turned there to catch up on what their colleagues were doing all over the country. According to sociologist Philip Ennis, who conducted one of the first studies of the profession in the early 1950s, from its inception the column "described the minutiae of disk jockey culture as it unfolded, perhaps the best teacher after all." One old timer called it "a must-read for anybody

in the music radio business, back when disc jockeying was still an art form."
When Ron Jacobs, a DJ since 1953, in 1971 recorded the *Cruisin'* series, which
recreated representative pop record programs from the 1950s and 1960s, his
assistants selected the most significant personalities by perusing every "Vox
Jox" column and tabulating jockey mentions by hand. The column "was to-
tally democratic," Jacobs remembered, all DJs "were acknowledged if they did
anything of note." Early on, the column featured one-line updates on everyone from top personalities like Dave Garroway or Al Benson to smaller, local
celebrities like Hoppy Adams of WANN.[11]

Disc jockeys' influence in the industry rested on their personal connection to listeners. Jocks took extreme pains to cultivate this connection. Between records, they read funnies and comics, sung lullabies, and performed
burlesque soap operas over the air. They broadcast recipes, style hints, local
news, weather reports, the correct time, and sports results "as often as possible." They gave away prizes, including show tickets, chickens, and live rabbits.
These prizes were not always doled out fairly—in 1948 a North Hollywood
restaurant refused service to a black contest winner, and offered her a dinner
in the kitchen instead.[12] But most of the time they served to cultivate the connection between the DJs and local audiences.

In the late 1940s, disc jockeys became a fixture of local cultural life. In
Michigan City, Indiana, Stew McDonnell announced amateur boxing fights.
In Chicago, Al Benson sponsored a basketball team. In New Orleans, Dick
Bruce emceed a Louis Jordan jump blues concert. Beverly Norberry, the "only
fem jock in the Detroit area," remotely broadcast interviews with people attending the show at the local Wyandotte Theater.[13] Community involvement
allowed DJs to stay close to their local constituencies.

Before the national music industry discovered its postwar youth audiences, jockeys courted teenagers' favor and opinions. In Washington, D.C.,
Hal Jackson spun records at high school dances. Johnny Russell of Albuquer-
que, New Mexico, served peanuts and cokes at the open house for teenagers on his "Disk Hop" show. DJs all over the country organized guest jockey
shows where local kids picked and announced records.[14] Contests allowed
DJs to study as well as shape the new youth music culture.

At WANN, Hoppy Adams became the most locally famous rhythm and
blues disc jockey. Adams recalled getting interested in radio while he was sick
with polio as a child. In 1952, while working as a cabby, he began his stint as a
disc jockey, instructed by Hal Jackson, a veteran black jockey known both in
New York and Washington, DC. Jackson came to WANN in 1950; at the time,

13. Hoppy Adams and his audience at Carr's Beach, ca. 1953. WANN Radio Station Records, Archives Center, National Museum of American History, Smithsonian Institution.

he juggled four shows on four different stations in Baltimore and Annapolis. Hoppy Adams had a huge following in part because he emceed live concerts at nearby Sparrow's Beach and Carr's Beach—two venues popular with black audiences. Located just outside Annapolis city limits, they operated from early spring through Labor Day, with a combined attendance of twenty thousand people on an average weekend. In 1956 a concert featuring Chuck Berry drew eight thousand spectators, with over seven thousand turned away. The throngs attending these concerts recalled the audience enthusiasm for the sports broadcasts of early radio. But in the earlier decades, while radio producers made use of the minstrel tradition, they frequently ignored black audiences. The Carr's Beach crowds showed that now black listeners and DJs had reinvented radio as a participatory medium (fig. 13).[15]

Adams's listeners made requests for music and shared their daily problems at the same time. One asked for numbers to be broadcast when she is tired after work: "I leave most time 4 oclock and sometime we use 7 oclock getting home and a few good spirituals or blues to cheer us up would be a great help." Some expected to convey their frustration over the air. Katherine Johnson requested that Adams play the Ruth Brown record "Mama He Treat Your Daughter Mean": "please play this request for my good for nothing husband, Walter Johnson, & his outside sweetheart Estel Hunter"; "please call husband & sweetheart name," she added. A blind listener writing in Braille mentioned a famous gospel group and asked Adams to "tell Ray Charles not to holler so loud when he is singing the alto." Because few DJs in the 1940s played blues and gospel records, such personal letters gave DJs like Adams a firsthand opportunity to study and represent the emerging rhythm and blues audience.[16]

Disc jockeys' informal ways of interacting with listeners gave rise to the new technologies of jockey polls and station log analysis. In network radio, live bands had performed music numbers chosen by the band leaders or program producers. As recorded music broadcasts gained prominence, music producers grew dissatisfied with radio ratings because they did not adequately describe the nuances of the music market. Beginning in the late 1930s, national surveys canvassed music airplay on four major networks. The developers of these polls, academics John Gray Peatman and Richard Himber, gave the most points to commercial live network performances. *Variety* and *Billboard* published weekly Peatman reports of the fifty songs with the largest listening audiences, calculated on the basis of Hooperatings; and Himber's weekly RH log sheets, which listed songs by the number and type of performances as scheduled on the four major networks. These "hit sheets" governed network broadcasting—major commercial radio shows would program a song only if it consistently appeared on the top of the Peatman list of "songs with greatest radio audiences."[17]

But music producers pointed out that the network charts did not track regional preferences and types of music. Himber, for example, distinguished between vocal and instrumental numbers but did not consider country, bebop, or jump blues music. Because the networks rarely aired hillbilly or "race" records, they reflected the music preferences of urban middle-class white audiences. In 1949 the talent agency United Music complained that *The Lucky Strike Hit Parade* radio program had shunned its rhythm and blues instrumental, "The Hucklebuck," in favor of songs published by its sponsor, Warner Brothers. Unlike Warner Brothers' songs, "The Hucklebuck" appeared on *Billboard* bestselling records charts for both pop and rhythm and blues. United Music charged that the *Hit Parade* ad agency cheated by "still compiling ratings mainly on the basis of air plugs."[18] Like United Music, many specialty musicians complained that the major networks rigged the results of these surveys in conspiracy with the major record companies.

In order to keep up with the changes, the *Billboard* charts began to track specialized as well as national markets. Starting in the early 1940s, *Billboard*, *Variety*, and *Cash Box* used weekly sales reports from record dealers and jukebox operators to correct the slant of network airplay logs. *Billboard* used three chart categories—record sales, jukebox play, and radio performances—and at the end of the year, calculated a cumulative list of best-selling records. The top ten songs in the "honor roll of hits" were determined by combining data from all three categories. At the same time, *Billboard* and *Cash Box* established separate charts for "the hit parade," "race," and "country and western" music. *Billboard* editors established the "Harlem Hit Parade" in October 1942, and renamed it "Race Records" in February 1945, and "Rhythm and Blues Records" in June 1949.[19] The "race" and "country and western" sections considered only record sales and jukeboxes, because independent stations remained beyond the scope of national radio surveys.

Despite these corrections and the accompanying scientific rhetoric, record producers read local social context into the national music charts' selection and ordering strategies. *Billboard* editors presented its "authentic," "accurate," and "exhaustive tabulation of song and record popularity." Yet when Ahmet Ertegun of Atlantic Records planned to replicate the popularity of his one bestselling record that had made the "race" charts, "Drinkin' Wine Spo-Dee-O-Dee" by Stick McGhee, he described the prospective music consumer to his partner Jerry Wexler in terms of locality, as a working poor black man living outside of Opelousas, Louisiana: "One morning he hears song on the radio. It's urgent, bluesy, authentic, irresistible . . . He drops everything, jumps in his pickup, and drives twenty-five miles to the first record store he finds.[20] Small-time producers like Ertegun drew on their racial imagination and personal observation rather than scientific procedure when they interpreted the charts and attempted to imitate the success of hit records.

DJs adopted blatantly unscientific methods of audience research. They invited phoned-in responses. Telephone switchboards overloaded with calls to DJs became a common occurrence. In 1948, the Hollywood branch of the Bell telephone company, "considerably concerned over the deluge of calls" black jockey Joe Adams pulled on his show at KOWL, requested that he change over to a different exchange "to relieve the pressure." DJs also interviewed men on the street. When Philip Morris was considering sponsoring

Hal Jackson's football broadcasts from Howard University, Jackson could not use Hooper ratings because the university did not subscribe to the service. "I just took the Philip Morris people out to the Black community and stopped people on the street and asked them who they listened to on the radio. In 7 cases out of 10 the answer was 'Hal Jackson.' That convinced them."[21]

The earliest disc jockeys established symbiotic relationships with local record stores and small record companies. They often ran "hit parades" of the records that sold the most copies in local record shops, or were most requested in local juke boxes—a practice later appropriated by the corporate "Top 40" format. They also regularly organized informal music polls, where national and specialty genres of music often clashed. In Graeme Zimmer's semi-annual poll in Columbus, Indiana, the black jazz singer Sarah Vaughan pulled more votes than the white singing movie actress Doris Day. As a result, Zimmer reported, Vaughan's records "will be featured in a daily segment of the show during the entire month of June." Because of such polls, disc jockeys had a unique opportunity to introduce a record on the air and test its local popularity on the spot.[22]

Jockeys offered their informal market research services to record producers and distributors. In 1942, Capitol Records became the first studio to provide free releases for promotional purposes. "We typed up special labels with their names on both sides," Glenn E. Wallichs, Capitol's chairman of the board, remembered, "pressed them on expensive, lightweight, unbreakable vinylite compound and then had our limited employee force drive around and distribute each sample personally." Six years later, every record company, including the majors, had a budget for DJ records. Warren Quade of Santa Maria, California aired all the platters sent to him by the record companies on one of his shows, and included only those that appealed to the listeners on the station's other record programs. He then sent listeners' comments about the records to the record salesmen. Record companies used such input directly. The Coleman label pressed a recording commercially after a jockey played a trial, acetate, record of the song and got enthusiastic response from listeners. In 1952 DJ Phil Maclean played an amateur record of a Cleveland Heights high school student, Don Howard. "The switchboard lighted up as a Christmas tree," Maclean remembered. Listener enthusiasm inspired the Essex label to record the song, which then spent fifteen weeks on *Billboard* top pop records chart.[23] DJs could make an individual record, and build a reputation for a record company.

Yet jockeys' connection to their audiences was not as direct as they liked to believe. They could not always convince their listeners to like the music they played on the air. For every DJ who claimed to make a hit record through constant airplay, there were several who complained that their audiences did not share their sophisticated tastes. "Most of my listeners tend toward hill-billy," a jockey from Spencer, Iowa confessed. "I've been trying to educate them otherwise, but it's a long, slow process." A Pittsfield, Massachusetts, spinner appealed to his colleagues to push bebop and big band jazz: "I think if more jocks would get with it there wouldn't be such an overwhelming demand for corn." Small-town bebop jockeys had a particularly hard time converting their listeners. "So far, efforts have been hopeless," one of them reported from Columbia, Georgia.[24] Such restive constituencies demonstrated that not all audiences could be constructed by the music industry's publicity efforts. It was disc jockeys' ability to conjecture existing emergent audiences, rather than scientifically construct them, that made their reports so valuable for the music industry.

The disc jockey culture mediated between the scientific and informal aspects of the music business. In 1949, performance rights group Broadcast Music Incorporated placed a full-page ad in *Variety*, a major trade entertainment weekly (fig. 14). In the ad, a team of doctors examines an anthropomorphic "log" in an operating room. Sedated, the log lies motionless, its "hand" dangling, while three physicians probe its body with tweezers, dividers and a small hammer. The fourth wields a large saw. In the meantime, an unaffected nurse checks the log's vitals against the BMI manual. In such a clinical way, the ad suggested, BMI analyzed more than 32,400 daily station music logs on IBM "electronic accounting and tabulating machines." To the radio stations, BMI promised to diagnose the "strength of the heart of your broadcasting . . . according to the first scientific and automatic system of checking actual broadcast use of music." The music industry read the music and its audience as a live body, as a physician would read a patient's symptoms. The mixed organic and technical metaphors revealed a fundamental contradiction in 1940s music audience research: the new powerful computer technology was measuring disc jockeys' ad hoc aesthetic choices, made to please their local listeners.

By the end of the decade, disc jockey reports far surpassed national airplay logs in significance. As a result, the performance rights organizations changed their polling system. BMI challenged the validity of paying royalties to composers and publishers on the basis of specious network reports. In August 1949 BMI dropped its "payment by plug system," claiming that the

Operation "Log"

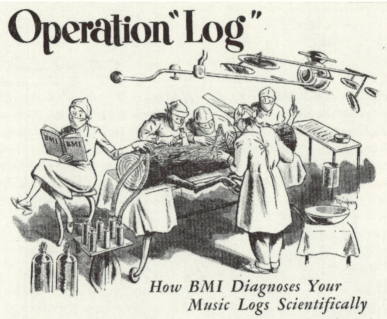

How BMI Diagnoses Your Music Logs Scientifically

Every 14 months your station supplies BMI with a log of the music you've performed each day for one month. This log, properly analyzed, determines the payment to composers and publishers, who are compensated by BMI on the basis of actual use of their music.

And, as important to you, your daily music log is the pulse of your station's musical programming. It is vital to you, for it charts the exact strength of the heart of your broadcasting. A study of your log helps you appraise the quality and selectivity of your music.

BMI will gladly send you a FEVER CHART, or analysis, of your station's log if you will simply ask for it.

In 1941 BMI instituted the first scientific and automatic system of checking actual broadcast use of music. Employing the very latest IBM electronic accounting and tabulating machines, BMI's "Operation Log" turns out a wealth of interesting facts and figures.

With more than 32,400 daily logs to be examined each year, the physical task of processing them is staggering. Every BMI licensee has been most cooperative in supplying its logs when asked to do so. This cooperation has resulted in standards of efficiency which amaze everyone who has seen BMI's logging system in operation.

You'll have an opportunity to see a typical BMI logging job at this year's NAB Convention when you visit the main exhibit hall at the Stevens for a look at BMI's "Operation Log" in action.

If unable to attend the NAB Convention, write to Station Relations Department at BMI for your copy of "Operation Log" in pamphlet form, illustrated.

AN INVITATION
You are cordially invited to visit the BMI Exhibit in the Main Exposition Hall and BMI Headquarters Rooms 535A—536A—537A at the Stevens During the NAB Convention

BROADCAST MUSIC, INC.
580 FIFTH AVENUE · NEW YORK 19, N. Y.
New York · Chicago · Hollywood

14. "Operation 'Log'—How BMI Diagnoses Your Music Logs Scientifically," BMI advertisement, *Daily Variety* (April 6, 1949). Copyright © 1949 Reed Business Information, a division of Reed Elsevier Inc. Courtesy of the BMI Archives.

Peatman and RH surveys "reflect forced and 'synthetic' popularity ratings." BMI paid royalties for record airplay as well as live music broadcasts. "Disk jockey request tune polls," BMI argued, "more clearly point out the true public reaction value of a melody." By the fall of 1950 even the monopolistic ASCAP announced plans for logging independent stations. Whereas previously "virtually all the credits were given to the [network] live plugs, with emphasis on commercials" now ASCAP would recognize and track local "recorded performances" of "specialty music."[25] ASCAP logged music record play on independent stations by tape recording. Insofar as disc jockeys spoke for their local constituencies, they undermined the authority of scientific polls and the uniformity of national music culture.

The music industry tried to manage local radio audiences by blending the scientific and practical methods of deciphering listener desires. Scientific knowledge relies on quantification and inference, whereas practical, or "conjectural," knowledge, as described by historian Carlo Ginzburg, draws upon the circumstantial interpretation of clues, symptoms, and signs.[26] Music radio audience research in the 1940s aspired to the scientific authority of the first method, but had to draw upon the informal judgment of the second. As middlemen between the emergent specialized music audiences and the national music industry, disc jockeys both interpreted and transformed the American musical and social landscape.

In promoting new music styles on their record shows, disc jockeys helped establish the status of the sound recording as a work of art. Indie radio stations transformed the music business, which had previously focused on live network plugs and sales of sheet music. When swing bands began to lose money in the early 1940s, the musicians had to break up into smaller groups or supplement their big band work with smaller gigs. According to white musician and disc jockey Johnny Otis, performers like himself, Roy Milton, or T-Bone Walker, with "former big band experience," also picked up on the Chicago blues coming from the Delta, "with harmonics and guitars." To preserve "some of the sound of jazz bands," the musicians "kept maybe a trumpet, a trombone, and saxes—this was a semblance of brass and reeds, and they continued to play the bop and swing riffs. And this superimposed on the country blues and boogie structure began to become rhythm and blues."[27]

In this period, pop, country, and rhythm and blues musicians recorded cover versions of successful records. Take, for example, the 1949 dance hit, "The Hucklebuck." According to Fred Mendelsohn, who cut "The Hucklebuck," the owner of Savoy Records, Herman Lubinsky, at first refused to issue the record when he realized that the basis for it was "Now's the Time," also a Savoy recording. Charlie Parker's early bebop hit record "Now's the Time" was cut in November 1945 in a jam session with Parker playing alto saxophone; Miles Davis, trumpet; Dizzie Gillespie, piano; Curley Russell, bass; and Max Roach on drums. In 1949, Paul Williams recorded "The Hucklebuck" with an eight-piece group: a four-piece rhythm section, tenor, baritone, trumpet, and trombone. Williams played tenor and baritone sax. Both were blues records, but "The Hucklebuck" was a slower, danceable riff instrumental. This type of genealogy of a popular tune was well known at the time. An instrumental recorded by Paul Williams for Savoy inspired covers by Roy Milton (with lyrics), Pearl Bailey and "Hot Lips" Page (sounded "like those old-fashioned house rent parties"); pop-sounding versions by Tommy Dorsey for Capitol (big band), Lionel Hampton for Decca, and Frank Sinatra for Columbia. *Variety* concluded that "'Hucklebuck' sets a Harlem trend" in the music market.[28]

In August 1949 bandleader Lucky Millinder sued composer Andy Gibson and publisher United Music for copyright of "The Hucklebuck." He claimed that the song really was "D' Natural Blues," a record that had appeared a little lower on rhythm and blues charts. According to Millinder, he had hired Andy Gibson to arrange the melody, which Gibson then took to Savoy and recorded as "The Hucklebuck;" Millinder later recorded it as "D' Natural Blues" with his orchestra. In February, Millinder tried to contest Gibson's authorship with the American Federation of Musicians. At that time Millinder agreed to retain "D' Natural" and give up rights to "The Hucklebuck." The popularity of the latter led Millinder to challenge Gibson's authorship again. There are various possible versions of the actual story: Millinder composed the melody himself and gave it to Gibson to arrange; Gibson created the melody as an assignment for hire and therefore lost his rights to it; or Gibson created both the melody and the arrangement.[29]

As one of the reporters pointed out, the confusion about ownership and origin was unique to the "jazz riff" style of music. The melody for both records was "unquestionably the same . . . a very primitive repeated two-bar riff." Williams's record was popular with both mainstream and black audiences. Parker's record was by far the most sophisticated, including several solo improvisations. Millinder's and Dorsey's renditions had a big band sound. Paul Williams emphasized the saxophone lead and the repetitive rhythm. Otis recalled that for many jazz musicians, the success of Charlie Parker's "Now's the Time" marked the beginning of a new democratic music-making era.[30]

The variety of the 1940s music scene made it necessary to consider different arrangements of the same tune copyrightable. Jazz, blues, and pop performers routinely borrowed each other's riffs—signature musical phrases. By the late 1940s, the practice of arranging other people's riffs had become so common that a more strict copyright was required, for different arrangements of the same melody. According to one legal scholar, an arranger's authorship of a tune included "the choice of instruments, voicing of chords, composition of backgrounds, introductions, modulations, and the addition of variations in rhythm and melody." In 1946 Harold Oxley wrested copyright for a swing number, "Be-Baba-Leba," from many other contenders by making a deal with the owner of the publishing rights and supposed author, Charlie Barnet. Oxley's singer Tina Dixon was the first to record the number, even though Helen Humes, a former singer with Count Basie, popularized it. "The ditty has many variations and just as many supposed authors," reported Billy Rowe, the *Pittsburgh Courier's* entertainment columnist. "Now the thing to do is just sit back and watch the feathers fly."[31]

This legal and stylistic confusion accompanied the transformation of "song" as a work of art, from sheet music to arrangement to recording. The first instance of copyright attached to the tune in its printed iteration—sheet music sold to be played on parlor pianos. By the 1940s, performances of music had become copyrightable also, but the artistic and copyright status of a recording still remained in doubt. When in 1940 bandleader Paul Whiteman and RCA sued a radio station for broadcasting Whiteman's recordings marked "for private use only," the U.S. Court of Appeals for the Second Circuit Judge ruled in favor of the plaintiff. In relation to copyright, Judge Learned Hand wrote: "We shall assume that it covers the performances of an orchestra conductor, and—what is far more doubtful—the skill and art by which a phonographic record maker makes possible the proper recording of those performances upon a disc."[32]

By the 1950s, the industry had accepted the status of recording as a work that stands on its own. Like the radio engineers who in the early 1920s had reinvented radio as a broadcasting medium, sound engineers at Sun, Chess, and King record companies reinvented recording as an art form, adding reverberation and echo to create a new ambient sound. Magnetic tape made it possible to cheaply produce several recording takes in the studio, experimenting with the sound without the give-and-take before a live audience. Instead, a neighborhood disc jockey would play a test acetate record and request immediate response from the radio public. Jockeys did not always approve of the new sound, but they were aware of it. Johnny Cash remembered that Sleepy Eye John, a Memphis DJ, once prefaced a Sun single, "Here's another Sam Phillips sixty-cycle hum record." Since the early 1940s, disc jockeys would indicate their displeasure with the recording by breaking records on the air, making the disc, and not the life performance it supposedly represented, an object of art criticism. "A phonograph record is a finished effort of many creative artists," Al Jarvis argued in 1953. "It represents the finest musical and engineering skill of many people striving for perfection."[33] By playing records, disc jockeys elevated recordings to the status of a distinct work of art.

The jockeys who helped to promote the new music styles took money for playing records—a practice that culminated in the payola scandals of the late 1950s. Payola in music was at least as old as vaudeville. In the 1930s, big bands collected it for playing songs on late night remotes, but by the late 1940s the trades reported the "devaluation of the live plug in favor of the recorded plug," and the money originally set aside for live remotes went to the DJs. Between 1948 and 1956 reporters maintained that rhythm and blues music encouraged much more payola than pop records. "Trouble appears to lie mainly with jocks specializing in race material," an investigative reporter explained in 1948. "Not too many spinners handle this category, with the result that there is terrific competition to get such platters aired. The smaller indies are the sufferers, and must often pay to get a play." Yet extralegal practices like payola provided the infrastructure for the rise of the 'indie' record companies and the development of rhythm and blues music. "When a small label owner," music producer Arnold Shaw argued, "lacking the promotional staffs and regional offices of the majors, felt confident about a record and was willing to pay a tariff, he knew that he could get this record heard."[34] At first glance, rhythm and blues in the 1940s appeared to be an outlaw province of music, where exploitation and corruption reigned despite the legal constraints of the modern music industry.

Rhythm and blues jockeys encouraged such interpretations when they crossed conventional lines of respectability. Mississippi-born Al Benson worked as a pastor, probation officer, WPA interviewer, railroad cook, and waiter before becoming the top rhythm and blues DJ in Chicago. Unlike refined black jockeys, such as Joe Adams in Los Angeles, Benson drew on his experience as a preacher and used the black vernacular. "If you've got plenty of geets on you, go right in the store," *Chicago Tribune* quoted one of his broadcasts. "Walk heavy and talk heavy. And that's for sure, from your old swingmaster." This "native talk" required translation: "Geets is money. To walk heavy means to throw your shoulders back, stride in as if you owned the place, and look the man right in the eye. Talk heavy means to speak right up. Don't be afraid; be confident." Like most black DJs and radio ministers, Benson reached both black and white listeners, yet his jive called up a core black urban audience for his shows. "My people know what I mean," he assured the *Tribune*'s white readers. By the 1950s, white rhythm and blues DJs like Hunter Hancock and Johnny Otis had adopted populist black urban styles on their shows.[35]

Some features of WANN programs seemed as corrupt as the practice of payola. In the late 1920s, white astrologist Rajah Raboid had broadcast from Mexico, along with other quacks like John Brinkley, and during the Great Depression he toured the East coast with his magic show. In September–October 1950, during another East coast tour, Raboid sponsored his own half-hour live religious show on WANN, and the show continued in transcription once he returned to Florida. In 1951, the FCC received a complaint about Raboid, claiming that "the program is operated entirely in behalf of the *colored people* A great many of whom *believe in fortune telling*, etc.!" Even though Blum claimed no fortune telling took place, listeners sent in questions such as "Will I be able to own my own home?" or "Please tell me where is my cousin that has been missing from his home since December 26, 1950. It has been such a heart breaking to his mother & family please tell me as soon as possible I will be listen to here the answer." At the same time, fortune telling seemed to provide a way for listeners to connect not just to Raboid but to each other: "Don't use on radio," another listener wrote, "I concede my turn to someone else." Blum participated in this personal relationship as well. When the FCC asked him for proof of Raboid's credentials, he replied that a reference from a friend was all he needed to hire the entertainer.[36]

Payola could also seem less of a crime to rhythm and blues musicians and DJs because at the time a bribe was often a useful way, and sometimes the only way, to overcome segregation. As a DJ Johnny Otis organized dances mixing Mexican, black, and white Los Angeles teenagers, but the police and local authorities used antiquated blue laws against mixed-age dancing to break up the couples, chasing Otis away from downtown and suburban venues. "It's really interesting how a little money can override concerns about racial purity and morality," Johnny Otis remarked later, "When we paid off the firemen and police, as we often did in Long Beach and other Southern California cities, we had no more trouble." Once Hoppy Adams and Morris Blum stopped for

the night in the only motel in a small South Carolina town. The owner offered
a room to Blum but not Adams. "The boss started putting the money down
in front of the guy, and the greener the money got, the whiter I got," Adams
remembered. Otis compared such moments to "the good old days of bootleg
liquor, only we weren't handling an illegal product."[37]

The informal payola system allowed many aspects of the music business
to flourish—record stores, songwriting, talent management, concert promotion, and interviews with musicians. In the late 1940s these were seen at once
as unjustified perks and as crucial building blocks of new music genres. Al
Benson filled Chicago's Civic Opera House for a bebop concert; 400 were
turned away by a special police detail mustered to control the crowd. He also
owned a record shop and was president of the Swingmaster Recording Company. Herb Abramson of Atlantic Records had a relationship with Randy's
Record Shop, which sold records by mail and sponsored a rhythm and blues
show on WLAC in Nashville. Every time he had a new record, he sent it to
Randy Wood to play on his show, along with two other records for Randy to
sell via mail-order, with "two dollars plus postage."[38]

Much of the payola in rhythm and blues in this period was informal, ranging from cash payments to theater tickets. Jerry Wexler of Atlantic records remembered: "We'd go on the road with an acetate of a new Ruth Brown record.
We'd see a transmitter, we'd walk in. The disc jockey would say, 'Hey! Sure,
what can I do for you?' He'd put the acetate right on! In other words, there was
no music director, there were no committees. You had something new? 'Here,
here you go.' And so we'd leave the guy a bottle of Jack or a sports shirt." This
was a typical distribution system for independent labels. One small Baltimore
record company, Howfum, distributed records in person to local DJs, including Hoppy Adams of WANN. Record company owners remembered that of
all the local DJs, he played their records most often.[39]

Nor was payola confined to the rhythm and blues field. In 1952, the Bureau of Applied Social Research conducted a survey for BMI, meant to determine how pop disc jockeys select their music. BMI executives assured the
researchers that they applied no pressure on jockeys to play records licensed
by the agency. However, a preliminary report showed that "several leading
disk jockeys . . . reveal that they have been requested by their superior in the
radio stations to give preferred treatment to BMI music." Researchers were
uncomfortable with the implication, "if even ten or twenty percent of the
leading disk jockeys operate under instructions to favor BMI music, they can
exert considerable influence on the entire music business."[40]

Rhythm and blues payola, then, was only the highest expression of payola practices everywhere. Pop jockeys, most of them underpaid at under $100 a week, saw "nothing immoral" in this system of recompense, for selling "time for the station, products for the advertiser, and records for the diskeries and publishers." Herb Abramson saw nothing wrong with "cultivating Randy"— only "later," he maintained, "that developed into payola." In 1948, an independent record producer complained to the FCC that "the diskery could not get its records played on certain stations unless the deejays were paid." The Commission replied that it was "not in a position to regulate the [alleged] practices." Such practices had become so commonplace by 1950 that one record company reportedly intended to use payola as a tax write-off. When in 1949–1951 *Billboard* published a series of exposés criticizing DJ payola, readers demanded that the magazine print the names of the worst offenders. But the editors refused to name names, and declared, "It is not within our province to be stool pidgeons." This statement recalled contemporaneous protests against the House Un-American Activities Committee's investigations of Communists in the entertainment industry. One of the reporters, Jerry Wexler, replaced Abramson at Atlantic Records in 1953, where his job was precisely the criminal kind he had investigated for the magazine. Adam Green has proposed calling enterprising disc jockeys like Al Benson, who admitted taking payola bribes during payola scandal in the late 1950s, "trickster figure[s] in relation to consumer capital" because they bent business rules to advance the black music industry. But Benson's achievement would have been impossible without the tacit moral approval of countless black and white players in the music business.[41] Like other moral media economies, disc jockeys' extralegal economies questioned the standards of property in the music industry.

In the early 1950s BMI organized a series of "program clinics," where independent station managers discussed strategies for surviving the competition with television. Some of the debates show how much the disc jockeys' relative autonomy frustrated industry officials. Echoing an earlier BMI ratings ad's focus on bodily harm, a 1953 BMI Clinic advertisement in *Billboard* showed a nurse feeding medicine to a microphone. In a canned speech at several such clinics, BMI's director of station relations Glenn Dolberg warned against the disc jockeys' penchant for broadcasting trial records, unless they were licensed by BMI or ASCAP. Dolberg declared unlicensed records "poison," citing legal consequences ranging from a fine of $250 plus court charges to bankruptcy. "Say there are four thousand bottles over there

and three or four of them contain poison," he warned, "Your chances of getting the poison would be three or four out of a thousand or more, still can you
afford to take that calculated risk?"[42] As jockeys invented their own broadcasting formats, many of their practices ran afoul of copyright restrictions
and established notions of authorship and control.

The use of audiences in programming, a widespread cultural practice, involved relations of reciprocity. For station managers, it was mainly
a matter of saving money. Hugh Smith, formerly a program director at
KPOJ, Portland, boasted of saving money by having customers at a local
drive-in chat with a DJ on the phone, or setting up a remote from the
YMCA: "You'll provide music for an informal dance, . . . get those kids
on the dance floor [and] let them to select the music for you . . . and the
YMCA I bet you ten to one will pay production costs." But when disc
jockeys invited high school students to spin records on the air, they also
offered them an opportunity to become cultural producers. Fred Robbins
in New York ran a typical teen contest, where high school students would
deliver a two-minute commentary on a record of their selection. The winner got an eight-week contract for his own show at the same station. Vivian Carter became a disc jockey after winning a contest organized by Al
Benson; then with her husband, she founded Vee-Jay Records, one of the
first black-owned record labels.[43] These practices walked a fine line between exploitation and collaborative invention.

Some enduring practices born in this period included elements that violated copyright restrictions. Testing and promoting new records was central
to the development of rhythm and blues, hillbilly, and Latin music and the
small independent record companies that produced it. Playing unlicensed
records was a side effect of testing records' popularity. In 1947, Roy Milton
sued black jockey War Perkins for $50,000 in damages for allegedly playing
an unauthorized transcription of one of Milton's broadcasts on his show. It
is this practice that BMI's Glenn Dolberg declared dangerous. He warned
station managers that "any unprincipled man" could "invent devious ways"
to get a DJ play his record, then "wait upon you later with an attorney" to
"collect from you in court" for airing unlicensed recordings.[44] Both extralegal
"piracy" and collaborative production were fundamental features of this transitional period in American music history.

Radio station managers needed DJs because they received several
thousand fan letters per week and helped to attract advertisers. Yet they
complained that jockeys had too much autonomy. They ad-libbed too much,

they stocked station music libraries only with records they liked, and they didn't clean the records properly. They needed to be controlled. "I don't particularly hate them," said Dick Redmond, program director at WHP, Harrisburg, Pennsylvania in 1951, "It's not the disc jockey's fault if he is ruining your station, it's your fault if you're letting him ruin your station." When Rex Dale, a Cincinnati DJ, set up a hit show playing advance copies of new releases ahead of his competitors, the station manager intervened and declared that station policy "specifically forbids his deejays from accepting and playing new records brought to them by distributors, artists, etc., that haven't cleared the regular station channels." In 1953, an amendment to copyright law forbidding the broadcast of any literary work in whole or in part further constrained DJs' ability to improvise. Several stations were immediately charged with "accidental infringement" because they could not "keep tabs" on "ad-lib deejays" used to "casual references to cartoon captions, anecdotal material," and magazine articles.[45]

By the late 1950s, the new radio formats had become standardized, and the national music industry had reasserted its control over radio. Station managers curtailed disc jockeys' relative autonomy in programming and promotional strategies. A new "Top 40" national music radio format reduced the role of the disc jockey to introducing national pop hits. In this format, radio no longer served as a public venue for the DJs' diverse local constituencies. Yet the "Top 40" format's success rested on practices and music styles that had emerged in the period of transition, experimentation, and "piracy."[46] Early DJs' practices opened up the airwaves to new local music styles and their constituencies, from bebop to rhythm and blues to hillbilly and Latin music.

Epilogue

In 2007, *New York Times* software reviewer David Pogue gave a speech to five hundred American college students. To demonstrate the importance of copyright, he asked who in the audience thought downloading a movie without paying for it was wrong. Only two hands went up in agreement, prompting him to declare an alarming "generational divide in copyright morality." In 1924, in another divide, listener petitions lined up behind "squatter" stations that violated radio transmitter patents against the patent owner, AT&T. Such stories render moot the idea, advanced by recent studies, that a sense of fairness is a universal phenomenon. Evolutionary biologists find that capuchin monkeys refuse unequal pay and economists report that students give up their own money to punish cheaters in classroom experiments. Yet a universal "moral instinct" cannot explain why British housewives see nothing "morally wrong" with downloading the latest episode of *Lost* from BitTorrent while the International Intellectual Property Alliance (IIPA), representing U.S. movie, music, software, and publisher lobbies, cries foul at Egypt for letting peddlers sell photocopied textbooks near university campuses.[1] A historical investigation that pays attention to the passions of the moment may be more useful for understanding today's economic moral sense than controlled experiments that presume that humans naturally behave as ethical beings. Insofar as radio's past helps us to understand American traditions of reciprocity, it illuminates the moral economy of digital culture today.

On the one side of the divide, corporate industries invoke morality to extend the reach of intellectual property. The Internet and digital media have made distribution and copying of creative works easier but have also led to more restrictive copyright legislation and "digital rights management" encryption technologies. In 1998, the Copyright Term Extension Act increased copyright terms to the life of the author plus 70 years and for corporate works to 120 years after creation or 95 years after publication, whichever is greater.

The same year, the Digital Millennium Copyright Act outlawed software that breaks encryption protections, and allowed owners to demand that copyrighted content posted without permission be taken offline without testing for "fair use" cases—for education or criticism, for example. Biotech and pharmaceutical industries have adopted this rhetoric as well. "Are you willing to sacrifice your morality for thirty dollars a bushel?" one radio commentator admonished soybean farmers in 2003 for storing hybrid seeds for next year's crop. These farmers, he argued, were thieves, just like peer-to-peer users, because they refused to pay annual royalties to the patent owner.[2]

On the other side, the "free and open source software" and "free culture" movements transform laws and institutions to collaborate and share information. Without CEOs or profit margins, free software projects such as Linux (an operating system) and Apache (a web server) bring together programmers who share expertise, resources, and code. The "geeks" participating in these projects follow the "hacker ethic"—an evolving and contradictory set of principles that include, but are not limited to, information sharing, decentralized collaborative governance, distrust of authority, and an understanding of programming as an art. This moral code draws on liberal doctrines of free speech and of copyright as a means to encourage innovation—written into the U.S. Constitution and the Bill of Rights—and thus seems to stand apart from the copyright-infringing music fans and soybean farmers in the United States and abroad.[3] Yet, much like the ethical sensibilities underlying innovation in early radio, the digital moral economies stretch across the line separating the "rule of law" from criminality, insurgency, and the so-called "developing world."

As history makes clear, media piracy has long thrived inside as well as outside of "developed" Western countries. In the 1920s, Americans tuned in pirate "wave jumping" radio stations. Today, users everywhere turn to BitTorrent and LimeWire, programs that allow users to share files over the web without storing them on one central server. The Electronic Frontier Foundation, a digital rights advocacy nonprofit based in the United States, estimated in 2003 that over sixty million Americans had used filesharing programs. By then, the Recording Industry Association of America and the Motion Picture Association of America had sued over 20,000 U.S. music and video downloaders. According to IIPA, as of early 2010, Canada was hosting four of the top ten filesharing sites in the world; Switzerland allowed downloading from international peer-to-peer sites; Russia had licensed several infringing pay-per-download music services; China had the most illicit music and video downloaders in the world; and street markets of pirated music, films, TV shows, software, and games flourished in Mexico, Argentina, and Chile. Citing data on financial losses that the U.S. government's own Accountability Office finds dubious, the Office of the U.S. Trade Representative has authorized sanctions against these and other infringing countries on its "watch list," thereby manufacturing global consumer audiences for U.S. pharmaceutical, biotech, and entertainment industries.[4]

Yet one executive's piracy is another user's justice. In 1922 the earliest radio fans saw nothing wrong in making and buying bootleg replacement tubes to keep their receivers going. Today, TV fans synchronize their bootleg viewing with American broadcasts. In 2005 Envisional, an Internet monitoring company, calculated that TV piracy had increased 150 percent from the previous year, Great Britain leading with 18 percent of the world's downloads. British viewers felt entitled to see episodes of *24* and *Battlestar Galactica* as soon as possible after they aired in the United States, seeing these shows as "legitimate material" for copying as long as they kept up their cable subscription. After surveying reports from public BitTorrent trackers, filesharing news blog TorrentFreak reported that in 2009, at the time the highest point of TV piracy, most downloaders resided in countries where American shows aired months later and thought it unfair to have to wait several months for an installment of *Heroes* or *Lost*. TorrentFreak suggested that the industry might want to experiment with TV-on-demand in response to viewers' desire for a new, globally live, television. Filesharing networks thus do for television what bootleg receivers and "squatter" stations did for radio in the 1920s—create an infrastructure and an international live audience for a reinvented entertainment medium.[5]

Peer-to-peer users assume that current intellectual property relations are unjust; fan fiction projects take this moral economy as a license for creative practice. *Star Trek* or *Buffy the Vampire Slayer* audiences communicate with producers directly in chat rooms, rewrite media stories in fanzines, and create communities around programs. As a result, much like the radio soap opera writers of the 1930s, some TV and film producers today opt for direct collaboration with fans instead of consulting ratings or survey data. Creators of the TV show *Battlestar Galactica* and *The Lord of the Rings* film trilogy consulted with fans while they were working on the new versions of these cult works. This reciprocal production process made both versions popular and profitable. Such authors still choose practical knowledge over scientific management of audiences.[6]

When producers prohibit fans from making art based on copyrighted shows, fans test the limits of corporate ownership. Their works inspire legal theories that extend doctrines of fair use in copyright to include derivative works, as well as new copyright licenses, like the Creative Commons license, that allow authors to share and remix creative material. Some creators side with audiences rather than the corporate owners on what is fair. In April 2010 Constantin Film tried to use Google's "Content ID" system to remove the innumerable YouTube parodies based on phony subtitles to a famous Hitler bunker scene from its film *Downfall*. "You couldn't get a better compliment as a director," the film's author Oliver Hirschbiegel had remarked about the videos just a few months earlier. Some parodists claimed fair use exceptions, allowing Google to restore the videos. As of this writing, many of the parodies are still online, including a version where Hitler fumes about Constantin Film's takedown of the videos. Precisely because these audiences do not have complete autonomy when they reinvent media stories, they propose a different, just relationship between media corporations and audiences.[7]

The audience's sense of entitlement seems even more justified when it comes to access to knowledge. In 2008, the *New York Times* reported, American students grew "angrier than ever before about the price of textbooks," hardly affordable at more than $200 a copy. This outrage inspired a range of nonproprietary solutions, from pirate sites such as the now defunct Textbook Torrents, to open-access journal publishing ventures, such as Public Library of Science, that make the latest academic research freely available for unrestricted use, to open source projects like Connexions, a collaborative site that lets members create free teaching "modules" that can be combined into textbooks. The scholarly entitlement extends across regional borders: the open-access movement expands the scholarly community to include unaffiliated researchers and scholars in non-Western universities who do not have access to commercial article databases. It also stretches across the digital divide. According to the IIRA, Egyptian government agencies "look the other way" while stalls selling photocopied textbooks and course packs operate near campuses, lecturers "encourage" copying, and universities "give pirate enterprises cover" and rent space to copy shops.[8]

Legal U.S. scholarly websites and illegal Egyptian copy shops may seem worlds apart; they are not. Although invented in the United States, open access transforms the ways scientists everywhere can claim authorship. At the turn of the nineteenth century, a self-taught English mathematician and engineer, Oliver Heaviside, came up with methods to overcome signal

distortion in telegraphy, but because he was not affiliated with a corporation or a university and did not patent his invention, AT&T appropriated and
profited from his theories. In 2002-2003, a reclusive and unemployed Russian
mathematician, Grigory Perelman, posted his own solution to the Poincaré
Conjecture on arXiv, an open-access repository of scientific preprints, and
received recognition for the discovery against the claims of published and
affiliated Chinese scholars. He also received offers of several million dollars
in prestigious prizes, which he refused.[9] The accepted practice of preprint
publishing served to ensure Perelman's credit, as did the concomitant moral
sensibility, the same sensibility that leads one to suspect that in going after
makeshift stalls on Egyptian campuses IIRA may have overreacted.

   In the United States, lay moral economies sometimes influence legal
thinking. The "copyleft" movement, which includes the Free Software Foundation and Creative Commons, among others, drew upon collaborative
practices in free software and fan communities to develop several licenses
that allow authors to waive some or all of their rights to users. FSF founder
Richard Stallman developed GPL (General Public License) informally, while
making software; Lawrence Lessig, a Constitutional legal scholar, consulted
open source developers when he first conceptualized Creative Commons. Although Stallman and Lessig disagree on the value of each other's approaches
to copyright, these and other "copyleft" projects draw upon the "pragmatist"
view of the Anglo-American common law tradition, articulated by Oliver
Wendell Holmes, Jr., who famously opined that "the life of law has not been
logic; it has been experience." This emphasis on practice, anthropologist
Chris Kelty argues, makes the free software and free culture movements a
"recursive public," which constantly reinvents its own technological, legal,
and moral conditions of existence.[10]

   U.S. government actions and court decisions, too, occasionally share or
take into account popular practices and moral views. In 1932, the Justice Department followed popular outrage when it broke up the radio trust. In 1986,
the U.S. Supreme Court agreed with VCR owners that recording television
programs on their machines was fair. In the 1970s, early video enthusiasts
had begun to "timeshift"—tape TV shows on their recorders to watch later.
When Universal sued Sony over its new Betamax copying technology in
1976, many videorecorder owners saw the lawsuit as an attack on their civil
liberties. By 1982, VCRs had supplanted Betamax machines and videorecord-
ing had become a common practice. The Supreme Court ruled in favor of
Sony, extending the fair use provisions of the 1976 Copyright Act to include

timeshifting, and arguing that Sony was not liable for potential infringement, given that many lawful uses of the technology were also possible. The Court's decision was not unanimous and, some say, was actually contradictory, yet it seemed to concur with Judge Holmes in that it relied not on logic alone but also on the practical knowledge of VCR users' experience.[11]

The moral economies embedded in free software, open-access, fan fiction, and filesharing practices may yet influence legal decisions on digital property. In 2005 in *MGM v Grokster*, the Supreme Court ruled that Grokster, a peer-to-peer filesharing service, was liable for its users' music piracy even though lawful uses of its services were also possible. This ruling contradicted the Betamax decision, and led to the development of takedown software systems like Google's Content ID, which made it easy for Constantin Films to remove the Hitler parodies from YouTube. Between 1999 and 2003, the MPAA and Adobe used DMCA to initiate high-profile arrests and lawsuits targeting a Norwegian, Jon Johansen, and a Russian, Dmitry Sklyarov, for authoring software that could break the content scrambling protection on DVD discs and Adobe e-books. These cases, later dismissed, inspired hacker protests that established a notion that software code qualifies for legal protection as free speech. This notion then informed legal arguments by Lessig, Yochai Benkler, and other digital rights advocates, in what anthropologist Gabriela Coleman, following legal theorist Robert Cover, calls "jurisgenesis"—a process whereby lay communities invent new legal meanings and institutions. In July 2010, the Copyright Office and the Librarian of Congress, charged by the 1976 copyright law to clarify fair use, declared that it is legal to jailbreak iPhones and to circumvent CSS encryption on DVDs to create remix videos. Both rulings chip away at DMCA restrictions and attendant legal reasoning.[12]

In the global context, however, digital moral economies often come into irreconcilable conflict with legal codes governing the relationships between the United States and the rest of the world. The IIPA, for example, condemns foreign nations for practices that would be legal in the United States: Israel, for "overly broad" fair use provisions; and Indonesia, Brazil, and India for using open source software to run government agencies. The anarchist antiglobalization movements, active since the anti-World Trade Organization protests in Seattle in 1999, have adopted the open-access model of decentralized collaborative governance. Meanwhile, human rights and environmentalist groups have been living in fear that their computers would be taken by local police for pirating Microsoft software. In September 2010 the Baikal Environmental Wave group in Russia had its computers confiscated in the midst of protesting the reopening of a paper factory that had polluted the world's largest fresh-water preserve, Lake Baikal. "Microsoft did not want to help us, which would have been the right thing to do," activists reported. In several such cases, Microsoft, whose formidable bootleg software tracking force of former FBI and Secret Service agents recalls RCA's anti-tube-bootlegging squads of the 1920s, claimed that they were required to assist the police under Russian law. Only after the *New York Times* published an exposé of its policies did Microsoft withdraw its support of Russian police raids and announce a free software licensing program for activists in Russia and several former Soviet republics, as well as China, Malaysia, and Vietnam, thereby admitting that it was not free market but free software that best served justice in those countries.[13]

The story of Wikileaks demonstrates on a global Internet-era scale the point that this book makes about early American radio: that reciprocity required by a new medium can inform a critique of larger power relations. Much like early radio and free software, the digital whistleblower organization took shape by trial and error. In July 2007, a small stateless group of hackers had first invited anonymous submissions of secret government and corporate documents, publishing files from a Kenyan political corruption study to email correspondence showing that British scientists fudged data to advocate for global warming. Wikileaks activists began by posting on their website documents as received; only a few journalists and bloggers paid attention. Then in 2010 Wikileaks published a vast collection detailing U.S. imperialism in diplomacy and war: in April of that year, a video showing a U.S. army helicopter killing several Iraqis and two Reuters journalists, and wounding two Iraqi children; in July, 76,607 military dispatches from Afghanistan; in September, 390,136 Iraq war dispatches; and starting in November, gradually, 251,287 U.S. State Department cables. They widely announced the release of the U.S. helicopter video and included their own edits along with the raw footage; major media outlets replayed it but criticized the group for partisan editorializing. Since then, Wikileaks has released documents simultaneously with analyses of them in established media sources, collaborating on the Afghan war logs with the *New York Times*, the British newspaper *Guardian*, and the German magazine *Der Spiegel*; then adding Al Jazeera and French *Le Monde*, for the Iraq logs, and Spanish *El Pais*, for the diplomatic cable release. After human rights organizations censured the group for revealing names of Afghan civilians, Wikileaks took care to redact every name in the Iraq logs and the diplomatic cables, in collaboration with journalists. "Wikileaks Evolves," one observer concluded in December 2010, noting the increasingly mature ways whereby the organization protected individual lives while focusing public attention on the civilian deaths, bribes, lies, torture, and other calamities witnessed and incited by U.S. agents.[14]

Wikileaks makes vernacular political economy—the subject of this book—possible on a global scale because it "crowdsources" interpretation. It allows its readers to form and express their own opinions based on the documents that usually get to the public second-hand, digested by journalists, politicians, and corporate publicists. Besides the Wikileaks websites, several interfaces have sprung up that make such popular political theory possible: online comment sections of Wikileaks partner news outlets, the *Guardian*'s "You Ask, We Search" feature for readers, the user analysis interface by the French nonprofit digital journalism organization OWNI, and the diplomatic cable search by the European Center for Computer Assisted Reporting, to name just a few. This direct public access to massive sets of classified materials "embodies all that is sacred to the hacker mentality," according to the veteran hacker newsletter *2600*; it has also been declared dangerous. The Pentagon likened document leaks to illegal file sharing; the State Department, to espionage; Amazon refused to host Wikileaks; MasterCard, Visa, and Paypal, to process donations; EveryDNS, to process the wikileaks.org domain name; even some Wikileaks members defected to form their own organization, Openleaks, that resolved "not to publish any document directly." Because, not despite, of this government and corporate onslaught, Wikileaks has maintained popular legitimacy, evident in over three hundred volunteer mirror sites hosting its files and several copycat organizations, such as Tradeleaks, Brusselsleaks, and Indoleaks.[15]

Although their politics belonged to a different age, that of the New Deal and World War II, early radio's moral economies have much in common with today's tenets of cooperation, reciprocity, and trial-and-error production in technology, ethics, and law. Aspects of hacker values and practices—values that now seem inseparable from contemporary computer communication networks—also applied in earlier eras in American history, especially at times when new technologies and cultural forms were emerging. Studying this history helps us make moral and political judgments in the present. The point of Wikileaks, one defender argued, is "to encourage in individuals the sense of justice which would embolden them to challenge the institutions that control our fate."[16] Nanny Roy, the radio listener whose own account of her sense of justice opened this book, would surely agree.

Abbreviations

AHC-FAH	Frank and Anne Hummert Papers, American Heritage Center, University of Wyoming, Laramie, Wyo.
AHC-PHL	Phillips H. Lord Papers, American Heritage Center, University of Wyoming, Laramie, Wyo.
AHC-TJM	Thomas J. McDermott Collection, American Heritage Center, University of Wyoming, Laramie, Wyo.
BG	*Boston Globe*
CD	*Chicago Defender*
CU-BASR	Bureau of Applied Social Research, Columbia University, New York, N.Y.
CU-PFL	Paul F. Lazarsfeld Papers, Columbia University, New York, N.Y.
CU-RPP	Radio Pioneers Project, Columbia University, New York, N.Y.
DSL-DS	David Sarnoff Papers, David Sarnoff Library, Princeton, N.J.
GB	*Gang Busters*
LAB-BMI	BMI Program Clinics Collection, Library of American Broadcasting, University of Maryland, College Park, Md.
LAB-HJS	Helen J. Sioussat Papers, Library of American Broadcasting, University of Maryland, College Park, Md.
LC-ES	Eric Sevareid Papers, Manuscript Division, Library of Congress, Washington, D.C.
LC-FA	Fred Allen Papers, Manuscript Division, Library of Congress, Washington, D.C.
LC-FSA	Farm Security Administration-Office of War Information Photograph Collection, Prints and Photographs Division, Library of Congress, Washington, D.C.

LC-NBC	National Broadcasting Company Collection, Motion Picture, Broadcasting, and Recorded Sound Division, Library of Congress, Washington, D.C.
LC-NPC	National Photo Company Collection, Prints and Photographs Division, Library of Congress, Washington, D.C.
LC-WOR	WOR Collection, Library of Congress, Washington, D.C.
NA-FCC	Federal Communications Commission Papers, Record Group 173, National Archives, College Park, Md.
NMAH-GHC	George H. Clark Radioana Collection, Archives Center, National Museum of American History, Smithsonian Institution, Washington, D.C.
NMAH-JA	Joe Adams Papers, National Museum of American History, Smithsonian Institution, Washington, D.C.
NMAH-WANN	WANN Collection, National Museum of American History, Smithsonian Institution, Washington, D.C.
NYT	*New York Times*
PIRE	*Proceedings of the Institute of Radio Engineers*
POQ	*Public Opinion Quarterly*
RAC-RFA	Series 200R, Record Group 1.1, Rockefeller Foundation Archives, Rockefeller Archive Center, Newark, N.J.
RB	*Radio Broadcast*
RD	*Radio Digest*
RG	*Radio Guide*
RL	*Radioland*
RM	*Radio Mirror*
RN	*Radio News*
RPW	*New York Radio Program Weekly*
RS	*Radio Stars*
RT-WHN	WHN Collection, *Ridgewood Times*, Queens, N.Y.
SMM	*The Story of Mary Marlin*
TI	*Tune In*
TOL-RV	Rudy Vallee Collection, Thousand Oaks Library, Thousand Oaks, Calif.
USC-CG	Charles Correll and Freeman F. Gosden Collection, University of Southern California, Los Angeles, Calif.
WA	*Wireless Age*
WHS-EPHJ	E. P. H. James Papers, Wisconsin Historical Society, Madison, Wisc.

WHS-IP	Irna Phillips Papers, Wisconsin Historical Society, Madison, Wisc.
WHS-JC	Jane Crusinberry Papers, Wisconsin Historical Society, Madison, Wisc.
WHS-NBC	National Broadcasting Company Records, Wisconsin Historical Society, Madison, Wisc.
WHS-WH	Wendell Hall Papers, Wisconsin Historical Society, Madison, Wisc.
WP	*Washington Post*

Notes

Preface

1. Mrs. W. W. Roy to Leonard Bass, October 18, 1942, box 16, folder GB 281, 2 of 2, LC-WOR; *Real Detective*, clipping, used for "Case of Virgil Harris," *GB*, September 18, 1942; box 16, folder GB 281, 1 of 2, LC-WOR. This book relies on thousands of letters, most of them handwritten. For the sake of clarity, I did not use "sic" to mark numerous spelling and grammatical errors and typos in listeners' letters and broadcasters' memos. Whenever I was in doubt about a possible error in a handwritten letter, I used the correct spelling in the quotation. Unless otherwise noted, occupation, age, ethnicity, and residential data on letter writers is taken from the U.S. federal census records for 1910, 1920, and 1930, available at Ancestry.com, http://www.ancestry.com/search/rectype/census/usfedcen/default.aspx.

2. See, for example, Thomas Bender, *Community and Social Change in America* (New Brunswick, N.J.: Rutgers University Press, 1978), on community; Alan Brinkley, *Voices of Protest: Huey Long, Father Coughlin and the Great Depression* (New York: Vintage Books, 1982), on populism; Lizabeth Cohen, *Making a New Deal: Industrial Workers in Chicago, 1919–1939* (Cambridge: Cambridge University Press, 1990), on workers; Roland Marchand, *Creating the Corporate Soul: The Rise of Public Relations and Corporate Imagery in American Big Business* (Berkeley: University of California Press, 1998), on corporations; James Sparrow, "'Buying Our Boys Back': The Mass Foundations of Fiscal Citizenship in World War II," *Journal of Policy History* 20, no. 2 (2008): 263–86; and Meg Jacobs, "'How About Some Meat?': The Office of Price Administration, Consumption Politics, and State Building from the Bottom Up, 1941–1946," *Journal of American History* 84 (December 1997): 910–41, on wartime government; and E. P. Thompson, "The Moral Economy of the English Crowd in the Eighteenth Century," *Past and Present* 50 (1971): 76–136, on the concept of "moral economy."

3. See Susan Douglas, *Inventing American Broadcasting, 1899–1922* (Baltimore: Johns Hopkins University Press, 1987), on amateurs; Robert McChesney, *Telecommunications, Mass Media, and Democracy: The Battle for the Control of U. S. Broadcasting, 1928–1935* (New York: Oxford University Press, 1993), on legislation; Susan Smulyan, *Selling Radio: The Commercialization of American Broadcasting, 1920–1934* (Washington, D.C., and London: Smithsonian Institution Press, 1994) and Thomas Streeter, *Selling the Air: A Critique of the Policy of Commercial Broadcasting in the United States*

(Chicago: Chicago University Press, 1996), on advertising and surveys; and Michele Hilmes, *Radio Voices: American Broadcasting, 1922-1952* (Minneapolis: University of Minnesota Press, 1997), on national culture. Yochai Benkler, *The Wealth of Networks: How Social Production Transforms Markets and Freedom* (New Haven: Yale University Press, 2006), 27, 196.

4. See, for example, Derek W. Vaillant, *Sounds of Reform: Progressivism and Music in Chicago, 1873-1935* (Chapel Hill: University of North Carolina Press, 2003), and Clifford J. Doerksen, *American Babel: Rogue Radio Broadcasters of the Jazz Age* (Philadelphia: University of Pennsylvania Press, 2005), on local stations; Michael J. Socolow, "To Network a Nation: N.B.C., C.B.S. and the Development of National Network Radio in the United States, 1925-1950" (Ph.D. diss., Georgetown University, 2001), on network coverage and the FCC; Alexander Russo, *Points on the Dial: Golden Age Radio Beyond the Networks* (Durham, N.C.: Duke University Press, 2010), on regional networks; Charles F. McGovern, *Sold American: Consumption and Citizenship, 1890-1945* (Chapel Hill: University of North Carolina Press, 2006), on citizenship; Kathy Newman, *Radio Active: Advertising and Consumer Activism, 1935-1947* (Berkeley: University of California Press, 2004), on boycotts; Jason Loviglio, *Radio's Intimate Public: Network Broadcasting and Mass-Mediated Democracy* (Minneapolis: University of Minnesota Press, 2005), Bruce Lenthall, *Radio's America: The Great Depression and the Rise of Modern Mass Culture* (Chicago: University of Chicago Press, 2007), and Susan Douglas, *Listening In: Radio and the American Imagination* (New York: Times Books, 1999), on intimacy. Claude Fischer, *America Calling: A Social History of the Telephone to 1940* (Berkeley: University of California Press, 1992), 22 (radio ownership); Erik Barnouw, *The Golden Web: A History of Broadcasting from 1933 to 1953* (New York: Oxford University Press, 1968), 6 (giving up necessities); George Washington Hill quoted in Charles A. Siepmann, *Radio, Television, and Society* (New York: Oxford University Press, 1950), 49.

5. Henry Jenkins, "Contacting the Past: Early Radio and the Digital Revolution," *MIT Communications Forum*, December 3, 1997, http://web.mit.edu/comm-forum/papers/jenkins_cp.html; Michael Denning, "The End of Mass Culture," *International Labor and Working-Class History* 37 (Spring 1990): 15-16.

6. See, for example, Jonathan Sterne, *The Audible Past: Cultural Origins of Sound Reproduction* (Durham, N.C.: Duke University Press, 2002); Emily Thompson, *The Soundscape of Modernity: Architectural Acoustics and the Culture of Listening in America, 1900-1933* (Cambridge, Mass.: MIT Press, 2002); and Steve J. Wurtzler, *Electric Sounds: Technological Change and the Rise of Corporate Mass Media, Film and Culture* (New York: Columbia University Press, 2007). This argument extends Rosalind Krauss's concept of "reinventing the medium" in visual arts; see Krauss, "'The Rock': William Kentridge's Drawings for Projection," *October* 92 (Spring 2000): 12.

7. For example, "active audience" theory celebrates audiences' power to reinterpret media narratives. It took as its starting point Stuart Hall's "Encoding/Decoding," in *Culture, Media, Language*, ed. Stuart Hall et al. (London: Hutchinson, 1980); for examples, see David Morley, *The Nationwide Audience: Structure and Decoding* (London: British

Film Institute, 1980); and Henry Jenkins, *Textual Poachers: Television Fans and Participatory Culture* (New York: Routledge, 1992). On parallels, or "homologies," between different social domains, see Raymond Williams, "Typification and Homology," in *Marxism and Literature* (Oxford: Oxford University Press, 1977), 104–5; and Pierre Bourdieu, "The Intellectual Field: A World Apart," in *In Other Words: Essays Toward a Reflexive Sociology* (Cambridge, Mass.: Polity, 1990), 140–41. Meg Jacobs, *Pocketbook Politics: Economic Citizenship in Twentieth-Century America, Politics and Society in Twentieth-century America* (Princeton, N.J.: Princeton University Press, 2004); Robert B. Westbrook, *Why We Fought: Forging American Obligations in World War II* (Washington, D.C.: Smithsonian Books, 2004) ("popular political theory," Betty Grable); Lawrence W. Levine, *The Unpredictable Past: Explorations in American Cultural History* (New York and Oxford: Oxford University Press, 1993) (Hollywood films).

8. Marcel Mauss, *The Gift: The Form and Reason For Exchange in Archaic Societies*, trans. W. D. Halls (New York: W.W. Norton, 1990), originally published as "Essai sur le don: Forme et raison de l'échange dans les sociétés archaïques," *L'année sociologique* n.s. 1 (1923–24): 30–186; Thompson, "The Moral Economy of the English Crowd"; Thompson, "Folklore, Anthropology and Social History," *Indian Historical Review* 3 (1977): 252-72 (Mauss and gift giving); Benkler, *The Wealth of Networks*; Yochai Benkler, "Coase's Penguin, or, Linux and The Nature of the Firm," *Yale Law Journal* 112 (2002): 33 (Mauss and gift giving); Jacobs, *Pocketbook Politics*; Jacobs, "'How About Some Meat?'" 913 (Thompson and moral economy). Mauss and Thompson inspired many followers and critics; one of many accounts that considers "gift economy" and "moral economy" as related concepts of reciprocity is Peter Burke, *History and Social Theory* (Ithaca, N.Y.: Cornell University Press, 2005), 68–70.

9. Useful starting points for the study of modernity and its varieties are Marshall Berman, *All That Is Solid Melts into Air: The Experience of Modernity* (New York: Penguin Books, 1988); Arjun Appadurai, *Modernity at Large: Cultural Dimensions of Globalization* (Minneapolis: University of Minnesota Press, 1996); and Dilip Parameshwar Gaonkar, ed., *Alternative Modernities* (Durham, N.C.: Duke University Press, 2001). Brian Larkin, *Signal and Noise: Media, Infrastructure, and Urban Culture in Nigeria* (Durham, N.C.: Duke University Press, 2008), ch. 7; Charles Hirschkind, *The Ethical Soundscape: Cassette Sermons and Islamic Counterpublics* (New York: Columbia University Press, 2006); and Peter Geschiere, *The Modernity of Witchcraft: Politics and the Occult in Postcolonial Africa* (Charlottesville: University Press of Virginia, 1997). This argument extends points made in Ann Laura Stoler, "Tense and Tender Ties: The Politics of Comparison in North American History and (Post) Colonial Studies," *Journal of American History* 88, no. 3 (December 2001): 829–65.

10. Sarah E. Igo, *The Averaged American: Surveys, Citizens, and the Making of a Mass Public* (Cambridge, Mass.: Harvard University Press, 2007) (Middletown, popular critique, then acceptance, of surveys); Susan Ohmer, *George Gallup in Hollywood* (New York: Columbia University Press, 2006); Streeter, *Selling the Air* (ratings); Herta Herzog, "Radio—The First Post-War Year," *POQ* 10 (Fall 1946): 311–12; Hans Zeisel, "The

Coincidental Audience Measurement," *Education on the Air* (1946): 387, 399. On population management, see Michel Foucault, "Governmentality," in *The Foucault Effect: Studies in Governmentality*, ed. Graham Burchell, Colin Gordon, and Peter Miller (Chicago and London: University Of Chicago Press, 1991), 87–104.

11. William E. Connolly, *Why I Am Not a Secularist* (Minneapolis: University of Minnesota Press, 1999); Carlo Ginzburg, "Morelli, Freud, and Sherlock Holmes: Clues and Scientific Method," in *Dupin, Holmes, Peirce: The Sign of Three*, ed. Umberto Eco and Thomas A. Sebeok (Bloomington: Indiana University Press, 1983), 81–118 (reasoning from the particular); James C. Scott, *Seeing Like a State: How Certain Schemes to Improve the Human Condition Have Failed* (New Haven: Yale University Press, 1998), 309–41 (practical knowledge); "Counterfeit Vacuum Tubes Now Made on Huge Scale," *BG*, September 23, 1923; Mrs. W. T. Oppemann to John Murray, June 4, 1944, box 46, folder 1, WHS-IP (advice to a character); Orrin E. Jr. Dunlap, "Listening-In," *NYT*, April 24, 1932 (gifts); Hugh M. Beville, "The ABCD's of Radio Audiences," *POQ* 4 (June 1940): 199; Jürgen Habermas *The Structural Transformation of the Public Sphere: An Inquiry into a Category of Bourgeois Society* (Cambridge, Mass.: MIT Press, 1989).

12. The *Spectator* is the key early example in Habermas's account of the public sphere; here I extend the more recent definition of "publics" in Michael Warner, *Publics and Counterpublics* (New York: Zone Books, 2005). Joseph Chaves, "Strangers and Publics," *Media History* 14, no. 3 (2008): 303 (*Spectator*); Julius Weinberger, "Broadcast Transmitting Stations of the Radio Corporation of America," *PIRE* 12, no. 6 (1924): 779 (telegraph and telephone); NBC Statistical Department, "A Brief Study of the Appeal and Popularity of 'The Goldbergs,'" July 25, 1932, box 13, folder 58, WHS-NBC (mail contests); "Radio Fans Found More Mail Minded," *RG*, January 28, 1932 (CBS); "Fan Mail," *Literary Digest*, May 22, 1937 (NBC); "Voice of the Listener," *RG*, February 6, 1937; "The Listener Speaks," *RPW*, April 7, 1927.

13. David M. Henkin, *The Postal Age: The Emergence of Modern Communications in Nineteenth-Century America* (Chicago and London: University of Chicago Press, 2006), 2–3; *Rates for Domestic Letters, 1863–2009* (United States Postal Service, May 2009), http://www.usps.com/postalhistory/_pdf/DomesticLetterRates1863–2009.pdf; *Pieces of Mail Handled, Number of Post Offices, Income, and Expenses, 1789 to 2008* (United States Postal Service, January 2009), http://www.usps.com/postalhistory/_pdf/Piecesof Mail1789to2008.pdf; Jennifer Hayward, *Consuming Pleasures: Active Audiences and Serial Fictions from Dickens to Soap Opera* (Lexington: University Press of Kentucky, 1997); Samantha Barbas, *Movie Crazy: Fans, Stars, and the Cult of Celebrity* (New York: Palgrave, 2001) (letters to theatrical and movie stars); William Thackeray, quoted in E. D. H. Johnson, *Charles Dickens: An Introduction to His Novels* (New York: Random House, 1969), ch. 3; Roland Marchand, *Advertising the American Dream: Making Way for Modernity, 1920–1940* (Berkeley: University of California Press, 1985), 93 ("friendly and personal letter," "personal touch," use of intimacy in advertising); Allison McCracken, "'God's Gift to Us Girls': Crooning, Gender, and the Re-creation of American Popular Song, 1928–1933," *American Music* 17, no. 4 (Winter 1999): 365–95 (microphones and

crooners); Loviglio, *Radio's Intimate Public* (personal address); Lawrence W. Levine and
Cornelia R. Levine, *The People and the President: America's Conversation with FDR* (Boston: Beacon Press, 2002) (court packing).

14. The best account of U.S. corporate campaigns to identify consumption with
citizenship in this period is McGovern, *Sold American*; for a relevant account of a later
period, see Lizabeth Cohen, *A Consumer's Republic: The Politics of Mass Consumption
in Postwar America* (New York: Knopf, 2003). On the power and eventual collapse of
the Soviet reeducation project, see Steven A. Barnes, *Death and Redemption: The Gulag
and the Shaping of Soviet Society* (Princeton, N.J.: Princeton University Press, forthcoming); and Alexei Yurchak, *Everything Was Forever, Until It Was No More: The Last Soviet
Generation* (Princeton, N.J.: Princeton University Press, 2005). On ideas embodied in
practices, see, for example, Raymond Williams, "Structures of Feeling," in *Marxism and
Literature* (Oxford: Oxford University Press, 1977), 128–35; and Charles Taylor, *Modern
Social Imaginaries* (Durham, N.C.: Duke University Press, 2004). For a great account,
one of many, of HMV trademark's history and meanings, see John M. Picker, *Victorian
Soundscapes* (New York: Oxford University Press, 2003), 142–43.

Chapter 1

1 Harold Warren to NAWA; "Voice-Broadcasting the Stirring Progress of the 'Battle
of the Century,'" *WA*, August 1921, 11–21, http://earlyradiohistory.us/century2.htm; "The
Radiophone on Roller Chairs," *RN*, August 1920, http://earlyradiohistory.us/1920roll.
htm; J. Andrew White, "Radiophone Broadcasting of Dempsey-Carpentier Fight on July
2, 1921," report to RCA, New York, July 14, 1921, box 1, DSL-DS. All extant letters to
NAWA in response to the Dempsey-Carpentier broadcast were summarized or quoted in
White's report and are cited from this report. The report gives no dates for letters; all must
have been written between the day of the broadcast, July 2, and the date of the report, July
14, 1921. Most of the summaries and quotes of letters from the report were published,
sometimes in an abridged form, in "Voice-Broadcasting the Stirring Progress of the 'Battle
of the Century.'"

2. White, "Radiophone Broadcasting" (RCA transmitter; 300,000 listeners). On the
Dempsey-Firpo fight, see Elliott J. Gorn, "The Manassa Mauler and the Fighting Marine,"
Journal of American Studies 19 (April 1985): 41–42; "Listening In," *WP*, September 4–9;
and documents in box 1, folder 3, WHS-EPHJ.

3. "Ringside Radio," *American Experience*, PBS, http://www.pbs.org/wgbh/amex/
fight/sfeature/sf_radio_pop_1938_intro.html; Lewis A Erenberg, *The Greatest Fight of
Our Generation: Louis vs. Schmeling* (New York: Oxford University Press, 2006); David
Margolick, *Beyond Glory: Joe Louis vs. Max Schmeling and a World on the Brink* (New
York: Knopf, 2005).

4. Hugh G. J. Aitken, *The Continuous Wave: Technology and American Radio, 1900–
1932* (Princeton, N.J.: Princeton University Press, 1985); Leonard S. Reich, "Research,
Patents, and the Struggle to Control Radio: A Study of Big Business and the Uses of Industrial Research," *Business History Review* 51 (Summer 1977): 208–35; Reich, *The Making of*

American Industrial Research: Science and Business at GE and Bell, 1876–1926 (Cambridge and New York: Cambridge University Press, 1985).

5. Douglas Gomery, *The Hollywood Studio System* (London: British Film Institute, 2005); Arthur Frank Wertheim, *Vaudeville Wars: How the Keith-Albee and Orpheum Circuits Controlled the Big-time and Its Performers* (New York: Palgrave Macmillan, 2006); David Suisman, *Selling Sounds: The Commercial Revolution in American Music* (Cambridge, Mass.: Harvard University Press, 2009). On boxing in the 1920s, see Elliott J. Gorn, *The Manly Art: Bare-Knuckle Prize Fighting in America* (Ithaca, N.Y.: Cornell University Press, 1986); Randy Roberts, *Jack Dempsey: The Manassa Mauler* (Baton Rouge: Louisiana State University Press, 1979); Jeffrey Sammons, *Beyond the Ring: The Role of Boxing in American Society* (Urbana: University of Illinois Press, 1988).

6. William Peck Banning, *Commercial Broadcasting Pioneer: The WEAF Experiment, 1922-1926* (Cambridge, Mass.: Harvard University Press, 1946), 134 ("squatters," AT&T); *Radio Service Bulletin*, February 1, 1923 (1923 stations); Charles Parlin, *The Merchandising of Radio* (Philadelphia: Curtis Publishing, 1925), 5 (1925 stations). See also Erik Barnouw, *A Tower in Babel* (New York: Oxford University Press, 1966), 4.

7. Reich, "Research, Patents, and the Struggle to Control Radio," 225–28 (patents and independent manufacturers); Charles Sloan, "'Bootleg' Tubes Cause Trouble to Radio Fans," *Chicago Tribune*, May 26, 1922 (RCA unable to satisfy the demand; small manufacturers make and sell their own tubes); I. M. Wisernow, "Radio Experiences of a Broadcast Listener," *BG*, July 1, 1923 (constructing sets with bootleg tubes); "Counterfeit Vacuum Tubes Now Made on Huge Scale," *BG*, September 23, 1923 (as profitable as rum smuggling); "Confesses He Spied on De Forest Radio," *NYT*, May 5, 1925 (RCA detectives secretly infiltrated other factories); Donald Monroe McNicol, *Radio's Conquest of Space: The Experimental Rise in Radio Communication* (New York: Murray Hill, 1946), 341–42 ($79.50 sets); "Plan Better Radio Goods," *NYT*, April 19, 1922, ($25 sets); "Million and Half Sets in U.S.," *RD*, January 27, 1923, 1 (1923 set sales); Parlin, *The Merchandising of Radio*, 5 (1925 set sales); "Total Retail Radio Sales—1922–1928 in Numbers and Dollars," *Sales Management* 19 (September 21, 1929): 91, sec 2 (1926 sales). See also Leslie J. Page, Jr., "The Nature of the Broadcast Receiver and Its Market in the United States from 1922 to 1927," *Journal of Broadcasting* 6 (Spring 1960): 176–77; and Richard Butsch, *The Making of American Audiences: From Stage to Television, 1750–1990* (New York: Cambridge University Press, 2000), 175–76.

8. Lloyd Espenschied, "The Origin and Development of Radiotelephony," *PIRE* 25 (September 1937): 1111 (Catalina Island); Harold Arlin quoted in Jennie Irene Mix, "The Listener's Point of View," *RB*, June 1925, 217–18; Mrs. John H. Gardner to WGY, August 1924, excerpted in "Excerpts from Letters Received at WGY," report #38, August 1924, series 134, box 379, folder 3, NMAH-GHC.

9. Credo Fitch Harris, *Microphone Memoirs* (New York: Bobbs Merrill, 1937) (WHAS); Thomas H. Cowan, interview by Frank Ernest Hill, 1950–51, CU-RPP, 13. Ben Gross, *I Looked and I Listened: Informal Recollections of Radio and TV* (New York: Random House, 1954) (Cowan); Roland Marchand, *Creating the Corporate Soul: The Rise of Public Rela-*

tions and Corporate Imagery in American Big Business (Berkeley: University of California Press, 1998).

10. On early radio programming, see Susan Smulyan, *Selling Radio: The Commercialization of American Broadcasting, 1920–1934* (Washington, D.C. and London: Smithsonian Institution Press, 1994); Michele Hilmes, *Radio Voices: American Broadcasting, 1922-1952* (Minneapolis: University of Minnesota Press, 1997). *Printer's Ink* (February 1927), 89, quoted in Roland Marchand, *Advertising the American Dream: Making Way for Modernity, 1920–1940* (Berkeley: University of California Press, 1985), 383 n13.

11. "Refuse to Allow Receipt of Bout Returns at Y.M.C.A.," *NYT*, June 29, 1921; "Pictures in Pulpit Fight as He Saw It," *NYT*, July 11, 1921; John Held, Jr., cover for "The Football Issue," *Life*, November 19, 1925; Edgar H. Felix, "Early Days in Radio," 1962, CU-RPP, 39. Felix misremembered the station as WHN and the game as the last in the World Series; for correct game and station, see "Today's Program," *NYT*, October 14, 1923; and "Broadcasting History: WEAF—Now WNBC," n.d., LC-NBC, 19.

12. This account is based on my analysis of 138 Carpenter letters excerpted in White, "Radiophone Broadcasting of Dempsey-Carpentier Fight;" and the following Firpo letters: 15 published in "Listening In" and "Broadcast News" columns, *WP*, September 4–16; and 18 preserved in WEAF files, box 1, folder 3, WHS-EPHJ.

13. On growing audiences for prizefights, see Gorn, *The Manly Art*, and Gorn, "The Manassa Mauler and the Fighting Marine." "Women 2,000 Strong," *NYT*, July 3, 1921 ("novelty"); "Crowd Early at Gates," *NYT*, July 3, 1921 (Carpentier audiences); "Crowd of 90,000 Below the Record," *NYT*, September 15, 1923 (Firpo audiences, "South Americans, Spaniards, Cubans"); "At the Ringside," *CD*, June 18, 1921 (three correspondents); "Will Witness Big Fight," *CD*, June 25, 1921 (black visitors from Seattle); "New York Society," *CD*, July 9, 1921 (visitors from other cities).

14. James G. Webster, Patricia F. Phalen, and Lawrence W. Lichty, *Ratings Analysis: The Theory and Practice of Audience Research* (Mahwah, N.J.: Lawrence Erlbaum Associates, 2000), 81–82 (Fessenden); Susan J. Douglas, *Inventing American Broadcasting, 1899–1922* (Baltimore: Johns Hopkins University Press, 1987), 156 (Fessenden), 294 (operator licenses); Espenschied, "The Origin and Development of Radiotelephony," 1111–13 (transmitters for China and Deal Beach tests); Espenschied, interview by Julian Tebo and Frank Polkinghorn, June 2, 1973, Institute of Electrical and Electronics Engineers History Center, 13 (Deal Beach), http://www.ieee.org/portal/cms_docs_iportals/iportals/aboutus/history_center/oral_history/pdfs/Espenschied011.pdf.

15. Lloyd Espenschied, "Beginning of Broadcasting," *Proceedings of the Institute of Electrical and Electronics Engineers* 51 (1963): 1791 (letter to De Forest); Espenschied, 1973 interview, 13 (ship-to-shore radio), 19 (early wireless companies); Carl Dreher, "Memoirs of a Radio Engineer, XI," *RB*, May 1926, 63; Steven Wurtzler, *Electric Sounds: Technological Change and the Rise of Corporate Mass Media* (New York: Columbia University Press, 2007), 265–68 (Dreher's role in sound engineering debates); Joseph E. Baudino and John M. Kittross, "Broadcasting's Oldest Stations: An Examination of Four Claimants," *Journal of Broadcasting* 21 (1977): 65–66 (Frank Conrad); Robert S. John-

son to NAWA and White, "Radiophone Broadcasting of Dempsey-Carpentier Fight" (Smith's equipment advice).

16. White, "Radiophone Broadcasting of Dempsey-Carpentier Fight on July 2, 1921," 7–8; F. William Boettcher, "*Ridgewood Times* 'Memory,'" Brooklyn, NY, 1980, RT-WHN.

17. Raymond F. Guy, interview by Frank Ernest Hill, February 1951, CU-RPP, 17, 51, 53; W.R.G. Baker, "Description of the General Electric Company's Broadcasting Station at Schenectady, New York," *PIRE* 11, no. 4 (1923): 339–74; William Easton quoted in George H. Clark, "Abstract of Notes on Station WJZ," August 23, 1945, box 139, folder 32, NMAH-GHC.

18. The argument about ideal sound standards in this and the following paragraph draws upon several groundbreaking studies that described the emergence of a modern, commodified, or what I here call "corporate," electronic sound; unlike these studies, here I trace the emergence of an alternative, "populist," modern sound. See Jonathan Sterne, *The Audible Past: Cultural Origins of Sound Reproduction* (Durham. N.C.: Duke University Press, 2002); Emily Thompson, *The Soundscape of Modernity: Architectural Acoustics and the Culture of Listening in America, 1900–1933* (Cambridge, Mass.: MIT Press, 2002); Wurtzler, *Electric Sounds*; James Lastra, *Sound Technology and the American Cinema: Perception, Representation, Modernity* (New York: Columbia University Press, 2000). "The 'Rule of Thumb' Is Over," Western Electric advertisement, *Scientific American*, December 1926, 447; E. L. Nelson, "Transmitting Equipment for Radio Telephone Broadcasting," *PIRE* 12, no. 5 (1924): 553–77 (microphones); Paul Sabine, "The Acoustics of Sound Recording Rooms," *Transactions of the Society of Motion Picture Engineers* 12 (1928): 809–22; Leon Alfred Duthernoy, "Singing to Tens of Thousands," *RB*, November 1922, 49 (potato sacks); Julius Weinberger, "Broadcast Transmitting Stations of the Radio Corporation of America," *PIRE* 12, no. 6 (1924): 748 (studio materials), 778 (placement of musicians); C.E. Le Massena, "How Opera Is Broadcast," *RB*, August 1922, 286.

19. "You Need a Headset," Brandes headphones advertisement, *WA*, May 1925, 5; Sigmund Spaeth, *Listening* (New York: Federal-Brandes, 1927) (Kolster radio); *Radio Enters the Home* (New York: RCA, 1922); "Plan Better Radio Goods," 27 (cheap sets); Alfred N. Goldsmith, "Picking Up Broadcast Music." *BG*, October 28, 1923 (RCA director of research); RCA Information Bureau to Radio Editor, form letter, October 1923, series 134, box 381, folder 1, NMAH-GHC (syndication).

20. H. V. Kaltenborn, interview by Frank Ernest Hill, 1950, CU-RPP, 157; Clark, "Abstract of Notes on Station WJZ," 2 (sopranos and cats); Guy, interview by Hill, 20 (condenser microphone), 32 (theater managers).

21. Guy, interview by Hill, 27 ("fading equipment"), 30–31 (Shubert Theatre); Weinberger, "Broadcast Transmitting Stations of the Radio Corporation of America," 786–88 (description and photograph of the portable amplifier). On early trial-and-error sound engineering, see also Susan Schmidt Horning, "Engineering the Performance: Recording Engineers, Tacit Knowledge and the Art of Controlling Sound," *Social Studies of Science* 34, no. 5 (October 2004): 703–31.

22. Herbert B. Higgins to WGI, 11 September 1923, series 8, box 139, folder 2, NMAH-GHC; John Gambling, interview by Frank Ernest Hill, January 1951, CU-RPP, 26 (chorus girl); Sabine, "The Acoustics of Sound Recording Rooms."

23. Lois Deppe quoted in Stanley Dance, *The World of Earl Hines* (New York: Scribner, 1977), 134; William Barlow, "Black Music on Radio During the Jazz Age," *African American Review* 29 (Summer 1995): 325–28; Jacob J. Podber, "Early Radio in Rural Appalachia: An Oral History," *Journal of Radio Studies* 8, no. 2 (2001): 388–410; Cohen, *Making the New Deal*, 133 (Chicago immigrants); Geoffrey T. Hellman, "Courtesy of Coca-Cola," *New Yorker*, August 9, 1930 (McNamee); Untitled report of an early WEAF radio survey, [1925], box 1, folder 5, WHS-EPHJ.

24. E. P. H. James to Sol Taishoff, July 22, 1970, box 1, folder 10, WHS-EPHJ (numbers for WEAF letters); William E. Harkness, "Reminiscences," St. Louis, 1951, CU-RPP, 25 (listeners invited to studios), 66 ("carefully read"), 41 ("soup to nuts"); S. E. Ripley to WGI, September 23, 1923, series 8, box 139, folder 2, NMAH-GHC.

25. George Shuyler, draft of an announcement about airing listener telegrams, December 26, 1922, RT-WHN; "WHN, Target of WEAF in Air Battle, Is Station of Pep," *Jersey Journal*, March 12, 1924; Clifford J. Doerksen, *American Babel: Rogue Radio Broadcasters of The Jazz Age* (Philadelphia: University of Pennsylvania Press, 2005), 21–48; on-air announcement from February 1923, quoted in "Broadcasting History: WEAF—Now WNBC," 10; Weinberger, "Broadcast Transmitting Stations of the Radio Corporation of America," 779.

26. For a good summary of scholarly debates about the two engineering tendencies, toward direct nonreverberant sound and toward acoustic effects, see Wurtzler, *Electric Sounds*, 364 (see n. 15).

27. Jonathan Sterne, "The MP3 as Cultural Artifact," *New Media and Society* 8, no. 5 (October 2006): 835–36 (telephone & MP3s); Sir James Jeans, *Science and Music* (Cambridge: Cambridge University Press, 1947), 241 (radio loudspeakers); Ingrid Monson, "Hearing, Seeing, and Perceptual Agency," *Critical Inquiry* 34, no. 2 (2008): 40 (orchestra recording).

28. Myra May, "Meet J. Andrew White, the Most Famous Announcer in Radio," *RB*, October 1924, 451 (Rickard); White, "Radiophone Broadcasting of Dempsey-Carpentier Fight" (crowd noise); James W. Cook, *The Arts of Deception: Playing with Fraud in the Age of Barnum* (Cambridge, Mass.: Harvard University Press, 2001); Michael Leja, *Looking Askance: Skepticism and American Art from Eakins to Duchamp* (Berkeley and Los Angeles: University of California Press, 2004); Tom Gunning, "The Aesthetic of Astonishment: Early Film and the (In)credulous Spectator," in *Viewing Positions: Ways of Seeing Film*, ed. Linda Williams (New Brunswick, N.J.: Rutgers University Press, 1995), 114–16.

29. "To Broadcast Fight News," *NYT*, July 25, 1922 (Leonard-Tendler fight); "2,000,000 Hear Bout Described by Radio," *NYT*, July 14, 1923 (Willard-Firpo fight); George B. Chadwick, "Football by Radio," *PR*, January 1923, 56–57 ("electric wave filter"). "Rickard Bans Radio in Garden; Says It Has Hurt Attendance," *NYT*, November 26, 1924.

30. J. G. Truesdell, "Report of Transmission of Dempsey-Firpo Boxing Exhibition

from the Polo Grounds," memorandum for William E. Harkness, Manager of Broadcasting, WEAF, September 14, 1923, box 1, folder 3, WHS-EPHJ.

31. Edward Hatton to WEAF, September 15, 1923, box 1, folder 3, WHS-EPHJ; Truesdell, "Report of Transmission;" Weinberger, "Broadcast Transmitting Stations of the Radio Corporation of America," 788.

32. B. D. Heller to NAWA; Charles H. Dugan to NAWA; "Crowd Early at Gates;" *Time*, October 4, 1926, 28, and *Chicago Tribune*, September 24, 1926, quoted in Gorn, "The Manassa Mauler and the Fighting Marine." See also Gorn, *The Manly Art* (see n. 5).

33. "Crowd Early at Gates" (field glasses); James R. Harrison, "Greatest Ring Spectacle," *NYT*, September 23, 1927 (radios at the stadium); "The Wayward Press," *New Yorker*, January 26, 1929 (Rickard's death).

34. These listeners acted in a way similar to early movie audiences, who, as film historian Tom Gunning argued, combined the appreciation of "realistic effects with a conscious awareness of artifice." Gunning, "The Aesthetic of Astonishment," 118; Cook, *The Arts of Deception*; Leja, *Looking Askance*; Dr. Gordon M. Christine to NAWA; Benjamin F. Cutler to NAWA.

35. Michael Warner, *Publics and Counterpublics* (New York: Zone Books, 2005) (style and public); Doerksen, *American Babel*, 25 (corporate announcing standards); Kaltenborn, interview, 59 (position vis-à-vis the mike); Graham McNamee, "Radio Broadcasting Has Grown from Game to Fun to National Institution," *Shreveport Journal*, December 31, 1929 (crooning and mikes); Harris, *Microphone Memoirs*, 129 (WHAS); Cowan, interview, 16–17.

36. Weinberger, "Broadcast Transmitting Stations of the Radio Corporation of America," 791; "2,000,000 Hear Bout Described by Radio;" "Qualifications Necessary to Be a Radio Announcer," *NYT*, November 16, 1924; W. B. Beals to J. G. Truesdell, September 18, 1923, box 1, folder 3, WHS-EPHJ (announcers' names); Douglas Gomery, *The Coming of Sound: A History* (New York: Routledge, 2005), 16 ("Wildflower" broadcast); Hector Fuller, *Abroad with Mayor Walker* (New York: Shields Publishing Co., 1928).

37. George F. McClelland to William E. Harkness, memorandum ("cordial," "technically correct," "stagy," "lifeless," "dead," newspaper clippings, "never pay attention," "his own importance"); WCAP to WEAF, telegram, 8:40 P.M. ("change position," "blurred"); W. L. Pierson, Washington, D.C., to Taylor, telegram ("sharpen up," "tubby"); Clarkson to J. G. Truesdell, telegram, 10:00 P.M. ("hard to make out"); WCAP to WEAF, telegram, 9:25 P.M. (long distance calls, "rotten"); J. G. Truesdell to Clarkson, telegram, 9:55 P.M. ("persists in talking too close"); Round Hills to WEAF, telegram, 10:15 P.M.; and WCAP to WEAF, telegram, 10:15 P.M. (better sound after McClelland took over); all from 14 September 1923, in box 1, folder 3, WHS-EPHJ; Don Dunphy quoted in David J. Halberstam, *Sports on New York Radio: A Play-By-Play History* (Lincolnwood, Ill.: Masters Press, 1999), 6; "Notices," *Time*, October 22, 1934 (McClelland's career and death).

38. Myra May, "Meet J. Andrew White, the Most Famous Announcer in Radio,"

RB, October 1924, 447; L. E. Dickinson to WEAF, September 15, 1923, box 1, folder 3, WHS-EPHJ.

39. Halberstam, *Sports on New York Radio*, ch. 1 (White's career); Graham McNamee with Robert G. Anderson, *You're On the Air* (New York and London: Harper & Brothers, 1926), 64 (tips from listeners), 66 (reviewer); Phillips Carlin, interview by Frank Ernest Hill, transcript, 1951, CU-RPP, 14 (partnering with McNamee on sportscasts); Norman Brokenshire, *This Is Norman Brokenshire: An Unvarnished Self-Portrait* (New York: David McKay, 1954), 41.

40. Marchand, *Advertising the American Dream*, 66 (women consumers), 93 (crooners); Smulyan, *Selling Radio*, 88 (1925 cooking shows); H. B. L., "Woman at the Ring Side," *NYT*, January 30, 1921 ("matinee idol"); McNamee, *You're On the Air*, 44–45 (women at ringside); Charles Popenoe quoted in John Wallace, "Men versus Women Announcers," *RB*, November 1926, 44; George H. Douglas, *The Early Days of Radio Broadcasting* (Jefferson, N.C.: McFarland, 1987), 123 ("honest enthusiasm," McNamee's career); Gross, *I Looked and I Listened*, 89 (boxing club); Heywood Broun, "Introduction," in *You're On the Air*, vi ("sense of movement"); "Voice of the '20s," *Time*, May 18, 1942.

41. Dickinson to WEAF; Hatton to WEAF; "Throng in Front of Post Building Hearing Dempsey-Firpo Battle Blow by Blow," *WP*, September 15, 1923 (photograph); "El público congregado frente a 'La Nación' al ser informado de ce los concrincantes acababan de subir al ring," *La Nación*, September 15, 1923 (photograph); "Times Sq. Crowd Roars for Both," *NYT*, July 3, 1921 (women); John White, "Argentine Weeps Then Tries to Forget Firpo," *Chicago Tribune*, September 16, 1923; William White, "Sidelights of the Fight," *CD*, September 22, 1923 (blacks).

42. Christine Ehrick, "'Savage Dissonance': Gender, Voice, and Women's Radio Speech in Argentina, 1930–1945," in *Sound in the Age of Mechanical Reproduction*, ed. David Suisman and Susan Strasser (Philadelphia: University of Pennsylvania Press, 2010), 69–93 ("shrill" voices); "Suffragist Halts Boxing Bout to Urge Votes for Women," *WP*, July 24, 1915; H. B. L., "Woman at the Ring Side," ("ladylike"); "Reserve Section for Women Boxing Fans," *WP*, April 26, 1922 (a separate section for single women); Jimmy Durante, *Night Clubs* (New York: Knopf, 1931), 115.

43. "Louis Firpo Robbed of the Heavyweight Crown," *CD*, September 22, 1923; Jewett Fisher to WEAF, September 15, 1923, box 1, folder 3, WHS-EPHJ ("unsportsman like," "the great majority"). For another example of listeners using political language to demand changes in programming, see also Derek W. Vaillant, "'Your Voice Came in Last Night . . . But I Thought It Sounded a Little Scared': Rural Radio Listening and 'Talking Back' during the Progressive Era in Wisconsin, 1920–1932," in *Radio Reader: Essays in the Cultural History of Radio*, ed. Michele Hilmes and Jason Loviglio (New York: Routledge, 2002), 63–88.

44. George J. Smith to NAWA (firehouse); Carroll T. Downes to NAWA (ticket seller); White, "Radiophone Broadcasting of Dempsey-Carpentier Fight," 22; F. S. Gostenhofer to NAWA and Malcolm J. Homan to NAWA ("public service").

45. "Dempsey-Firpo Bout Radioed to Argentine in 15 Seconds," *BG*, September 23,

1923; Robert H Claxton, *From Parsifal to Perón: Early Radio in Argentina, 1920–1944* (Gainesville: University Press of Florida, 2007), 15–16 (amateurs); James Schwoch, *The American Radio Industry and Its Latin American Activities, 1900–1939* (Urbana: University of Illinois Press, 1990) (receiver market); Barnouw, *A Tower in Babel*, 80–81, gives credit to Sarnoff and White and does not mention NAWA, citing two earlier histories; White, "'Battle of the Century,'" details discrepancies between all contemporary and historical accounts and restores credit to amateurs and Hopp. White, "Radiophone Broadcasting of Dempsey-Carpentier Fight," 2 (Hopp), 22 (Smith); White, "The First Big Radio Broadcast," *Reader's Digest*, December 1955, 81–85; David Sarnoff to George S. DeSousa et al., July 14, 1921, box 1, DSL-DS; David Sarnoff, "Radio," *Saturday Evening Post*, August 7, 1926; Julius Hopp to David Sarnoff, December 27, 1935, series 134, box 381, folder 1, NMAH-GHC.

46. James G. Massey to RCA, September 13, 1923, reproduced in "Broadcast News," *WP*, September 16, 1923.

47. Mark J. Woods to William E. Harkness, September 15, 1923, box 1, folder 3, WHS-EPHJ.

48. W. P. Marmon to WEAF, September 18, 1923 ("large-minded"); Jewett Fisher to WEAF, September 15, 1923; 1. G. H. Blaker to WEAF, September 17, 1923, all in box 1, folder 3, WHS-EPHJ.

49. Carl Dreher, "What Business Kills," *Harper's*, June 1939, 45–46; Hugh R. Slotten, "Radio Engineers, the Federal Radio Commission, and the Social Shaping of Broadcast Technology: Creating 'Radio Paradise,'" *Technology and Culture* 36 (October 1995): 950–86; Espenschied, 1973 interview (see n. 14), 18.

Chapter 2

1. "Protest Suit of WEAF," *New Jersey Evening Journal*, March 1924, RT-WHN; "WEAF Rules the Air Is Whalen's Charge," *NYT*, March 1, 1924; "Monopoly in Radio by Eight Concerns Charged in Action," *NYT*, January 28, 1924 (Federal Trade Commission); William E. Harkness, "Reminiscences," St. Louis, 1951, CU-RPP, 98 (Apocalypse); "Hoover Condemns Private Monopoly of Broadcasting," *NYT*, March 11, 1924; "WHN Gets License, Ending Radio Suit," *NYT*, April 11, 1924; William Peck Banning, *Commercial Broadcasting Pioneer: The WEAF Experiment, 1922-1926* (Cambridge, Mass.: Harvard University Press, 1946), 136 (public outcry as AT&T motive).

2. Marvin R. Bensman, "The Zenith-WJAZ Case and the Chaos of 1926–1927," *Journal of Broadcasting* 13 (Fall 1970): 423–40; Table 1-A, "AM Radio Stations through 1940," and Table 3-A, "Radio Advertising: 1927–2000," in Christopher H. Sterling and John M. Kittross, *Stay Tuned: A Concise History of American Broadcasting* (Mahwah, N.J.: Lawrence Erlbaum Associates, 2002), 838. On the decline of nonprofit radio, see Robert W. McChesney, *Telecommunications, Mass Media, and Democracy: The Battle for the Control of U. S. Broadcasting, 1928–1935* (New York: Oxford University Press, 1993), 20, 228; On experts, see Hugh Richard Slotten, "Radio Engineers, the Federal Radio Commission, and the Social Shaping of Broadcast Technology: Creating 'Radio Paradise,'" *Technology and*

Culture 36 (October 1995): 950–86; on "corporate liberalism," a collusion between corporate broadcasters and the FRC, see Thomas Streeter, *Selling the Air: A Critique of the Policy of Commercial Broadcasting in the United States* (Chicago: Chicago University Press, 1996), 59–112; on the FRC's ideology of modernization, see Bill Kirkpatrick, "Localism in American Media Policy, 1920–34: Reconsidering a 'Bedrock Concept,'" *Radio Journal* 4, no. 1 (January 2006): 87–110.

3. On the broadcast reform movement, see McChesney, *Telecommunications, Mass Media, and Democracy*; and Susan Smulyan, *Selling Radio: The Commercialization of American Broadcasting, 1920–1934* (Washington and London: Smithsonian Institution Press, 1994); for the range of listener opinion, see letters to NBC and fan magazine correspondence discussed below; FCC General Correspondence, box 497, FCC Mss; and letters and petitions stored in United States Senate Interstate Commerce Committee Manuscripts, National Archives, Washington, D.C., Sen 73A-J28, tray 155. Table 6-A, "Ownership of Radio Receivers: 1922–1959," in Sterling and Kittross, *Stay Tuned*, 862 (audience size).

4. On legal interpretations of "public interest, convenience, and necessity," see Louis G. Caldwell, "The Standard of Public Interest, Convenience or Necessity as Used in the Radio Act of 1927," *Air Law Review* 1 (July 1930): 295–330; and "Federal Control of Radio Broadcasting," *Yale Law Journal* 39 (1929): 245–75. "Hearing Before the Federal Radio Commission in the Conference Room of the Department of Commerce in re: Application of Station WMSG," Washington, D.C., June 21, 1927, box 3, docket 13A, NA-FCC (radio magazine polls); this summary is based on my survey of Docket Files in NA-FCC.

5. Bill Jaker, Frank Sulek, and Peter Kanze, *The Airwaves of New York: Illustrated Histories of 156 AM Stations in the Metropolitan Area, 1921–1996* (Jefferson, N.C.: McFarland, 1998), 41–42 (WBKN history); Morris J. Lasowitz, to WBKN, November 4, 1927, box 3, docket 16A, NA-FCC. On Yiddish radio, see Ari Y. Kelman, *Station Identification: A Cultural History of Yiddish Radio in the United States* (Berkeley: University of California Press, 2009).

6. Herman Silverberg to WBKN, November 24, 1927; Isaak Axelrod and family to WBKN, November 24, 1927; both in docket 16A, FCC. On the use of the language of political rights in listener correspondence, see also Derek Vaillant, "'Your Voice Came in Last Night ... But I Thought It Sounded a Little Scared': Rural Radio Listening and 'Talking Back' during the Progressive Era in Wisconsin, 1920–1932," in *Radio Reader: Essays in the Cultural History of Radio*, ed. Michele Hilmes and Jason Loviglio (New York: Routledge, 2002), 77.

7. Clarence F. Nelson to WBIO, September 30, 1928, docket 307, FCC; Derek W. Vaillant, "Sounds of Whiteness: Local Radio, Racial Formation, and Public Culture in Chicago, 1921–1935," *American Quarterly* 54, no. 1 (March 2002): 35, 37

8. Amanda Sund to A. E. Nelson, September 23, 1928; Mrs. Jos. E. Swanson to A. E. Nelson, September 23, 1928; Gustav A. Almgren to A. E. Nelson, September 24, 1928; all in docket 307, NA-FCC.

9. Mrs. Anna Goodman to WBKN, November 4, 1927 (*Jewish Forward*); Mrs. M. Lichtenstein to WBKN, November 8, 1927 (tickets); M. B. Schear to WBKN, November 3,

1927; Hilda Levine to WBKN, June 6, 1927, all in box 3, docket 16A, NA-FCC; Lizabeth Cohen, *Making a New Deal: Industrial Workers in Chicago, 1919–1939* (Cambridge: Cambridge University Press, 1990); Nathan Godfried, *WCFL: Chicago's Voice of Labor, 1926–78* (Chicago: University of Illinois Press, 1997); Vaillant, "Sounds of Whiteness," 25–66.

10. For Clansmen on 1920s radio, see Erik Barnouw, *A Tower in Babel* (New York: Oxford University Press, 1966), 102; for quacks, see Godfried, *WCFL*, 64; Mrs. Edith C. Leech to FRC, November 2, 1929, box 398, file 89–6, NA-FCC (Henderson). On Henderson, see also Derek W. Vaillant, "Bare-knuckled Broadcasting: Enlisting Manly Respectability and Racial Paternalism in the Battle against Chain Stores, Chain Stations, and the Federal Radio Commission on Louisiana's KWKH, 1924–33," *Radio Journal* 1, no. 3 (2004): 193–211.

11. Scots For A to *RPW*, March 31, 1927, 35; H. E. Lindquist to Nelson Brothers Bond & Mortgage Co., September 25, 1928, docket 307, NA-FCC; Rowland L. Field to WDAF, March 7, 1924, box 1, folder 3, WHS-WH; Barnouw, *A Tower in Babel*, 167.

12. Rev. Merrill T. MacPherson, testimony, "Hearing before the Federal Radio Commission in the Conference Room of the Department of Commerce in re Application of Station WDWM," June 1, 1927, box 1, docket 3A, NA-FCC, 116; Kirkpatrick, "Localism in American Media Policy, 1920–34," 100 (black and Japanese-language stations); *Annual Report of the Federal Radio Commission to the Congress of the United States for the Fiscal Year Ended June 30, 1927* (Washington, D.C.: United States Government Printing Office, 1927), 8; Louis G. Caldwell quoted in Godfried, *WCFL: Chicago's Voice of Labor, 1926–78*, 86; Orestes H. Caldwell, "Reminiscences of Orestes H. Caldwell," 19, CU-RPP (emphasis in original).

13. O. E. Roberts, Jr., "Correspondence from Readers: The Itch for Distance," *RN*, August 1923, 161.

14. Orange Edward McMeans, "The Great Audience Invisible," *Scribner's*, April 1923, 410.

15. On maps and social perception, see Denis E. Cosgrove, "Introduction: Mapping Meaning," in *Mappings*, ed. Denis E. Cosgrove (London: Reaktion Books, 1999), 4–5; Armand Mattelart, "Mapping Modernity: Utopia and Communication Networks," in Cosgrove, ed., *Mappings*, 169.

16. De Forest advertisement, *RB*, January 1923; Frances Pott to Wendell Hall, March 27, 1924, box 1, folder 2, WHS-WH; Mr. Irving Moulton, Jr., to WGY, December 18, 1923, in "Excerpts from Letters Received from Radio Listeners," report #30, December 1923, series 134, box 379, folder 3, NMAH-GHC; McMeans, "The Great Audience Invisible," 410–11.

17. Albert [Kumfe] to WGI, November 10, 1923; Francis J. Harris to WGI , September 12, 1923; F. C. Gardner to WGI, November 15, 1923; John Chesleigh to WGI, October 5, 1923; R. H. De Vlieger to WGI, September 3, 1923; all in series 8, box 139, folder 2, NMAH-GHC.

18. N. S. Young to WGI, October 13, 1923; R. H. De Vlieger to WGI; U.S. Marshall Dickerson to WGI, September 19, 1923; all in series 8, box 139, folder 2, NMAH-GHC.

19. Hiram L. Jome, *Economics of the Radio Industry* (Chicago and New York: A. W.

Shaw, 1925); worker quoted in Robert Lynd and Helen M. Lynd, *Middletown: A Study in American Culture* (San Diego: Harvest, 1957), 269–70; A. E. Hutchins to Wendell Hall, March 21, 1924, box 1, folder 3, WHS-WH; "Early N. W. Ayer & Son Radio Clients, from 1924–1929," ca. October 1934, AHC-TJM (tour for National); Genevieve R. Bier to WGY, [1924], in "Excerpts from Letters Received at WGY," report #38, August 1924, series 134, box 379, folder 3, NMAH-GHC.

20. Barnouw, *A Tower in Babel*, 229–30; G. C. Ruble to Wendell Hall, January 17, 1924, box 1, folder 2; Mr. & Mrs. L. E. Wulfert to WOC, March 19, 1924, box 1, folder 3; Miss Helen B. Penny to Wendell Hall, April 2, 1924, box 1, folder 3 ("where do you go"); Mrs. J. R. Marr to Wendell Hall, March 11, 1924, box 1, folder 2 ("keep up"); Mrs. Latham Hull Ayer to Wendell Hall, March 21, 1924, box 1, folder 2 ("around via Radio"); C. W. Mapes to WSAI, February 7, 1926, box 2, folder 1 ("watch for his appearances"); Mildred A. Pearl to Wendell Hall, March 9, 1923, box 1, folder 2; Mrs. J. R. Marr to Wendell Hall, March 11, 1924, box 1, folder 2; Miss Helen B. Penny to Wendell Hall, April 2, 1924, box 1, folder 3; all in WHS-WH.

21. Richard Butsch, *The Making of American Audiences: From Stage to Television, 1750–1990* (Cambridge and New York: Cambridge University Press, 2000), 181 (attempts by experimenter magazines to cross over to lay radio audiences); *RB*, May 1927, 15–16; Godfried, *WCFL*, 62; *Standard Rate and Data Service*, September 1930, 365; Michael Brown, "Radio Magazines and the Development of Broadcasting: Radio Broadcast and Radio News, 1922–1930," *Journal of Radio Studies* 5 (1998): 68–81; Keith Massie and Stephen D. Perry, "Hugo Gernsback and Radio Magazines: An Influential Intersection in Broadcast History," *Journal of Radio Studies* 9, no. 2 (December 2002): 264–81.

22. On readers' columns in pulp magazines, see Harold B. Hersey, *Pulpwood Editor: The Fabulous World of the Thriller Magazines Revealed by a Veteran Editor and Publisher* (New York: Frederick A. Stokes Company, 1937), 87–102.

23. I examined all issues of *Radio Digest* and *Radio Program Weekly* available to me at the Library of Congress, and these contained a total of 59 letters and several dozen excerpts; not every issue for these years was available at the library, and the letters to the editor column in *Radio Digest* was suspended for several months in 1928.

24. *Radio Guide* quoted in Harold E. Hill, *The National Association of Educational Broadcasters: A History* (Urbana, Ill.: The National Association of Educational Broadcasters, 1954), 21; "Broadcasters on Their Guard," *RD*, March 1931, 61; "Kill the Fess Bill," *RD*, September 1931; Ray Bill, "A Plea for Continued Freedom of the Air," *RD*, November 1930, 65; H. A. Bellows, "Chaos!" *RD*, November 1931, 18; Robert W. McChesney, "Press-Radio Relations and the Emergence of Network, Commercial Broadcasting in the United States, 1930–1935," *Historical Journal of Film, Radio and Television* 11, no. 1 (1991): 51–52; "Radio Digest against Fess Bill," *Broadcasters' News Bulletin*, September 19, 1931; John F. Royal to Frank Mason, January 4, 1932, box 13, folder 37, WHS-NBC; Phillips Carlin to John Royal, December 31, 1931, box 13, folder 37, WHS-NBC; Royal to Mason, January 4, 1932.

25. Helen Walker to Hampson Gary, December 1934; Curtis Mitchell to Eugene Sykes,

November 30, 1934; E. O. Sykes to Curtis Mitchell, Editor, December 6, 1934, 201–4, FCC General Correspondence, box 497, NA-FCC; Curtis Mitchell to Frank Mason, September 27, 1934, box 31, folder 57, WHS-NBC; Curtis Mitchell to Richard C. Patterson, Jr., May 16, 1934, box 31, folder 30, WHS-NBC.

26. V. C. Shive to *RD*, March 1, 1928, 96; Ben F. Redmann to *RD*, March 1, 1928, 96; E. G. Tate to *RD*, March 1, 1927, 30; Irwin Matheny to *RD*, March 1, 1928, 96. On progressivist antimonopoly rhetoric, see Daniel T. Rodgers, "In Search of Progressivism," *Reviews in American History* 10 (December 1982): 113–32.

27. Harold A. Lafount to G. F. McClelland, May 3, 1928, box 398, file 89–6, NA-FCC.

28. FRC to Seattle resident, April 27, 1928, box 398, file 89–6, NA-FCC.

29. William J. Perry to FRC, October 2, 1929; C. G. Powell to M. H. Aylesworth, April 27, 1928; all in box 398, file 89–6, NA-FCC; Wm. J. Perry to *RD*, March 15, 1927.

30. M. H. Aylesworth to Judge Ira E. Robinson, May 9, 1928; E. C. Chamberlin to NBC, April 30, 1928; M. H. Aylesworth to Ira E. Robinson, December 12, 1928 ("great number"); M. H. Aylesworth to O. H. Caldwell, August 9, 1928 ("several thousand"); M. H. Aylesworth to Judge E. O. Sykes, January 28, 1928 ("eighty thousand nine hundred and ninety"); M. H. Aylesworth to Judge Ira E. Robinson, May 9, 1928 ("ninety thousand"); M. H. Aylesworth to Judge Ira E. Robinson, August 6, 1928 ("more than a million"); M. H. Aylesworth to O. H. Caldwell, November 22, 1928 ("pouring in"); all in box 398, file 89–6, NA-FCC; E. P. H. James to Sol Taishoff, July 22, 1970, box 1, folder 10, WHS-EPHJ.

31. Sister Ethel Mary to Walter Damrosch, September 23, 1928 (nun); Mrs. Carl L. Sherburne to M. H. Aylesworth, November 14, 1928; Mrs. W. P. Hanson, Russell, Iowa, to M. H. Aylesworth, November 12, 1928; Lorrain E. Watters to RCA Executive Department, November 16, 1928; Herbert J. Day, M.D. to M. H. Aylesworth, November 9, 1928; M. H. Aylesworth to Judge E. O. Sykes, 28 February 1928; all in box 398, file 89–6, NA-FCC; Day to Aylesworth, 9 November 1928; Sherburne to Aylesworth, November 14, 1928; Hanson to Aylesworth, November 12, 1928.

32. "What the Listener Likes and How He Likes It," *RB*, May 1927, 32; *Amos 'n' Andy's* Charles Correll and Freeman Gosden switched from WGN to WMAQ in March 1928, and to NBC Blue in August 1929. Melvin Patrick Ely, *The Adventures of Amos 'n' Andy: A Social History of an American Phenomenon* (New York: Free Press, 1991), 57–59; James L. Palmer, "Radio Advertising," *Journal of Business of the University of Chicago* 1 (1928): 495–6, cited in Cohen, *Making a New Deal*, 142–43.

33. Daniel Starch, "A Study of Radio Broadcasting Based Exclusively on Personal Interviews with Families in the United States East of the Rocky Mountains, Confidential and for Private Use Only," made for NBC, New York, 1928, box 8, folder 4, WHS-EPHJ; the quote is from a note accompanying the report; see also Daniel Starch, *Revised Study of Radio Broadcasting* (New York: National Broadcasting Co., 1930). Neil H. Borden, "Daniel Starch," *Journal of Marketing* 21, no. 3 (January 1957): 265–67; Barbara Campbell, "Daniel Starch, Ad Analyzer, at 95," *NYT*, February 10, 1979; Daniel Starch, *Principles of Advertising* (Chicago: A. W. Shaw, 1923), 38; Frank N. Stanton, interview by Michael J. Socolow, transcript in author's possession, April 6, 2004.

34. John Wallace, "The Listeners' Point of View: What Many Listeners Think about Broadcasting," *RB*, April 1927; "What the Listener Likes and How He Likes It," *RB*, May 1927, 32; United States Federal Radio Commission, *Second Annual Report of the Federal Radio Commission* (Washington, D.C.: GPO, 1928).

35. Malcolm Willey and Stuart Rice, *Communication Agencies and Social Life* (New York: McGraw-Hill, 1933), 187; for a persuasive critique of radio surveys in this period that argues this point, see Godfried, *WCFL*, 61–62.

36. Frederick H. Lumley, *Measurement in Radio* (New York: Arno Press and the New York Times, 1934), 35 (leading questions); Lumley cites several advertising articles that came to this conclusion shortly after 1928; see also Roland Marchand, *Advertising the American Dream: Making Way for Modernity, 1920–1940* (Berkeley: University of California Press, 1985), 92, 383 n. 17.

37. Frank A. Arnold, interview by Frank Ernest Hill, transcript, 1950, CU-RPP; Edgar H. Felix, "Early Days in Radio," 1962, CU-RPP, 26–27, 46–47; Edgar H. Felix, *Using Radio in Sales Promotion; a Book for Advertisers, Station Managers and Broadcasting Artists* (New York: McGraw-Hill, 1927). On Goldsmith, see Chapter 1.

38. "Big Increase in Farm Radio Sets," *Printers' Ink*, May 5, 1927, 160–61; Reynold Wik, "The Radio in Rural America During the 1920s," *Agricultural History* 55 (October 1981): 341; Butsch, *The Making of American Audiences*, 208–18; J. Steven Smethers and Lee B. Jolliffe, "Singing and Selling Seeds: The Live Music Era on Rural Midwestern Radio Stations," *Journalism History* 26 (Summer 2000): 61–70; On the debate about direct and indirect radio advertising in the 1920s, see Marchand, *Advertising the American Dream*, 89–94; Smulyan, *Selling Radio*, 65–92; and Charles F. McGovern, *Sold American: Consumption and Citizenship, 1890–1945* (Chapel Hill: University of North Carolina Press, 2006), 49–50. On carnivalesque advertising, see T. J. Jackson Lears, *Fables of Abundance: A Cultural History of Advertising in America* (New York: Basic Books, 1994).

39. M. H. Aylesworth to Orestes H. Caldwell, September 22, 1928, box 398, file 89–6, NA-FCC; Francis St. Austell, "Direct Selling by Radio," *RB*, May 1928, 58–59.

40. Powell to Aylesworth, April 27, 1928; Mrs. Edith C. Leech to FRC, November 2, 1929; E. C. Chamberlin to NBC, April 30, 1928; Stephen A. Cocks to NBC, February 1, 1928; M. H. Aylesworth to Judge E. O. Sykes, February 28, 1928; all in box 398, file 89–6, NA-FCC.

41. Mrs. C. V. N. to *RD*, January 1, 1927, 30; J. P. to *RD*, December 15, 1926, 15.

42. C. S. to *RD*, December 15, 1926, 15, 28.

43. R. W. Jones to *RPW*, April 21, 1927, 38; V. U. to *RD*, December 1, 1926, 19; O. E. S. to *RD*, January 1, 1927, 30.

44. Edgar H. Cox to *RD*, March 1, 1927, 29.

45. For an argument that listeners did welcome direct advertising specifically, see Doerksen, *American Babel*.

46. Clifford J. Doerksen, in *American Babel*, shows that local stations pioneered the advertising style that broadcasters later adopted. Lears, *Fables of Abundance*, 194,

233, 238–39, 334–35 ("carnivalesque" advertising and the Great Depression); Michael J. Socolow, "Psyche and Society: Radio Advertising and Social Psychology in America, 1923–1936," *Historical Journal of Film, Radio, and Television* 24, no. 4 (October 2004): 524 (critics buy products), 530 (radio surveys); Kathy M. Newman, *Radio Active: Advertising and Consumer Activism, 1935–1947* (Berkeley: University of California Press, 2004), 41 (brand recognition). "Disease Marches On," *Printers' Ink*, August 13, 1936, 12–14, cited in Lears, *Fables of Abundance*, 194 (mythical diseases); "Cameron Raps Bad Reporting, Blatant Radio," *Advertising Age*, February 21, 1938, 24, cited in Lears, *Fables of Abundance*, 238 ("impertinent," "insistent," "unmannerly"); "Neither Sponsors nor Stations Hear Radio Listeners' Grumblings," *Business Week*, February 10, 1932, 18–19, cited in Lears, *Fables of Abundance*, 468 ("sophisticated hokum").

47. "Advertising Is Basis of Radio Existence," *Federation News*, August 5, 1933, 6; Godfried, *WCFL*, 70.

48. Myrtle Denny quoted in KMM Program Guide (Shenandoah, Iowa: Tom Thumb Publishing Company, August 1952); Smethers and Jolliffe, "Singing and Selling Seeds."

49. Smethers and Jolliffe, "Singing and Selling Seeds"; Butsch, *The Making of American Audiences*, 212–13.

50. Harriet W. Stothard to Herbert Jewelry Shop, May 8, 1928, 1928 scrapbook, TOL-RV.

51. John Fitzpatrick, President of Chicago Federation of Labor, to Hon. Joseph D. Beck, House of Representatives, January 5, 1929, docket 342, NA-FCC, quoted in Vaillant, "Sounds of Whiteness," 54–55; McChesney, *Telecommunications, Mass Media, and Democracy*.

52. Robert McChesney, "Conflict, Not Consensus: The Debate over Broadcast Communication Policy, 1930–1935," in *Ruthless Criticism: New Perspectives in US Communication History*, ed. William Solomon and Robert W. McChesney (Minneapolis: University of Minnesota Press, 1993), 248; Smulyan, *Selling Radio*, 167; Cohen, *Making a New Deal*, 142–43.

53. On local and regional radio in the network era, see Alexander Russo, *Points on the Dial: Golden Age Radio Beyond the Networks* (Durham, N.C.: Duke University Press, 2010).

Chapter 3

1. Mrs. Leland Zollinger to Jane Crusinberry, March 30, 1937, box 3, folder 10, WHS-JC; Jane Crusinberry to Mrs. Robert J. Hoffman, August 4, 1941, box 3, folder 10, WHS-JC.

2. Richard Henderson to *RG*, February 13, 1937, 19 ("lives of stars," engineers); Herman Francis Kissel to *RG*, May 29, 1937, 18 (screenwriters, "spinning wheel"). On the national intimate culture of Depression-era network radio, see Jason Loviglio, *Radio's Intimate Public: Network Broadcasting and Mass-Mediated Democracy* (Minneapolis: University of Minnesota Press, 2005); Bruce Lenthall, *Radio's America: The Great Depression and the Rise of Modern Mass Culture* (Chicago: University of Chicago Press, 2007); and

Michele Hilmes, *Radio Voices: American Broadcasting, 1922–1952* (Minneapolis: University of Minnesota Press, 1997).

3. On pulp magazines, see especially Sean McCann, *Gumshoe America: Hard-Boiled Crime Fiction and the Rise and Fall of New Deal Liberalism* (Durham, N.C.: Duke University Press, 2000); Erin A. Smith, *Hard-Boiled: Working Class Readers and Pulp Magazines* (Philadelphia: Temple University Press, 2000); John Cheng, "Amazing, Astounding, Wonder: Popular Science, Culture, and the Emergence of Science Fiction in the United States, 1926–1939" (Ph.D. diss., University of California, Berkeley, 1997).

4. Edgar H. Felix, "Early Days in Radio," 1962, CU-RPP; Keith Massie and Stephen D. Perry, "Hugo Gernsback and Radio Magazines: An Influential Intersection in Broadcast History," *Journal of Radio Studies* 9, no. 2 (December 2002): 264–81.

5. Circulation data in this chapter is taken from *N. W. Ayer & Son's Directory of Newspapers and Periodicals* (Philadelphia: N. W. Ayer & Son, 1920–50); Massie and Perry, "Hugo Gernsback and Radio Magazines."

6. This list is based on ABC reports, letterheads, and library catalog searches.

7. Margaret MacMullen, "Pulps and Confessions," *Harper's Monthly*, June 1937; Ann Fabian, "Making a Commodity out of Truth: Speculations on the Career of Bernarr Macfadden," *American Literary History* 5, no. 1 (Spring 1993): 51–76; Robert Ernst, *Weakness Is a Crime: The Life of Bernarr Macfadden* (Syracuse, N.Y.: Syracuse University Press, 1991).

8. "Click," *Time*, January 10, 1938 ("profitable pulp"); "Radio: Presidential Timbre," *Time*, June 19, 1939 (most alert); "Quick Revival," *Time*, July 20, 1953 (Moe Annenberg's bio); "The Successful Upstart," *Time*, September 12, 1955 (paper shortage); Jack Shafer, "Citizen Annenberg," *Slate*, October 2, 2002; Christopher Ogden, *Legacy: A Biography of Moses and Walter Annenberg* (Boston: Little, Brown, 1999).

9. "Shaking the Empire," *Time*, December 31, 1951; Curtis Mitchell to Richard C. Patterson, Jr., May 16, 1934, box 31, folder 30, WHS-NBC; "News from the Army," *Time*, March 31, 1941.

10. Miss Sylvia Grill to *RM*, March 1938, 84; *Variety Radio Directory, 1937–1938* (New York: Variety, 1937), 856–57.

11. On *Amazing Stories* and pulp science fiction, see Cheng, "Amazing, Astounding, Wonder"; on *Down Beat* and jazz periodicals, see John R. Gennari, *Blowin' Hot and Cool: Jazz and Its Critics* (Chicago and London: University of Chicago Press, 2006), 61–116.

12. The estimate for combined circulation is based on ABC reports; "Circulation Analysis - Radio Magazines (ABC net paid circulation first 6 months)," chart, 1934, box 31, folder 57, WHS-NBC; Paul F. Lazarsfeld, ed., *Radio and the Printed Page* (New York: Duell, Sloan & Pearce, 1940), 323 (*True Story*); Dr. D. M. Hoffman to *RG*, September 10, 1938, inside front cover (*Radio Guide*).

13. Douglas Waples, *Research Memorandum on Social Aspects of Reading in the Depression* (Reprint, New York: Arno Press, 1970), 100–102; William F. Rasche, *The Reading Interests of Young Workers* (Chicago: University of Chicago Libraries, 1937); Frederick H. Lumley, *Measurement in Radio* (New York: Arno Press and the New York Times, 1934), 186–87; Lazarsfeld, *Radio and the Printed Page*, 29–47; Hugh M. Beville,

"Social Stratification of the Radio Audience" (Princeton: Princeton Radio Research Project, 1939); Charles Hall Wolfe, *Modern Radio Advertising* (New York: Funk and Wagnalls, 1949), 101–78; "Chain Advertisers to Use Listener Magazines," *Broadcast Advertising*, June 1932, 26; On lower-class audiences for radio during the Depression, Roland Marchand, *Advertising the American Dream: Making Way for Modernity, 1920–1940* (Berkeley: University of California Press, 1985), 91, 93; Lizabeth Cohen, *Making a New Deal: Industrial Workers in Chicago, 1919–1939* (Cambridge: Cambridge University Press, 1990), 325.

14. "Channels of NBC Service to Broadcast Advertising Clients," NBC Chart, 1932, box 1, folder 11, WHS-EPHJ; "The Successful Radio Program, Merchandised through Direct and Indirect Advertising Channels, and Itself a Merchandising Aid," in *Broadcast Advertising*, vol. 2, *The Merchandising of a Broadcast Advertising Campaign* (New York: NBC, 1932).

15. R. C. Patterson, Jr. to John Royal, September 3, 1935, box 40, folder 60; Wayne L. Randall to John F. Royal, July 10, 1934, box 31, folder 30; John F. Royal to Frank Mason, June 19, 1934, box 31, folder 30; M. H. Aylesworth to Barrett Andrews, June 4, 1934, box 31, folder 30; Kobak's notes on M. H. Aylesworth's memo to Edgar Kobak, June 21, 1935, box 40, folder 56; Wayne L. Randall to M. H. Aylesworth, April 13, 1934, box 31, folder 30; Curtis Mitchell to Richard C. Patterson, Jr., May 16, 1934, box 31, folder 30; all in WHS-NBC.

16. *Radio Guide*, February–March 1936; John Dunning, *On the Air: The Encyclopedia of Old-Time Radio* (New York and Oxford: Oxford University Press, 1998), 427–28.

17. M. H. Aylesworth to Frank E. Mason, March 22, 1934, box 31, folder 30; Curtis Mitchell to M. H. Aylesworth, May 31, 1934, box 31, folder 57; M. H. Aylesworth to Curtis Mitchell, June 7, 1934, box 31, folder 57; M. H. Aylesworth to Curtis Mitchell, November 23, 1934, box 31, folder 57; M. H. Aylesworth to H. Krancer, March 26, 1934, box 31, folder 30; all in WHS-NBC.

18. M. H. Aylesworth to R. C. Patterson, Jr., May 21, 1934, box 31, folder 30, WHS-NBC; *Broadcast Advertising*, vol. 2.

19. Helen J. Sioussat to Phillips H. Lord, September 18, 1935, LAB-HJS.

20. John O. Ives to Joseph H. Neebe, July 22, 1935, folder G-Men, LC-WOR; Richard G. Powers, *G-Men: Hoover's FBI in American Popular Culture* (Carbondale: Southern Illinois University Press, 1983); Richard G. Powers, *Secrecy and Power: The Life of J. Edgar Hoover* (New York and London: Free Press and Collier Macmillan, 1987); Claire B. Potter, *War on Crime: Bandits, G-Men, and the Politics of Mass Culture* (New Brunswick, N.J.: Rutgers University Press, 1998); For telegrams from radio station managers and endorsements from the Parent-Teacher Association, see folder G-Men, LC-WOR.

21. On cross-marketing in this period, see Edward L. Bernays, *Crystallizing Public Opinion* (New York: Boni and Liveright, 1923); and Edward L. Bernays, *Biography of an Idea: Memoirs of Public Relations Counsel Edward L. Bernays* (New York: Simon and Schuster, 1965); Ernest V. Heyn, New York, to George Tormey, November 13, 1939, box 1A, folder Second Husband—General, AHC-FAHC.

22. M. H. Aylesworth to Wayne Randall, April 14, 1934, box 31, folder 30, WHS-NBC; Frank E. Mason to A. H. Morton, September 28, 1934, box 31, folder 57, WHS-NBC; Curtis Mitchell to Richard C. Patterson, Jr., May 16, 1934, box 31, folder 30, WHS-NBC; "Radio Guide Broadcasting!" *RG*, September 1931.

23. On consumption and citizenship in the 1930s, see Charles F. McGovern, *Sold American: Consumption and Citizenship, 1890–1945* (Chapel Hill: University of North Carolina Press, 2006); "Your Favorites—They're Radio's Stars," *RG*, February 13, 1937, 2; "Radio Fan Mail July 12th to 26th Inclusive," July 1935, box 4, folder 1, WHS-JC; "Radio's Winners in 1935," advertisement proofs, June 1934, box 40, folder 56, WHS-NBC.

24. Editor in reply to A. W. A. to *RG*, June 25, 1938, inside front cover; "Is There Too Much Swing?" *RG*, October 1, 1938, 10; "Do You Approve of Studio Applause during a Broadcast?" *RG*, November 6, 1938, 13; Meg Jacobs, *Pocketbook Politics: Economic Citizenship in Twentieth-Century America* (Princeton, N.J.: Princeton University Press, 2004); Robert B. Westbrook, "Fighting for the American Family: Private Interests and Political Obligations in World War II," in *The Power of Culture: Critical Essays in American History*, ed. Richard W. Fox and T. J. Jackson Lears (Chicago and London: Chicago University Press, 1993), 195–222.

25. "The Open Circuit," *Broadcast Weekly*, February 28, 1931, 16–19; "Voice of the Listener," *RG*, February 6, 1937, 19; "The Reader's Voice," *RL*, March 1935, 47; "The Fan Mailbag," *RL*, August 1934, 6; Harold B. Hersey, *Pulpwood Editor: The Fabulous World of the Thriller Magazines Revealed by a Veteran Editor and Publisher* (New York: Frederick A. Stokes Company, 1937), 87.

26. "The Loudspeaker Speaks Out," *RL*, May 1935, 33; "The Loudspeaker Speaks Out," *RL*, June 1935, 33; Howard E. Stanley to *RPW*, March 31, 1927, 35; John W. Mackela to *RPW*, April 21, 1927, 38; Hersey, *Pulpwood Editor*, 97–98; David Grimsted, "Gods, Gentlemen, and Groundlings," in *Melodrama Unveiled: American Theater and Culture, 1800–1850* (1968; Berkeley and Los Angeles: University of California Press, 1987), 62.

27. Carlton E. Morse to *RG*, December 17, 1938, Inside Front Cover; E. R. Johnstone to *RL*, August 1934, 6; Maxine Sullivan to *RG*, December 17, 1938, inside front cover; Benny Goodman to *RG*, December 17, 1938, inside front cover; Miss H. M. Johnson to *RL*, December 1933, 6, 76 ("won't dare"); (Unsigned), Cincinnati, OH, to *RG*, February 20, 1937, 19 ("don't suppose"); George H. Davis to *RL*, March 1935, 47 ("long-suffering listeners"); Hersey, *Pulpwood Editor*, 98–99.

28. Hersey, *Pulpwood Editor*, 102. For anti-communist letters, see Kenneth Tottenhoff to *RG*, May 22, 1937, 19; and Miss Elma L. Morris to *RG*, October 13, 1939, 12; Regina G. Kunzel, "Pulp Fictions and Problem Girls: Reading and Rewriting Single Pregnancy in the Postwar United States," *American Historical Review* 100 (December 1995): 1487.

29. See *The Story of Mary Marlin* fan mail summaries in box 4, folder 1, WHS-JC.

30. "Become a Contributing Editor to Radioland," *RL*, September 1933, 6; Mrs. Anne E. Anderson to *RL*, November 1933, 8; Mary Kay to *RL*, June 1935, 33; "Fan Mail—September 12th to 25th Incl.," September 1935, box 4, folder 1, WHS-JC.

31. "Fan Mail—September 12th to 25th Incl"; Rosse Fowlkes to *RG*, May 29, 1937, 18

(strike); Mrs. George Meyers to *RG*, May 8, 1937, 19 (WPA); Eldora Shellenbarger to *TI*, January 1944, 2 ("bomber plant"); Alice Ornan to *TI*, September 1945, 2 ("equal rights").

32. Joseph Julian, *This Was Radio: A Personal Memoir* (New York: Viking Press, 1975), 232; see also Susan J. Douglas, *Listening In: Radio and the American Imagination* (New York: Times Books, 1999); Rosanne Knight to *RG*, June 30, 1939, 17.

33. Mrs. R. H. Gleason to *RG*, May 22, 1937, 19.

34. See Paul M. Dennis, "Chills and Thrills: Does Radio Harm Our Children? The Controversy over Program Violence During the Age of Radio," *Journal of the History of the Behavioral Sciences* 34, no. 1 (1998): 33–50; Mrs. Herbert Johnson to *RG*, April 17, 1937, 19.

35. Johnson to *RG*; Mrs. Mabel H. Cozzens to *RL*, May 1935, 33 (long commercials); Bob Keeley to *RG*, May 1, 1937, 19 ("sneaked-in"); Annette Darklin to *TI*, March 1945, 2 (overwrought); Ellen A. Sewart to *TI*, September 1945, 2; Mrs. Kathleen Clarke to *RG*, April 3, 1937, 19; John M. Barton to *TI*, March 1944, 1; Mrs. Joe Miller to *RG*, February 27, 1937, 19 ("thrilling part"); Mrs. F. A. Rossetter to *RG*, March 27, 1937, 17 (six minutes); Marion Bevens, to *TI*, June 1944, 2.

36. George H. Davis to *RL*, March 1935, 47 ("spurious letters"); Louise Peterson to *RM*, March 1938, 85 (testimonials); Harry Dettefs to *RL*, March 1935, 47; Annette Darklin to *TI*, March 1945, 2. Examples such as these confirm Kathy M. Newman's point that radio advertisements, as well as the discourse about them, led listeners to critique the commercial radio system; see Newman, *Radio Active: Advertising and Consumer Activism, 1935–1947* (Berkeley: University of California Press, 2004). On the consumer movement in this period, see also McGovern, *Sold American*; and Lenthall, *Radio's America*, 17–52.

37. R. C. O'Brien to *RG*, February 6, 1937, 19; Hazel E. Hartman to *RG*, June 5, 1937, 19; Willard D. Hamilton to *RG*, February 27, 1937, 19.

38. Lauritz Melchio to *RG*, December 24, 1938, 16.

39. N. A. Beatty to *RG*, May 1, 1937, 19.

Chapter 4

1. Susan Smulyan, *Selling Radio: The Commercialization of American Broadcasting, 1920–1934* (Washington, D.C.: Smithsonian Institution Press, 1994), 110; Mae Douglas Drown to Wendell Hall, January 8, 1924, box 1, folder 2, WHS-WH; Francis Gerald Fritz, "Wendell Hall: Early Radio Performer," in *American Broadcasting: A Source Book on the History of Radio and Television*, ed. Lawrence W. Lichty and Malachi C. Topping (New York: Hastings House, 1976), 276–83; "Early N. W. Ayer & Son Radio Clients, from 1924–1929," ca. October 1934, AHC-TJM (tour for National).

2. J. F. Steiner, "Recreation and Leisure Time Activities," in *Recent Social Trends in the United States*, vol. 2 (New York: McGraw-Hill, 1933), 942; Arthur F. Wertheim, *Radio Comedy* (New York: Oxford University Press, 1979), 46; and Harvey Green, *The Uncertainty of Everyday Life* (New York: Harper Collins, 1992), 188. Radio ownership varied from region to region, and African-Americans were less likely than any other group to own radio sets. Malcolm M. Willey and Stuart A. Rice, "The Agencies of Communication," in *Recent Social Trends in the United States*, vol. 1, 211–15; Jeanette Sayre, "Progress in Radio Fan Mail

Analysis," *POQ* 3 (April 1939): 272 ("transgress the barrier"), 276 (women); Kenneth M. Goode, *What About Radio?* (New York: Harpers, 1937), 102–3 (women and the poor write more); Frederick H. Lumley, *Measurement in Radio* (New York: Arno Press, 1934), 48 ("universally used"). See also Herman S. Hettinger, *A Decade of Radio Advertising* (New York: Arno Press, 1971).

3. Gertrude Berg to *RG*, December 24, 1938, 16.

4. On "love and theft," see Eric Lott, *Love and Theft: Blackface Minstrelsy and the American Working Class* (New York: Oxford University Press, 1993).

5. On blackface radio in the 1920s, see Noah Arceneaux, "Blackface Broadcasting in the Early Days of Radio," *Journal of Radio Studies* 12, no. 1 (May 2005): 61–73. On minstrel shows in the nineteenth century, see Alexander Saxton, *The Rise and Fall of the White Republic: Class Politics and Mass Culture in Nineteenth-Century America* (London: Verso, 1990); David Roediger, *The Wages of Whiteness: Race and the Making of the American Working Class* (London: Verso, 1991); W. T. Lhamon, Jr., *Raising Cain: Blackface Performance from Jim Crow to Hip Hop* (Cambridge, Mass.: Harvard University Press, 1998); M. C. Anderson, to Wendell Hall, March 21, 1924, box 1, folder 3, WHS-WH. On imitation in vaudeville, see also Susan A. Glenn, "'Give an Imitation of Me': Vaudeville Mimics and the Play of the Self," *American Quarterly* 50 (March 1998): 47–76.

6. C. R. Beatty to Wendell Hall, March 15, 1924, box 1, folder 3, WHS-WH; Ted Fox, *Showtime at the Apollo* (New York: Holt, Rinehart, and Winston, 1983); Brenda Dixon Gottschild, *Waltzing in the Dark: African American Vaudeville and Race Politics in the Swing Era* (New York: St. Martin's Press, 2000); Melvin Patrick Ely, *The Adventures of Amos 'n' Andy: A Social History of an American Phenomenon* (New York: Free Press, 1991), 164; Edith Mary [Bitauf] to Wendell Hall, October 11, 1923, box 1, folder 2, WHS-WH; Jm. T. Steele to Wendell Hall, March 19, 1924, box 1, folder 3, WHS-WH; Dotty Wainwright to Wendell Hall, February 14, 1924, box 1, folder 2, WHS-WH.

7. E. C. Pendleton to Wendell Hall, March 25, 1924, box 1, folder 3. WHS-WH; Frank [P.] Taylor to Wendell Hall, January 10, 1924, box 1, folder 2, WHS-WH; "Little Willie" to Wendell Hall, April 3, 1924, box 1, folder 3, WHS-WH.

8. Stella F. Leonard to Wendell Hall, January 30, 1924, box 1, folder 2, WHS-WH; B[ing] F. Dawson to Wendell Hall, January 31, 1924, box 1, folder 2, WHS-WH.

9. "A negro listener-in" to Wendell Hall, February 16, 1924, box 1, folder 2, WHS-WH; Mrs. Charles F. Reid to Wendell Hall, March 26, 1926, box 2, folder 1, WHS-WH; draft of the response, written on Reid to Wendell Hall, March 26, 1926.

10. Miss Anna Shumaker to Wendell Hall, February [1926], box 2, folder 1, WHS-WH.

11. Mary Justine Dutt to *Amos 'n' Andy*, [1929], scrapbook 1929, USC-CG.

12. H. P. W. Dixon, "Amos 'n' Andy," *RN*, April 1930, 897, 951; James Whipple, *How to Write for Radio* (New York: Whittlesey House, 1938), 22; *AFTRA Guide* (Los Angeles: AFTRA, Los Angeles Local, 1954).

13. "An Appraisal . . . of Radio Advertising Today," *Fortune*, September 1932, 44; H. P. W. Dixon, "Amos 'n' Andy," *RN*, April 1930, 897; "March of Radio," *RB*, March 1929, 296–97;

Smulyan, *Selling Radio*, 115, 202; Waldo Freeman, *New York Evening World*, reprinted in *Hartford Courant*, April 6, 1930.

14. Jacquelyn Dowd Hall, James Leloudis, Robert Korstad, Mary Murphy, Lu Ann Jones, and Christopher B. Daly, *Like a Family: The Making of a Southern Cotton Mill World* (New York: W. W. Norton, 1987), 258.

15. William Benton interview in Studs Terkel, *Hard Times: An Oral History of the Great Depression* (New York: Pantheon Books, 1986), 61; Carlton E. Morse, "One Man's Radio Program," in *Off Mike: Radio Writing by the Nation's Top Radio Writers*, ed. Jerome Lawrence (New York: Duell, Sloan and Pearce, 1944), 116 (quote), 120.

16. Robert S. Lynd, *Middletown in Transition: A Study in Cultural Conflicts* (New York: Harcourt, Brace, 1937); Benedict Anderson, *Imagined Communities: Reflections on the Origin and Spread of Nationalism* (London: Verso, 1991), 35; Michele Hilmes, *Radio Voices: American Broadcasting, 1922–1952* (Minneapolis: University of Minnesota Press, 1997), 11; Jason Loviglio, *Radio's Intimate Public: Network Broadcasting and Mass-Mediated Democracy* (Minneapolis: University of Minnesota Press, 2005), 1–2.

17. Rudolf Arnheim, "The World of the Daytime Serial," in *Radio Research, 1942–43*, ed. Paul F. Lazarsfeld and Frank N. Stanton (New York: Duell, Sloan and Pearce, 1944), 34–35.

18. Hugh M. Beville, "The ABCD's of Radio Audiences," *POQ* 4 (June 1940): 196.

19. Claude S. Fischer, *America Calling: A Social History of the Telephone to 1940* (Berkeley: University of California Press, 1992), 22; Hugh M. Beville, *Audience Rating: Radio, Television, and Cable* (Hillsdale, N.J.: L. Erlbaum Associates, 1988), 10, 11; On the history of ratings, see also Karen Buzzard, *Chains of Gold: Marketing the Ratings and Rating the Markets* (Metuchen, N.J.: Scarecrow Press, 1990); Donald L. Hurwitz, "Broadcast 'Ratings': The Rise and Development of Commercial Audience Research and Measurement in American Broadcasting" (Ph.D. diss., University of Illinois at Urbana-Champaign, 1983).

20. William J. Buxton and Charles R. Acland, "Interview with Dr. Frank N. Stanton: Radio Research Pioneer," *Journal of Radio Studies* 8, no. 1 (2001): 202 (furniture); Lumley, *Measurement in Radio*; Frank N. Stanton, interview by Michael J. Socolow, transcript in author's possession, April 6, 2004, 8; Katherine Pandora, "'Mapping the New Mental World Created by Radio': Media Messages, Cultural Politics, and Cantril and Allport's *The Psychology of Radio*," *Journal of Social Issues* 54, no. 1 (Spring 1998): 7–27; Herman S. Hettinger, "Some Fundamental Aspects of Radio Broadcasting Economics," *Harvard Business Review* 14, no. 1 (1935), 26, cited in Michael J. Socolow, "Psyche and Society: Radio Advertising and Social Psychology in America, 1923–1936," *Historical Journal of Film, Radio, and Television* 24, no. 4 (October 2004): 530. See also Michael J. Socolow, "The Behaviorist in the Boardroom: The Research of Frank Stanton, Ph.D.," *Journal of Broadcasting & Electronic Media* 52, no. 4 (December 2008): 526–43.

21. Emmons C. Carlson to Irna Phillips, October 13, 1938, box 62, folder NBC Correspondence, WHS-IP. On commodity audiences, see Dallas W. Smythe, *Dependency Road: Communications, Capitalism, Consciousness, and Canada* (Norwood, N.J.: Ablex Pub.

Corp., 1981); and, most recently, Thomas Streeter, "Viewing as Property: Broadcasting's Audience Commodity," in *Selling the Air: A Critique of the Policy of Commercial Broadcasting in the United States* (Chicago: Chicago University Press, 1996), 275–308; Kathy M. Newman, *Radio Active: Advertising and Consumer Activism, 1935–1947* (Berkeley: University of California Press, 2004).

22. N. W. Ayer & Son, Inc., "A Confidential Statement of Policy and Practice in Radio Broadcasting," January 5, 1938, box 6, AHC-TJM, 20; Sidney Strotz to Irna Phillips, February 17, 1937, box 62, folder NBC Correspondence, WHS-IP.

23. Painter to Phillips, June 30, 1944.

24. See Igor Kopytoff, "The Cultural Biography of Things: Commoditization as Process," in *The Social Life of Things: Commodities in Cultural Perspective*, ed. Arjun Appadurai (Cambridge: Cambridge University Press, 1986), 64–91.

25. Lumley, *Measurement in Radio*, 48; Jack Benny, "Gags Have Grown Up," *TI*, April 1945, 11; "Fan Mail Complaints, Week of 10–9–38," October 17, 1938, box 4, folder 2, AHC-PHL.

26. Don E. Gilman to George Trato, December 26, 1934; Bertha Brainard to R. H. White, January 25, 1935 ("no cigarette or medecine sponsorship"); Vernon H. Pribble to John F. Royal, January 25, 1935 (Cleveland); William Burke Miller to Phillips Carlin, January 23, 1935 (Asheville); all in box 40, folder 7, WHS-NBC.

27. Entire telegram from Don Gilman reproduced in Isabella Hurst to R. C. Witmer, February 20, 1935, box 40, folder 7, WHS-NBC.

28. George Isaac to Jane Crusinberry, August 5, 1935, box 3, folder 2, WHS-JC.

29. A Fan to SMM, July 17, 1935, Mrs. T. J. B. to SMM, July 18, 1935, and Marian Louise to SMM, July 11, 1935, all in "Radio Fan Mail July 12th to 26th Inclusive," July 26, 1935, box 4, folder 1, WHS-JC; M. I., Elgin to SMM, October 31, 1935, in "Fan Mail 10/29 to 11/19 Inclusive," November 19, 1935, box 4, folder 1, WHS-JC ("most interesting"); Mrs. Joseph M. Meyers to SMM, September 3, 1935 ("more Cedar Springs"), and Mrs. P. Jones to SMM, September 6, 1935 (Paradise Pent House), both in "Fan Mail 8/28 to 9/11 Inclusive," September 11, 1935, box 4, folder 1, WHS-JC.

30. Jane Crusinberry, "Ratings and Facts of Interest," draft, [1944], box 5, folder 7, WHS-JC.

31. Jane Crusinberry to Lord & Thomas, 1935, box 3, folder 2, WHS-JC.

32. Mrs. Patrick Healy to SMM, October 14, 1935, "Fan Mail - Sept. 26 to Oct. 14 Inclusive," October 14, 1935, box 4, folder 1, WHS-JC (new station); Mrs. J. S. Pelletier to SMM, July 22, 1935 (a word now and then), Mrs. Ed Fenton to SMM, July 26, 1935 (admirers); Mrs. Nona Johnston to SMM, July 22, 1935 (never misses), Mrs. Minnie W. Porter to SMM, July 18, 1935 (best program), all in "Radio Fan Mail July 12th to 26th Inclusive." Rose Nehill to SMM, September 26, 1935, in "Fan Mail - Sept. 26 to Oct. 14 Inclusive" ("loweard"); Mrs. Fred Smith to SMM, October 19, 1935, in "Fan Mail 10/15/35–10/28/35 Inclusive," October 28, 1935, box 4, folder 1, WHS-JC (shopping); Mrs. B. Brotherson to SMM, November 8, 1935, in "Fan Mail 10/29 to 11/19 Inclusive" (Polish station); Mrs. G. E. Petkere to SMM, July 18, 1935, in "Radio Fan Mail July 12th to 26th Inclusive," July 26,

1935, box 4, folder 1, WHS-JC (confession); Mrs. J. A. Morelang to SMM, November 11, 1935, in "Fan Mail 10/29 to 11/19 Inclusive" (sit in radio).

33. Edgar H. Felix, "Early Days in Radio," 1962, CU-RPP, 11 (Conrad); JWT Representatives Meeting, April 16, 1930, quoted in Charles F. McGovern, *Sold American: Consumption and Citizenship, 1890–1945* (Chapel Hill: University of North Carolina Press, 2006), 50–51 (confidential results); *Broadcast Advertising*, April 1932.

34. T. J. Sabin to E. P. H. James, February 13, 1935, box 60, folder 26, WHS-NBC; P. G. Parker to Edgar Kobak, February 5, 1935, box 60, folder 26, WHS-NBC.

35. William Ramsey to Jane Crusinberry, February 18, 1943, box 3, folder 5, WHS-JC.

36. Carl Wester to Irna Phillips, April 22, 1936, box 62, folder NBC Correspondence, WHS-IP.

37. Mrs. Leland Zollinger, Providence to J.C., March 39, 1937 (not an affair); Jane Crusinberry to Mrs. Leland Zollinger, April 5, 1937 (not an affair); Carolyn Lee to Jane Crusinberry, February 12, 1938 (don't write out of script); Mrs. A. J. Zimmer to Jane Crusinberry, January 18, 1938 (Russia); Jane Crusinberry to Carolyn Lee, March 11, 1938 ("need not worry"); Jane Crusinberry to Mrs. A. J. Zimmer, March 11, 1938, ("not leaving"); all in box 3, folder 10, WHS-JC. Anne Hummert to Lloyd Rosamond, September 10, 1943, box 1A, AHC-FAHC.

38. George Isaac to Jane Crusinberry, December 13, 1935, box 3, folder 2, WHS-JC.

39. H. King Painter to Irna Phillips, June 30, 1944, box 62, folder Knox Reeves Correspondence, WHS-IP.

40. Painter to Phillips, June 30, 1944; H. King Painter to Irna Phillips, June 2, 1944, box 62, folder Knox Reeves Correspondence, WHS-IP ("don't write the way they used to"); Jason Loviglio, *Radio's Intimate Public: Network Broadcasting and Mass-Mediated Democracy* (Minneapolis: University of Minnesota Press, 2005), 83 (live audience).

41. Mrs. W. T. Oppemann to John Murray, June 4, 1944, box 46, folder 1, WHS-IP; Bertha May Hembling to To-Days Children, May 29, 1944, box 46, folder 1, WHS-IP; Mrs. W. M. Jackson to *Today's Children*, June 1944, box 46, folder 1, WHS-IP.

42. Hanna Rosin, "Life Lessons," *New Yorker*, June 5, 2006; Elizabeth A. Fones-Wolf, *Waves of Opposition: Labor and the Struggle for Democratic Radio* (Urbana: University of Illinois Press, 2006), 52 (labor and business soaps); Herta Herzog, "On Borrowed Experience: An Analysis of Listening to Daytime Sketches," *Studies in Philosophy and Social Science* 9 (February 1941): 90 (interviews); Vrinda Dalmiya and Linda Alcoff, "Are 'Old Wives Tales' Justified?" in *Feminist Epistemologies*, ed. Linda Alcoff and Elizabeth Potter (New York and London: Routledge, 1993), 220–39 (knowing how).

43. Mrs. H. G. Blakeslee (Mary T. Hawkes) to Jane Crusinberry, January 8, 1936, box 4, folder 1, WHS-JC; "Americus Girl Bride of San Francisco Man," *Atlanta Constitution*, December 12, 1920 (Theron Hawkes, father); "Theron Hawkes, Americus," *Atlanta Constitution*, December 25, 1917 (Theron Hawkes' wife, formerly Annie L. Hawkins); "Personal Mention," *Atlanta Constitution*, March 3, 1880 (Annie L. Hawkins, daughter of Colonel Willis A. Hawkins); "The State Campaign," *Atlanta Constitution*, September 7, 1880 (Colo-

nel Willis A. Hawkins appointed Associate Justice, Georgia Supreme Court); Alan Anderson, *Remembering Americus, Georgia: Essays on Southern Life* (Charleston, S.C.: History Press, 2006), 44 (Willis A. Hawkins votes for secession as a delegate to the Georgia Secession Convention of 1861). On slaveholders' worth as determined by their slaves, see Walter Johnson, *Soul by Soul: Life Inside the Antebellum Slave Market* (Cambridge, Mass.: Harvard University Press, 1999).

44. Miss Lynne Hofstetter to SMM, October 22, 1940, box 3, folder 5, WHS-JC.

45. Mrs. Grace Squires to SMM, April 11, 1940, box 3, folder 10, WHS-JC.

46. Jane Crusinberry to Mrs. Wm. H. Squires, October 4, 1940, box 3, folder 10, WHS-JC.

47. Jane Crusinberry to William Ramsey, November 8, 1940, box 3, folder 5, WHS-JC.

48. Robert T. Colwell to John U. Reber, January 13, 1944, box 62, folder JWT, WHS-IP; Irna Phillips to Robert T. Colwell, March 6, 1944, box 62, folder JWT, WHS-IP; Hugh M. Beville, "The ABCD's of Radio Audiences," *POQ* 4 (June 1940): 203–4; Miss Maxine Bachman to SMM, November 14, 1935, in "Fan Mail 10/29 to 11/19 Inclusive;" Lizabeth Cohen, *Making a New Deal: Industrial Workers in Chicago, 1919–1939* (Cambridge: Cambridge University Press, 1990), 328 (Lithuanian).

49. Lynd, *Middletown in Transition*, 124–25, 128–30; Esther Joan Norman to Jane Crusinberry, April 5, 1941, box 3, folder 9, WHS-JC (labor paper); Mrs. Roy Robins to Procter and Gamble, March 27, 1939, box 3, folder 9, WHS-JC (stay-at-home scriptwriter); Mrs. Pete George to Jane Crusinberry, April 4, 1941, box 3, folder 10, WHS-JC (Siberia); Betty to SMM, September 17, 1935, in "Fan Mail - September 12th to 25th Inclusive," September 25, 1935, box 4, folder 1, WHS-JC.

Chapter 5

1. Adorno's plan for the music study is outlined in "Study of Likes and Dislikes in Light Popular Music," December 1939, box 272, folder 3242, RAC-RFA; Theodor W. Adorno, "Scientific Experiences of a European Scholar in America," in *The Intellectual Migration: Europe and America, 1920–1960*, ed. Donald Fleming and Bernard Bailyn (Cambridge, Mass.: Harvard University Press, 1969), 347; Max Horkheimer and Theodor W. Adorno, *Dialectic of Enlightenment*, trans. John Cumming (New York: Herder and Herder, 1972). For a comprehensive analysis of Adorno's stay in the United States, see David Jenemann, *Adorno in America* (Minneapolis: University of Minnesota Press, 2007). Adorno's manuscript writings from this period have been published in Theodor W. Adorno, *Current of Music*, ed. Robert Hullot-Kentor (Cambridge: Polity, 2009).

2. On NBC's interest in the Ohio and Princeton projects, see Franklin Durham to Hugh M. Beville, Jr., February 21, 1938, box 63, folder 48, WHS-NBC ("in touch"); Herman S. Hettinger, *A Study of Habits and Preferences of Radio Listeners in Philadelphia* (Philadelphia: Printed by Universal Broadcasting Company, 1930); Herman S. Hettinger and Richard R. Mead, *The Summer Radio Audience: A Study of the Habits and Preferences of Summer Radio Audiences in Philadelphia and Vicinity* (Philadelphia: Printed by Universal

Broadcasting Company, 1931). See also Irvin Stewart and Herman S. Hettinger, *Radio: Selected AAPSS Surveys, 1929–1941* (New York: Arno Press and the New York Times, 1971); Michael J. Socolow, "Psyche and Society: Radio Advertising and Social Psychology in America, 1923–1936," *Historical Journal of Film, Radio, and Television* 24, no. 4 (October 2004): 517–34. Martin Jay and others have shown how the Radio Project fueled Adorno's critique of radio music, radio listening, and "administrative research." Martin Jay, "Aesthetic Theory and the Critique of Mass Culture," in *The Dialectical Imagination: A History of the Frankfurt School and the Institute of Social Research, 1923–1950* (Berkeley and Los Angeles: University of California Press, 1996), 173–218; T. Y. Levin and M. Vonderlinn, "Elements of a Radio Theory: Adorno and the Princeton Radio Research Project," *Musical Quarterly* 78, no. 2 (1994): 316–24; David E. Morrison, "Kultur and Culture: The Case of Theodor W. Adorno and Paul F. Lazarsfeld," *Social Research* 45, no. 2 (Summer 1978): 331–55. See also Rolf Wiggershaus, *The Frankfurt School: Its History, Theories, and Political Significance*, trans. Michael Robertson (Cambridge, Mass.: MIT Press, 1994); Richard D. Leppert's commentaries in Theodor W. Adorno, *Essays on Music*, trans. Susan H. Gillespie (Berkeley: University of California Press, 2002).

3. Adorno, *Essays on Music*, 1–8 (Adorno's early years); Virgil Thomson to Theodor W. Adorno, 4 June 1941, folder 3243, box 272, RAC-RFA; Virgil Thomson, "How Popular Music Works," *New York Herald Tribune* (15 June 1941), 6; Virgil Thomson, "The 'Hit' Trade," *New York Herald Tribune* (26 January 1943), 6; Charles F. McGovern, *Sold American: Consumption and Citizenship, 1890–1945* (Chapel Hill: University of North Carolina Press, 2006), 48–58 (managers and advertisers).

4. Roland Marchand, *Advertising the American Dream: Making Way for Modernity, 1920–1940* (Berkeley: University of California Press, 1985), 66; Socolow, "Psyche and Society"; James H. Collins, "The Eternal Feminine," *Printer's Ink* 35, no.13 (June 26, 1901): 3; Charles McGovern, "Consumption and Citizenship in the United States, 1900–1940," in *Getting and Spending: European and American Consumer Societies in the Twentieth Century*, ed. Susan Strasser, Charles McGovern, and Matthias Judt (Cambridge and New York: Cambridge University Press, 1998), 45; David Segal, "Are We a Nation of 12-Year-Olds?" *School Life* 19 (December 1933): 79; Marchand, *Advertising the American Dream*, 67; Charles H. Stamps, *The Concept of the Mass Audience in American Broadcasting: An Historical-Descriptive Study* (New York: Arno Press, 1979); S. H. Bliss, "The Local Station and National Advertising," *Broadcasting* (November 1, 1932), 11; Elmo Roper, "Classifying Respondents by Economic Status," *POQ* 4, no. 2 (June 1940): 272; Maurice Zolotow, "Washboard Weepers," *Saturday Evening Post* (May 29, 1943), 48.

5. John F. Royal to Miss Janet MacRorie, memo, May 1, 1935; NBC to employees, December 8, 1938; Miller Wm. Burke to Edna Turner, December 9, 1938; Thomas H. Belviso to Phillips Carlin, May 25, 1937; all in folder 245, LC-NBC.

6. Henry Volkening, "Abuses of Radio Broadcasting," *Current History* 33 (December 1930): 397, 398; A. M. Sullivan, "Radio and Vaudeville Culture," *Commonweal* 23 (December 13, 1935): 177; Merrill Denison, "Why Isn't Radio Better?" *Harper's Monthly* 168 (April 1934): 580.

7. William Orton, "The Level of Thirteen-Year-Olds," *Atlantic Monthly* 147 (January 1931): 1–10; "Gang Busters Writing Rules," [1940], LC-WOR; James Whipple, *How to Write for Radio* (New York: Whittlesey House, 1938), 23–24; William Strunk and E. B. White, *The Elements of Style* (1918; rev. ed., New York: Macmillan, 1979). See also George Orwell, "Politics and the English Language" (1942), in *The Orwell Reader* (New York: Harcourt, Brace, and World, 1956), 365–66. On a history of language and rhetoric in American politics, see Kenneth Cmiel, *Democratic Eloquence: The Fight over Popular Speech in Nineteenth-Century America* (Berkeley and Los Angeles: University of California Press, 1990). On efficiency and modernism, see Emily Thompson, *The Soundscape of Modernity: Architectural Acoustics and the Culture of Listening in America, 1900–1933* (Cambridge, Mass.: MIT Press, 2002), 157; Terry E. Smith, *Making the Modern: Industry, Art, and Design in America* (Chicago: University of Chicago Press, 1993); and Cecelia Tichi, *Shifting Gears: Technology, Literature, Culture in Modernist America* (Chapel Hill: University of North Carolina Press, 1987).

8. Chester B. Bowles, "Agency's Responsibility in Radio," *Printers' Ink Monthly* (July 1936), 81; Willis Cooper to Sidney Strotz, August 8, 1934, box 62, folder NBC Correspondence, WHS-IP.

9. "Minutes of the Meeting of the Executive Committee of the Rockefeller Foundation," May 21, 1937, box 271, folder 3233, RAC-RFA; The Rockefeller Foundation funded the National Advisory Council on Radio and Education since 1930, and chose to further focus on radio to reorient its Humanities Division "to influence contemporary taste in large masses of population." Quoted in William J. Buxton, "The Political Economy of Communications Research: Commercial Broadcasting, the Rockefeller Foundation and the Princeton Radio Research Project," in *Information and Communication in Economics*, ed. R. Babe (Boston: Kluwer, 1994), 154–55. On the history of the Princeton Radio Research Project in all its guises, see also Todd Gitlin, "Media Sociology: The Dominant Paradigm," *Theory and Society* 6, no. 2 (September 1978): 205–53; Elihu Katz, "Communication Research Since Lazarsfeld," *POQ* 51 (1989): 525–45; Daniel Czitrom, "The Rise of Empirical Media Study: Communications Research as Behavioral Science, 1930–1960," in *Media and the American Mind: From Morse to McLuhan* (Chapel Hill: University of North Carolina Press, 1982), 122–46; David E. Morrison, "The Transference of Experience and the Impact of Ideas: Paul Lazarsfeld and Mass Communications Research," *Communication* (1988): 185–210.

10. John Marshall, untitled memorandum on the Radio Research Project, May 1937, box 271, folder 3234, RAC-RFA; Hadley Cantril to John Marshall, May 11, 1937, box 271, folder 3234, RAC-RFA; George Gallup to John Marshall, May 19, 1937, box 271, folder 3234, RAC-RFA; Frank Stanton, interview by John Marshall, summary, November 6, 1936, box 271, folder 3233, RAC-RFA; John Marshall, untitled memorandum on the Radio Research Project, May 1937, box 271, folder 3234, RAC-RFA.

11. "RF Program in broadcasting," [1936], box 271, folder 3234, RAC-RFA; Hugh M. Beville, Jr. to Walter G. Preston, Jr., October 5, 1938, box 63, folder 48, WHS-NBC; Paul F. Lazarsfeld to John Marshall, March 4, 1940, box 222, folder 2661, RAC-RFA; Paul

F. Lazarsfeld to John Marshall, September 6, 1940, box 222, folder 2661, RAC-RFA. Hugh M. Beville, "Social Stratification of the Radio Audience" (Princeton: Princeton Radio Research Project, 1939). The summary was published as Hugh M. Beville, "The ABCD's of Radio Audiences," *POQ* 4 (June 1940): 195–206. Former employees also found jobs in government agencies and universities. Paul F. Lazarsfeld to John Marshall, November 23, 1943, box 222, folder 2665, RAC-RFA. Beville, "The ABCD's of Radio Audiences"; Paul F. Lazarsfeld and Frank N. Stanton, eds., *Radio Research, 1941* (New York: Duell, Sloan & Pearce, 1942); Paul F. Lazarsfeld and Frank N. Stanton, eds., *Radio Research, 1942–1943* (New York: Duell, Sloan & Pearce, 1944); Paul F. Lazarsfeld and Frank N. Stanton, eds., *Communications Research, 1948–1949* (New York: Harper, 1949). On the speech, see Paul F. Lazarsfeld to John Marshall, October 19, 1946, box 222, folder 2667, RAC-RFA. Justin Miller to John Marshall, November 19, 1946, box 222, folder 2667, RAC-RFA; Paul F. Lazarsfeld, "How Can Industry Use the NORC Survey," [1946], box 222, folder 2667, RAC-RFA.

12. Hadley Cantril to John Marshall, December 31, 1936, box 271, folder 3233, RAC-RFA; Princeton Radio Research Project, "Inventory of Materials," [1939], box 272, folder 3239, RAC-RFA; Frank Stanton, "Listener Research Techniques," rev. ed., July 1939, box 272, folder 3241, RAC-RFA, 5; "On the Use of Elaborate Personal Interviews for the Princeton Radio Research Project," [1937], box 221, folder 2654, RAC-RFA, 3. The study was published as Paul F. Lazarsfeld and Harry N. Field, *The People Look at Radio* (Chapel Hill: University of North Carolina Press, 1946); Justin Miller to John Marshall, November 19, 1946, box 222, folder 2667, RAC-RFA; Paul F. Lazarsfeld, "How Can Industry Use the NORC Survey," [1946], box 222, folder 2667, RAC-RFA.

13. Adorno, "On a Social Critique of Radio Music," paper read at the Princeton Radio Research Project, October 26, 1939, box 1, folder B0076, CU-BASR, 1, 3, 5; Paul F. Lazarsfeld to John Marshall, December 27, 1939, box 272, folder 3242, RAC-RFA; Lazarsfeld describes Adorno's plans in Paul F. Lazarsfeld to John Marshall, December 27, 1939, box 272, folder 3242, RAC-RFA; Hugh M. Beville, Jr. to John Royal, May 25, 1938, box 63, folder 48, WHS-NBC. On Stanton, see Lazarsfeld cited in David E. Morrison, "Kultur and Culture: The Case of Theodor W. Adorno and Paul F. Lazarsfeld," *Social Research* 45, no. 2 (Summer 1978): 349; Adorno refers to these letters in Theodor W. Adorno, "On a Social Critique of Radio Music," paper read at the Princeton Radio Research Project by T. W. Adorno, October 26, 1939, box 1, folder B0076, CU-BASR 11. Papers include: Theodor W. Adorno, "Lecture Delivered by Theodore Wiesengrund-Adorno," January 1938, box 1, folder B0072, CU-BASR (a later version published as Adorno, "The Radio Symphony: An Experiment in Theory," in Lazarsfeld and Stanton, eds., *Radio Research, 1941*, 110–39); Adorno, "On a Social Critique of Radio Music" (a later version published as Adorno, "A Social Critique of Radio Music," *Kenyon Review* 8, no. 2 [Spring 1945]: 208–17); and a paper published much later as Adorno, "Analytical Study of the NBC Music Appreciation Hour," *Musical Quarterly* 78, no. 2 (1994): 325–77. The book-length study is Adorno, "Memorandum: Music in Radio," Princeton Radio Research Project, June 26, 1938, series 1, box 26, folder Subject File PRRP 4,

Microfilm #7970–1, CU-PFL. Another publication coming out of Adorno's work at the project is Adorno, "On Popular Music," *Studies in Philosophy and Social Science* 9, no. 1 (1941): 17–48.

14. Paul F. Lazarsfeld to Theodor W. Adorno, [1939], series 1, box 25, folder Subject File. Princeton Radio Research Project 3, CU-PFL; Morrison, "Kultur and Culture," 349; "Music expert" quoted in Walter G. Preston to John Marshall, December 18, 1939, box 272, folder 3242, RAC-RFA; "Discussion of the Columbia University Request for a Grant Toward the Expenses of Lazarsfeld's Research in Radio Listening," report, January 5, 1940, box 272, folder 3243, RAC-RFA; the last attempt to get funding for Adorno is discussed in John Marshall, Report of a conversation with T. W. Adorno, June 19, 1941, box 272, folder 3243, RAC-RFA.

15. Frederick H. Lumley, *Measurement in Radio* (New York: Arno Press, 1934), 85; and *Broadcast Advertising* 5 (June 1932): 8, 9 (early broadcasters); Hazel Gaudet to Mrs. Lazarsfeld, December 16, 1938, series 1, box 26, folder PRRP 6, CU-PFL.; the study came out as Hadley Cantril, *The Invasion from Mars: A Study in the Psychology of Panic* (1940; Reprint, New York: Harper & Row, 1966).

16. Herta Herzog, "Professor Quiz—A Gratification Study," in *Radio and the Printed Page*, ed. Paul F. Lazarsfeld (New York: Duell, Sloan & Pearce, 1940), 76 n9; see also Herta Herzog, "What Do We Really Know About Daytime Serial Listeners?" in Lazarsfeld and Stanton, eds., *Radio Research, 1942–43*, 23; Herzog, "Professor Quiz—A Gratification Study," 64–93; and Herta Herzog, "On Borrowed Experience: An Analysis of Listening to Daytime Sketches," *Studies in Philosophy and Social Science* 9 (February 1941): 65–91; Herta Herzog cited in Susan J. Douglas, *Listening In: Radio and the American Imagination* (New York: Times Books, 1999), 139 ("dearie" and accent). Lumley, *Measurement in Radio*, 293–309, includes a comprehensive list of local radio studies up to 1934; some of these are cited in this book. Theodor W. Adorno, "The Essay as Form," *New German Critique* (1984): 161. Of several accounts of "practical knowledge" cited in this book Carlo Ginzburg specifically offers Adorno's aphorisms as an example; see "Morelli, Freud, and Sherlock Holmes: Clues and Scientific Method," in *Dupin, Holmes, Peirce: The Sign of Three*, ed. Umberto Eco and Thomas A. Sebeok (Bloomington: Indiana University Press, 1983), 109.

17. Herzog, "Professor Quiz—A Gratification Study," 65 n8; Lazarsfeld, "An Episode in the History of Social Research," 312–13; Hadley Cantril to Paul F. Lazarsfeld, 1939, series, 1, box 26, folder PRRP 6, CU-PFL; Paul F. Lazarsfeld to Hadley Cantril, October 12, 1939, series 1, box 26, folder PRRP 6, CU-PFL; Cantril, *The Invasion from Mars*, iv; Herta Herzog, *Survey of Research on Children's Radio Listening* (New York: Columbia University, Office of Radio Research, 1941); Lazarsfeld and Stanton, eds., *Radio Research, 1942–1943*, 588. For a different interpretation of Herta Herzog's work, see Douglas, *Listening In*, 139. My analysis in this paragraph also draws upon the work of feminist oral historians and anthropologists who based their "dialogic" interview techniques on a belief that their subjects "can see with the greatest clarity not only their own position but also . . . the shape of social systems as a whole." See Ruth Frankenberg,

White Women, Race Matters: The Social Construction of Whiteness (Minneapolis: University of Minnesota Press, 1993 (quote on p. 8).

18. Theodor W. Adorno, "A Typology of Music Listening," draft, [1939], series 1, box 25, folder Subject File. Princeton Radio Research Project 2, CU-PFL; a later version came out as Theodor W. Adorno, "Types of Musical Conduct," in *Introduction to the Sociology of Music*, trans. E. B. Ashton (New York: Seabury Press, 1976), 1–20; Adorno, "Scientific Experiences of a European Scholar in America," 344; Theodor W. Adorno to Paul F. Lazarsfeld, memorandum "Reply to Dr. Gora's Letter," [1939], series 1, box 25, folder Subject File. Princeton Radio Research Project 2, CU-PFL; Adorno, "A Typology of Music Listening;" Adorno, "On a Social Critique of Radio Music," 18; Lazarsfeld describes the plan to use typology to guide interviews in Paul F. Lazarsfeld to John Marshall, December 27, 1939, box 272, folder 3242, RAC-RFA.

19. Adorno, "The Radio Symphony"; Julia Hufford, interview, July 3, 1939; Ed Hufford, interview, typescript, July 3, 1939, box 1, folder Musical Listening, CU-BASR; Helen Perriam, interview, typescript, July 3, 1939, box 1, folder Musical Listening, CU-BASR; Ed Hufford, interview, July 3,1939 (waltz); Louise Berger, interview, typescript, July 3, 1939, box 1, folder Musical Listening, CU-BASR (Sousa and waltz); Julia Hufford, interview, July 3, 1939 (sopranos).

20. Adorno, "A Typology of Music Listening," 3; Louise Berger, interview, typescript, July 3, 1939, box 1, folder Musical Listening, CU-BASR; Julia Hufford, interview, July 3, 1939; Adorno, "Scientific Experiences of a European Scholar in America," 347.

21. Theodor W. Adorno, "A Social Critique of Radio Music," *Kenyon Review* 8, no. 2 (Spring 1945): 208–17; Theodor W. Adorno, "Lecture Delivered by Theodore Wiesengrund-Adorno," January 1938, box 1, folder B0072, CU-BASR, 9. A later version was published as Adorno, "The Radio Symphony"; Samuel Zucker, Brooklyn, N.Y., to Colonel Schwarzkoff, November 4, 1940; Bass to Zucker, November 14, 1940, box 11, folder GB 212, 2 of 2, LC-WOR.

22. Adorno, "Scientific Experiences of a European Scholar in America," 347; Paul F. Lazarsfeld to Theodor W. Adorno, [1939], series 1, box 25, folder Subject File. Princeton Radio Research Project 3, CU-PFL; Jeanette Sayre, "Progress in Radio Fan Mail Analysis," *POQ* 3 (April 1939): 272; Adorno, "On a Social Critique of Radio Music," 11.

23. Tore Hollonquist and Edward A. Suchman, "Listening to the Listener: Experiences with the Lazarsfeld-Stanton Analyzer," in Lazarsfeld and Stanton, eds., *Radio Research, 1942–43*, 320 (see n. 12); Jack Peterman, "The 'Program Analyzer,'" *Journal of Applied Psychology* 24 (1940): 728–29; "'Easy Aces' (Broadcast October 12, 1945) Summary of Listener Reactions," Program Analysis Division confidential report, CBS, June 1947, LC-MPBRS.

24. Ryan quoted in Charles A. Siepmann, *Radio's Second Chance* (Boston: Little, Brown, 1946); Hill quoted in Charles A. Siepmann, *Radio, Television, and Society* (New York: Oxford University Press, 1950); "Study of Likes and Dislikes in Light Popular Music," December 1939, box 272, folder 3242, RAC-RFA; Christopher H. Sterling and John M. Kittross, *Stay Tuned: A History of American Broadcasting* (Mahwa, N.J.: Lawrence Erlbaum Associates, 2002), 830–31.

25. Niles Trammell to John F. Royal, April 29, 1940, box 95, folder 24, WHS-NBC; N. W. Ayer & Son, Inc., "The Telephone Hour," March 13, 1945, box 6, AHC-TJM; On wartime radio, see Gerd Horten, *Radio Goes to War: The Cultural Politics of Propaganda During World War II* (Berkeley: University of California Press, 2001).

26. H. L. McClinton to T. J. McDermott et al., March 14, 1945, box 6, AHC-TJM; N. W. Ayer & Son, Inc., "The Telephone Hour."

27. H. L. McClinton, "Radio Entertainment Since 1935," *Annals of the American Academy of Political and Social Science* (January 1941): 26; Barry T. Rumple to John W. Swallow, May 14, 1940, LC-NBC; Edward F. Evans to Sidney Strotz, August 5, 1941, LC-NBC; "Radio Handbook," sec. 9, p. 8.

28. Ernest Bornemann, "The Public Opinion Myth," *Harper's* (July 1947), 30–33, quoted in Susan Ohmer, "Measuring Desire: George Gallup and Audience Research in Hollywood," *Journal of Film and Video* 43, nos. 1–2 (March 1991): 20. The information on Gallup's film research in this paragraph is taken from this article. On Gallup's methods, see also "Increasing Profits Through Continuous Audience Research," *Gallup Looks at the Movies: Audience Research Reports, 1940–1950* (Princeton, N.J.: American Institute of Public Opinion; Wilmington, Del.: Scholarly Resources, 1979); Ranald MacDougall, "Reactions to Audience Research," *Screen Writers* 2 (April 1947): 30, quoted in Ohmer, "Measuring Desire," 21; Everett M. Rogers, *A History of Communication Study: A Biographical Approach* (New York: Free Press, 1994), 277.

29. John Steinbeck, quoted in "Radio: The World's Worst Juggler," *Time*, April 7, 1947; *Fred Allen Show*, script, January 9, 1949, LC-FA; "A Certain Mr. Allen Rates Raters' Labors as Worthy of Rating," *Variety*, March 27, 1946, 51; Alan Havig, *Fred Allen's Radio Comedy* (Philadelphia: Temple University Press, 1990), 96–97; Erik Barnouw, *The Golden Web: A History of Broadcasting from 1933 to 1953* (New York: Oxford University Press, 1968), 287; Carl Van Doren, "Preface," in *Thirteen by Corwin: Radio Dramas by Norman Corwin* (New York: Henry Holt, 1942), vii–ix; *Variety*, January 7, 1948, 95, cited in J. Fred MacDonald, *Don't Touch That Dial: Radio Programming in American Life from 1920 to 1960* (Chicago: Nelson-Hall, 1979), 60; James Thurber, "The Listening Women" (July 24, 1948), in *The Beast in Me and Other Animals* (New York: Harcourt Brace, 1973), 258–59.

30. Irna Phillips to William Ramsey, draft of unsent letter, September 13, 1947, box 62, folder Proctor & Gamble Correspondence, WHS-IP; Irna Phillips to William Ramsey, July 26, 1947, box 62, folder Proctor & Gamble Correspondence, WHS-IP; Irna Phillips to William Ramsey, 17 February 1948, box 62, folder Proctor & Gamble Correspondence, WHS-IP.

31. For examples of World War II broadcasts, see audio CD with Mark Bernstein, Alex Lubertozzi, and Dan Rather, *World War II on the Air: Edward R. Murrow and the Broadcasts That Riveted a Nation* (Naperville, Ill.: Sourcebooks MediaFusion, 2003). Michael J. Socolow, "'News Is a Weapon': Domestic Radio Propaganda and Broadcast Journalism in America, 1939–1944," *American Journalism* 24, no. 3 (Summer 2007): 109–31 (style and impact of wartime news); Paul W. White, "Covering a War for Radio," *Annals of the American Academy of Political and Social Science* 213 (January 1941): 83–92 (war news re-

porting methods), 89 (Bordeaux); Harry Romer to Eric Sevareid, November 5, 1940, box
1A folder Correspondence 1940, LC-ES; Nora Adams to Sevareid, September 6, 1946, box
1A, folder Fan Mail Jul-Dec 1946, LC-ES; Sevareid to Mrs. David L. Adams Sr., September
10, 1946, box 1A, folder Fan Mail 1946, LC-ES; Myra Finn to CBS, mimeographed copy,
March 24, 1947, box 1A, folder Fan Mail 1947 Ja-Ju, LC-ES; Myra Finn to Sevareid, March
25, 1947, box 1A, folder Fan Mail 1947 Ja-Ju, LC-ES; Esther J. Schreurs to Sevareid, March
24, 1947, box 1A, folder Fan Mail 1947 Ja-Ju, LC-ES. Finn and Schreurs also protested the
firing of Shirer. On wartime radio, radicalism, and anticommunism, see Nathan Godfried,
"'Fellow Traveler of the Air': Rod Holmgren and Leftist Radio News Commentary in
America's Cold War," *Historical Journal of Film, Radio, and Television* 24 (June 2004):
233–251; Barbara Dianne Savage, *Broadcasting Freedom: Radio, War, and the Politics of
Race, 1938–1948* (Chapel Hill: University of North Carolina Press, 1999); and Howard
Blue, *Words at War: World War II Era Radio Drama and the Postwar Broadcasting Industry
Blacklist* (Lanham: Scarecrow Press, 2002).

32. Socolow, "'News Is a Weapon'" (networks using war correspondents to gain public
trust); *Fortune*, August 1938, 75; Paul Lazarsfeld and Harry Field, *The People Look at Radio*
(Chapel Hill: University of North Carolina Press, 1946), 5–6, 82, 96–97, 100–101 (1945
survey); Paul Lazarsfeld and Harry Field, *Radio Listening in America: The People Look at
Radio—Again* (New York: Prentice-Hall, 1948), 46 (1947 survey); *Billboard*, December 6,
1947, 5, 9 (independent stations); N. W. Ayer, "Bell System Radio Program 'The Telephone
Hour,'" program proposal, April 1940, box 6, folder 46, AHC-TM; "Million Letters Set
All-Time Record for NBC Audience Mail," New York, April 30, 1936, series 134, box 381,
folder 2, NMAH-GHC; "WEAF Gets a Letter," August 7, 1942, box 139, folder 1, WHS-
NBC; and William Paley, "Broadcasting and American Society," *Annals of the American
Academy of Political and Social Science* 213 (January 1941): 67.

Chapter 6

1. "Sands-Siler," *GB*, episode 154, final script, CBS, February 15, 1939; George Norris
to Leonard Bass, January 15, 1939 (farm's location); both in box 7, folder GB 154, LC-
WOR.

2. Berniece Medrano to Leonard Bass, February 16, 1939, box 7, folder GB 154, LC-
WOR.

3. This summary is based on my research in the WOR collection. For histories of the
Gang Busters radio program, see Kathleen Battles, *Calling All Cars: Radio Dragnets and the
Technology of Policing* (Minneapolis: University of Minnesota Press, 2010); Martin Grams,
Gang Busters: The Crime Fighters of American Broadcasting (New York: OTR Publishing,
2004); and John Dunning, *On the Air: The Encyclopedia of Old-Time Radio* (New York:
Oxford University Press, 1998), 277–78.

4. Claire Potter, *War on Crime: Bandits, G-Men, and the Politics of Mass Culture* (New
Brunswick, N.J.: Rutgers University Press, 1998); K. H. Baker, "Radio Listening and Socio-
Economic Status," *Psychological Record* 1 (1937): 140 (Minnesota); I. K. Tyler, "Radio Stud-
ies in the Oakland Schools," in *Education on the Air* (Columbus: Ohio State University,

1934), 5, 297–312, cited in Herta Herzog, *Survey of Research on Children's Radio Listening* (New York: Columbia University, Office of Radio Research, 1941), 25 (California); St. Clair Drake and Horace Cayton, *Black Metropolis: A Study of Negro Life in a Northern City* (Chicago: University of Chicago Press, 1993), 608–9 (Chicago); and Hugh M. Beville, "Social Stratification of the Radio Audience" (Princeton: Princeton Radio Research Project, 1939), 39, 41, 42.

5. "Sands-Siler," script.

6. Phillips Lord, quoted in Richard Powers, *G-Men: Hoover's FBI in American Popular Culture* (Carbondale: Southern Illinois University Press, 1983), 210 ("left out all the color"); Hoover quoted in Powers, *G-Men*, 208–11 ("too sensational"); "The Eddie Doll Case," *G-Men*, episode 13, October 12, 1935, script, box 58, folder G-Men 13, LC-WOR; Powers, *G-Men*, 211–13; John Ives to Joseph Neebe, July 22, 1935, LC-WOR.

7. "Sands-Siler," script.

8. "Gang Busters Writing Rules," [1940], LC-WOR ("moralize"); Phillips Lord to Leonard Bass, September 14, 1942, box 16, folder GB 281, 2 of 2, LC-WOR (brakes); Phillips Lord, "Comments on Sands-Siler Rehearsal," January 1939, box 7, folder GB 154, LC-WOR ("shots"); Herzog, *Survey of Research*, 77–79; Harold Wentworth and Stuart Flexner, eds., *Dictionary of American Slang* (New York: Crowell, 1967), 117; Alfred Hitchcock quoted in John Taylor, *Hitch: The Life and Times of Alfred Hitchcock* (New York: Pantheon, 1978), 119 ("dull bits").

9. On detective pulps and gangster movies, see, for example, Erin Smith, *Hard-Boiled: Working Class Readers and Pulp Magazines* (Philadelphia: Temple University Press, 2000); and Jonathan Munby, *Public Enemies, Public Heroes: Screening the Gangster from Little Caesar to Touch of Evil* (Chicago: University of Chicago Press, 1999). Claire Potter, "'I'll Go the Limit and Then Some': Gun Molls, Desire, and Danger in the 1930s," *Feminist Studies* 21 (Spring 1995): 41–66 (autobiographies); "Pretty Boy Floyd," *G-Men*, episode 11, September 28, 1935; song quoted in Potter, *War on Crime*, 9.

10. "Gang Busters Writing Rules" (guidelines and "minor characteristics"); Lord, "Comments on Sands-Siler Rehearsal" ("tough quality"); Herzog, *Survey of Research*, 77–79 ("scars"), 65 ("catch bandits"); "Listen Flatfoot," *Time*, April 8, 1940, 10 ("lexicon").

11. Joseph Kovon to Mayor LaGuardia, May 6, 1937, box 3, folder GB 69, LC-WOR ("plates"); Phillips Lord to Byrnes MacDonald, May 20, 1937, box 3, folder GB 69, LC-WOR ("method" and "lesson"); "Listen Flatfoot" ("sermon" and "busters"); and Mrs. M. J. McCall to *RG*, June 11, 1938, 16 ("blood-and-thunder").

12. Phillips Lord to Gang Busters Department, April 15, 1940, folder GB 1, LC-WOR (advertisers' demands); John Franchey to Phillips Lord, February 21, 1937, box 3, folder GB 79, LC-WOR ("libel"). For a pulp article used for *Gang Busters*, see *Real Detective*, clipping, used for "Case of Virgil Harris," *GB*, episode 281, September 18, 1942; box 16, folder GB 281, 1 of 2, LC-WOR. Lord to MacDonald, May 20, 1937 ("in no instance"); B. L. Mitchell, "The Home Radio Listening of Wilmette Grade School Children," Wilmette, IL, 1940, quoted in Herzog, *Survey of Research*, 14.

13. Dunning, *On the Air*, 278; Samuel Zucker to Colonel Schwarzkopf, November 4, 1940, box 11, folder GB 212, 2 of 2, LC-WOR.

14. John Ives to Joseph Neebe, July 26, 1935, LC-WOR ("critical angles"); John Ives to Joseph Neebe, July 22, 1935, LC-WOR (editors); Joseph Neebe to Phillips Lord, July 30, 1935, LC-WOR (chords, cars, guns, dead air, and dialogue color); John Ives to Joseph Neebe, July 30, 1935, LC-WOR (music); "Seth Parker Fan Mail Analysis—Week 10–2–38," October 10, 1938, box 4, folder 2, AHC-PHL; "List of Stations Now Being Used On 'Gang Busters' Network" (1938); "Gang Busters Network Season 1939–1940" (1939); "Gang Busters Network 1941–1942" (1941); "Gang Busters 1943 Network (Crossley Cities)" (1943); Tevis Hunh to Leonard Bass, September 20, 1943; all in LC-WOR. For *Gang Busters* ratings, see Harrison Summers, ed., *A Thirty Year History of Programs Carried on National Radio Networks in the United States, 1926–1956* (New York: Arno, 1971).

15. Sands-Siler," final script, 2 ("office"); Phillips Lord to Lewis Valentine, January 24, 1936, box 1, folder GB 2, LC-WOR ("calls"); and J. Edgar Hoover to Homer Cummings, May 22, 1934, quoted in Potter, *War on Crime*, 115.

16. Tom Revere to Phillips Lord, March 29, 1937, box 3, folder GB 63, LC-WOR; Leonard Bass to Phillips Lord, September 12, 1942, box 16, folder GB 281, 2 of 2, LC-WOR; and Lord to Gang Busters Department, April 15, 1940 ("horror").

17. W. F. Byrd, Jr., to Phillips Lord, March 24, 1937, box 3, folder GB 63, LC-WOR ("servant"); W. E. Agee to Leonard Bass, January 21, 1939, box 7, folder GB 154, LC-WOR ("misrepresented" and "handcuffed"); Leonard Bass to George Norris, April 29, 1942, box 16, folder GB 281, 2 of 2, LC-WOR ("stationery"); Leonard Bass to George Norris, April 14, 1942, box 16, folder GB 281, 2 of 2, LC-WOR ("clips").

18. Description of James Hillard Houser; H. H. Houser to *Gang Busters*, November 4, 1940; Leonard Bass to H. H. Houser, November 13, 1940; release form signed by parents of James Hillard Houser, November 18, 1940; Rev. W. J. Roof to Leonard Bass, November 17, 1940; all in box 14, folder GB 220, LC-WOR. U.S. Federal Census records show that the Housers owned a farm in 1930.

19. Donato Cugino to Phillips Lord, June 28, 1936 (emphasis in the "self-defense" quote by broadcasters; emphasis in the "victim" quote by Cugino); and "Tony 'The Stinger' Cugino," *GB*, episode 25, July 1, 1936, script; both in box 1, folder GB 25, LC-WOR.

20. "Sands-Siler," final script, 21–27 (three children); Medrano to Bass, February 16, 1939 (one child); Leonard Bass to George Norris, February 7, 1939; George Norris, "Sands-Siler," resume, 1939 ("part Indian"); George Norris to Leonard Bass, January 20, 1939 ("family history"); all in box 7, folder 154, LC-WOR. For interviews, see Waldo Wedel's interview with Post Oak Jim, July 17, 1933, cited in Curtis Marez, "Signifying Spain, Becoming Comanche, Making Mexicans: Indian Captivity and the History of Chicana/o Popular Performance," *American Quarterly* 53, no. 2 (June 2001): 267–307. On Bonnie Medrano's parents, see 1930 U.S. federal census. On white Americans' attitudes towards Indians, see, for example, Philip Deloria, *Playing Indian* (New Haven, Conn.: Yale University Press, 1998).

21. Leonard Bass to George Norris, February 7, 1939; Waymond Ramsey to Leonard

Bass, February 1, 1939; Chester MacCracken to John Ives, February 6, 1939; and "Sands-Siler," final script, 3–4 (Chief's lines); all in box 7, folder GB 154, LC-WOR.

22. Norris to Bass, January 20, 1939 ("bitter"); "Admits Robbery," newspaper clipping [1935]; and George Norris to Leonard Bass, January 30, 1939 ("Indian"); all in box 7, folder GB 154, LC-WOR; Marez, "Signifying Spain," 278; and "Sands-Siler" script, 26.

23. Norris to Bass, January 30, 1939; and Leonard Bass to Berniece Medrano, March 3, 1939; all in box 7, folder GB 154, LC-WOR.

24. Norris to Bass, January 20, 1939 ("bullet holes" and Ambroses' testimony); Medrano to Bass, February 16, 1939 ("fatherless children"); and George Norris to Leonard Bass, January 28, 1939 (Apachee and New Mexico); all in box 7, folder GB 154, LC-WOR.

25. Norris to Bass, January 30, 1939; Leonard Bass to Mrs. C. L. Ambrose, January 26, 1939; Leonard Bass to Berniece Medrano, January 26, 1939; Mrs. C. L. Ambrose to Manager of Gang Busters, January 19, 1939; and Medrano to Bass, February 16, 1939; all in box 7, folder GB 154, LC-WOR.

26. Zucker to Schwarzkopf, November 4, 1940; and Leonard Bass to Samuel Zucker, November 14, 1940, box 11, folder GB 212, 2 of 2, LC-WOR. Elsie Detrich to Palmolive Company, June 6, 1939; and Leonard Bass to Elsie Detrich, June 28, 1939; both in box 9, folder GB 168, LC-WOR; *St. Louis City Directory* (1935) (Detrich's occupation).

27. Detrich to Palmolive Company, June 6, 1939. On radio and women consumers, see Kathy M. Newman, *Radio Active: Advertising and Consumer Activism, 1935–1947* (Berkeley: University of California Press, 2004); Michele Hilmes, *Radio Voices: American Broadcasting, 1922–1952* (Minneapolis: University of Minnesota Press, 1997), 315–16.

28. On the investigation and criticism of the networks between 1938 and 1946, see Michael Socolow, "Questioning Advertising's Influence Over America Radio: The Blue Book Controversy of 1945–1947," *Journal of Radio History* 9 (2004): 282–302; Susan J. Douglas, *Listening In: Radio and the American Imagination* (New York: Times Books, 1999); and Newman, *Radio Active*.

Chapter 7

1. "WANN Program Log," January 1, 1947, box 3, NMAH-WANN; Jeff Nelson, "An on-Air Risk Paid Off for WANN and Its Listeners," *Capital* (Annapolis, Md.), January 12, 1997; "WANN: $250,000,000 Negro Market Coming Up!" 1953, box 3, NMAH-WANN.

2. Adam Green, *Selling the Race: Culture, Community, and Black Chicago, 1940–1955* (Chicago: University of Chicago Press, 2007), 53; Tom McCourt and Eric W. Rothenbuhler, "Burnishing the Brand: Todd Storz and the Total Station Sound," *Radio Journal* 2, no. 1 (June 2004): 4.

3. Christopher H. Sterling and John M. Kittross, *Stay Tuned: A History of American Broadcasting* (Mahwah, N.J.: Lawrence Erlbaum Associates, 2002), 830–31; Scott DeVeaux, *The Birth of Bebop: A Social and Musical History* (Berkeley and Los Angeles: University of California Press, 1997), 299; Russell Sanjek and David Sanjek, *Pennies from Heaven: The American Popular Music Business in the Twentieth Century* (New York: Da Capo Press,

1996); Mary M. Austin, "The American Federation of Musicians' Recording Ban, 1942–1944, and Its Effect on Radio Broadcasting in the United States" (master's thesis, University of North Texas, 1980).

4. "Indies' Growing Audience," *Billboard*, December 6, 1947; Jerry Franken, "Come the Revolution: Radox!" *Billboard*, July 9, 1949; "Incomes Rule Tuner Tastes," *Billboard*, November 15, 1947; Susan J. Douglas, *Listening In: Radio and the American Imagination* (New York: Times Books, 1999); Philip H. Ennis, *The Seventh Stream: The Emergence of Rocknroll in American Popular Music* (Middletown, Conn.: Wesleyan University Press; Hanover, N.H.: University Press of New England, 1992); and James L. Baughman, *The Republic of Mass Culture: Journalism, Filmmaking, and Broadcasting in America since 1941* (Baltimore, Md.: Johns Hopkins University Press, 1992).

5. *Rev. LeRoy Brown, Pastor, First Baptist Church, Annapolis, Maryland*, photograph, January 10, 1947, box 3, NMAH-WANN; "WANN Sets Record for Return to Air," *County Chronicle*, February 20, 1948; "WANN: $250,000,000 Negro Market."

6. "WANN: $250,000,000 Negro Market Coming Up!" "WANN serves the largest Negro Market in America . . . outside New York!" *Printer's Ink*, September 11, 1953.

7. Irene Hall to WANN, January 15, 1950, box 3, NMAH-WANN; Bertha Thomas to WANN, February 16, 1956, box 3, NMAH-WANN; "The Forgotten 15,000,000 Part 1," *Sponsor*, October 10, 1949; Kathy M. Newman, "The Forgotten Fifteen Million: Black Radio, the 'Negro Market' and the Civil Rights Movement," *Radical History Review* 76 (Winter 2000): 115–35.

8. "Disc Jockeys," *Ebony*, December 1947, 44. On Latin DJs in Los Angeles in this period, see Anthony F. Macias, *Mexican American Mojo: Popular Music, Dance, and Urban Culture in Los Angeles, 1935–1968* (Durham: Duke University Press, 2008). Examples of Latin disc jockeys from other parts of the country writing to "Vox Jox" columns abound: see Don Eduardo to *Billboard*, November 10, 1951, 93; Ted Duran to *Billboard*, February 4, 1950, 26; Paul Britt and Eugenio de la Pena to *Billboard*, March 1, 1952, 42; Alan Boal to *Billboard*, August 12, 1950, 26; Jim Hodge to *Billboard*, March 10, 1951, 18; Joe McCauley to *Billboard*, August 6, 1949, 39; Pedro Albani to *Billboard*, March 19, 1949, 24–25; Max Cole to *Billboard*, December 24, 1949, 26; Steve Allison to *Billboard*, November 4, 1950, 28; Los Chicos to *Billboard*, March 12, 1955, 48.

9. Philip Hamburger, "Socko!" *New Yorker*, July 29, 1944, 27; "Roy Milton Band Debuts at Apollo Friday,'" *New York Amsterdam News*, November 9, 1946; "High-School Students Label-Wise," *Billboard*, June 17, 1944; "G.I.'s Tab Favorite Disks," *Billboard*, September 23, 1944.

10. "First Annual Billboard Jockey Poll," *Billboard*, August 2, 1947.

11. "Vox Jox," *Billboard*, March 13, 1948 (first column); Ennis, *The Seventh Stream*, 397; Doc Searls, "Hall Monitor," *Doc Searl's Weblog*, July 21, 2003, http://doc-weblogs.com/2003/07/21; Ron Jacobs, interview, *Rock Radio Scrapbook*, http://www.rockradioscrapbook.ca/jacobs.html; Dave Garroway et al. to *Billboard*, March 20, 1948, 36; Al Benson to *Billboard*, December 18, 1948, 40; Hoppy Adams to *Billboard*, May 24, 1952, 30.

12. Bette-Lou Purvis and Ed Bartell to *Billboard*, November 27, 1948, 44–45; Larry

Wayne to *Billboard*, December 11, 1948, 38 (soaps); Ed Weston and Bill Martin to *Billboard*, November 20, 1948, 43; Bob King to *Billboard*, December 18, 1948, 40; Arty Kay to *Billboard*, December 25, 1948, 37; "Radio Fan Wins; Refused Service," *Los Angeles Sentinel*, March 11, 1948.

13. Stew McDonnell to *Billboard*, May 28, 1949, 40; Al Benson to *Billboard*, December 18, 1948, 40; Dick Bruce to *Billboard*, December 25, 1948, 37; Beverly Norberry to *Billboard*, May 28, 1949, 40.

14. Johnny Russell to *Billboard*, February 26, 1949, 47; Harold Craven to *Billboard*, December 4, 1948, 20.

15. "WANN: $250,000,000 Negro Market"; "Jackson Scores on Maryland Radio Station," *Pittsburgh Courier*, June 24, 1950; Galen Gart, ed., *First Pressings: The History of Rhythm & Blues, Vol. 6, 1956* (Milford, N.H.: Big Nickel, 1993), 91; Bruce Pegg, *Brown-Eyed Handsome Man: The Life and Hard Times of Chuck Berry, an Unauthorized Biography* (New York: Routledge, 2005), 62.

16. Bessie Lee to WANN, December 3, 1955, box 3, NMAH-WANN; Katherine Johnson to WANN, 1951, box 3, NMAH-WANN; Jennie Johnson to WANN, January 19, 1956, box 3, NMAH-WANN.

17. Duncan MacDougald, "The Popular Music Industry," in *Radio Research, 1941*, ed. Paul F. Lazarsfeld and Frank N. Stanton (New York: Duell, Sloan and Pearce, 1941), 65–109. Arnold Shaw, "The Vocabulary of Tin-Pan Alley Explained," *Music Library Association Notes* (December 12, 1949), 33–53. On Richard Himber's method, see *Variety*, August 31, 1949, 45; on Peatman surveys, see John Gray Peatman, "Radio and Popular Music," in *Radio Research, 1942–43*, ed. Paul F. Lazarsfeld and Frank N. Stanton (New York: Duell, Sloan and Pearce, 1944), 335–93.

18. "United Music Charges Cheating," *Variety*, September 7, 1949, 43.

19. "Harlem Hit Parade," *Billboard*, October 24, 1942; "Most Played Juke Box Race Records," *Billboard*, February 17, 1945; "The Billboard Music Popularity Charts, Part VII: Rhythm and Blues Records," *Billboard*, June 25, 1949. On the history of *Billboard* black music charts, see "Billboard Adopts 'R&B' as New Name for 2 Charts," *Billboard*, October 27, 1990.

20. On listing strategies, see Marilyn Robinson Waldman, " 'The Otherwise Noteworthy Year 711': A Reply to Hayden White," in *On Narrative*, ed. W. J. T. Mitchell (Chicago and London: University of Chicago Press, 1981), 242; and Hayden V. White, "The Value of Narrativity in the Representation of Reality," in Mitchell, ed., *On Narrative*, 1–23; "The *Billboard* Fourth Music Record Poll," *Billboard*, January 14, 1950, 13; Ahmet Ertegun quoted in Jerry Wexler and David Ritz, *Rhythm and the Blues: A Life in American Music* (New York: St. Martin's Press, 1994),78–79.

21. Paula to Arthur H. Croghan, August 11, 1948, NMAH-JA; Hal Jackson and James Haskins, *The House That Jack Built: My Life as a Trailblazer in Broadcasting and Entertainment* (New York: HarperCollins, 2001), 95.

22. Dick Olson to *Billboard*, November 27, 1948, 44–45 (juke boxes); "Sarah Wins First Place, Stafford Next," *Pittsburgh Courier*, June 11, 1949, 29.

23. Dave Dexter, "Disk Jockey: Origin of the Species, 1930–1945," *Billboard*, December 27, 1969; Warren Quade to *Billboard*, December 4, 1948, 20; Bill Cook to *Billboard*, December 4, 1948, 20; Ennis, *The Seventh Stream*, 159.

24. Tim Edwards to *Billboard*, November 27, 1948, 44–45; Mac McGarry to *Billboard*, May 7, 1949, 37; Howard Garland to *Billboard*, May 7, 1949, 37.

25. "Disk Jock Polls Key to 'Action' Sought by BMI," *Variety*, August 3, 1949, 37; "ASCAP in Plan to Expand Logging of Indie Stations," *Billboard*, October 7, 1950, 12; Sanjek and Sanjek, *Pennies from Heaven*, 286–287.

26. Carlo Ginzburg, "Morelli, Freud, and Sherlock Holmes: Clues and Scientific Method," in *Dupin, Holmes, Peirce: The Sign of Three*, ed. Umberto Eco and Thomas A. Sebeok (Bloomington: Indiana University Press, 1983), 81–118;

27. Duncan MacDougald, "The Popular Music Industry," in Lazarsfeld and Stanton, eds., *Radio Research, 1941*, 65–109; Michael Erdélyi, "The Relation between 'Radio Plugs' and Sheet Sales of Popular Music," *Journal of Applied Psychology* 24, no. 6 (December 1940): 696–702; G. D. Wiebe, "A Comparison of Various Ratings Used in Judging the Merits of Popular Songs," *Journal of Applied Psychology* 23 (February 1939): 18–22; Johnny Otis quoted in Jannette L. Dates and William Barlow, eds., *Split Image: African-Americans in the Mass Media* (Washington, D.C.: Howard University Press, 1993), 66–67.

28. Arnold Shaw, *Honkers and Shouters: The Golden Years of Rhythm and Blues* (New York: Macmillan, 1978), 357; Fred Mendelsohn interview in Shaw, *Honkers and Shouters*, 357. For a musicological comparison of "Now Is the Time" and "The Hucklebuck," see Samuel A. Floyd, *The Power of Black Music: Interpreting Its History from Africa to the United States* (New York: Oxford University Press, 1995), 144–45. Liner notes to "D'Natural Blues," *Blues Masters: The Essential Blues Collection*, vol. 13, *New York City Blues*, Rhino, 1993; *New York Age*, August 13, 1949, 21; "The Billboard Fourth Annual Music Record Poll," *Billboard* (January 14, 1950), 13–17; *Variety*, August 31, 1949, 45.

29. "The Hucklebuck," by Roy Alfred and Andy Gibson, © United Music, 1948; "Millinder Sues over Hucklebuck," *Melody Maker*, September 17, 1949, 4, and "Millinder Suit," *Variety*, August 31, 1949, 45 (first version); "Lucky Would Extract Bucks from out 'The Hucklebuck,'" *Billboard*, September 3, 1949, 34 (first and second version); all three articles mention the third possibility.

30. "Millinder Sues over Hucklebuck"; Johnny Otis, *Upside Your Head! Rhythm and Blues on Central Avenue* (Hanover, N.H.: University Press of New England, 1993), xxv–xxvi.

31. John H. Merryman, "Copyright Law and the Modern Jazz Arrangement," *Notre Dame Lawyer* 23 (May 1948): 481–500; "Billy Rowe's Note Book," *Pittsburgh Courier*, February 2, 1946.

32. *RCA Manufacturing Co., Inc., v. Whiteman*, 114 F.2d 86 (2d Cir. 1940), at 6. On the sound recording as a work of art, see Theodore Gracyk, *Rhythm and Noise: An Aesthetic of Rock* (Durham, N.C. and London: Duke University Press, 1996); and Albin Zak, *I Don't Sound Like Nobody: Remaking Music in 1950s America* (Ann Arbor: University of Michigan Press, 2010).

33. Peter Doyle, *Echo and Reverb: Fabricating Space in Popular Music Recording, 1900–1960* (Middletown, Conn.: Wesleyan University Press, 2005), 167 (Johnny Cash quote), (reinvention of sound at Sun and Chess); Gracyk, *Rhythm and Noise* (Sun sound and recordings as art); "Jockeying Is a Fine Art," *Billboard Music Yearbook,* 1944 (breaking records on the air); Al Jarvis, "The Disk Jockey," *Billboard,* April 25, 1953.

34. Jerry Wexler and Hal Webman, "Pluggers War on Payola," *Billboard,* October 29, 1949; "Hungry DJs a Growing Headache," *Billboard,* December 23, 1950; "Payola Deejays Jeopardize Licensees," *Billboard,* December 11, 1948; Shaw, *Honkers and Shouters,* 511. For an overview of payola in the music industry, see Kerry Segrave, *Payola in the Music Industry: A History, 1880–1991* (Jefferson, N.C.: McFarland, 1994). On "infrastructures of piracy" in another context, see Brian Larkin, *Signal and Noise: Media, Infrastructure, and Urban Culture in Nigeria* (Durham, N.C.: Duke University Press, 2008).

35. "Meet Al Benson, the Wizard of Weird Words," *Chicago Tribune,* March 4, 1951. For more on Benson and other black disc jockeys' performance style, see Nelson George, *The Death of Rhythm and Blues* (New York: Plume, 1988), 39–57.

36. Gene Fowler and Bill Crawford, *Border Radio* (Austin: Texas Monthly Press, 1987), 9, 89, 109 (astrologist on Mexican radio); "'Rajah' to Appear in Stage Show," [1937] (throwing knives blindfolded), and "Rajah Raboid and His Miracles of 1937," [1937] (sawing a man in half), "Miracles of 1937," advertisement, [1937] (India), clippings, Johnny Eck Museum website, http://www.johnnyeckmuseum.com/magic/rajah-raboid.html; "Cover," *Vaudeville News and New York Star,* November 26, 1927 (turban); copy of a letter of complaint to the FCC, in T. J. Slowie to Annapolis Broadcasting Corporation, January 3, 1951 ("on behalf of the colored people"); Anthon Sawage to WANN, January 14, 1951 ("own home"); Mary C. Ray to WANN, January 17, 1951 (missing cousin); W. Chester Carey to WANN, January 13, 1951 (concedes turn); Morris H. Blum to the Federal Communications Commission, January 20, 1951; all in box 3, NMAH-WANN.

37. Otis, *Upside Your Head,* 60–61; Adam Katz-Stone, "WANN of a Kind," *Baltimore Jewish Times,* March 7, 1997.

38. "Hungry DJs a Growing Headache"; "Meet Al Benson, the Wizard of Weird Words"; Herb Abramson quoted in Chip Deffaa, *Blue Rhythms: Six Lives in Rhythm and Blues* (Urbana: University of Illinois Press, 1996), 37. For more on Benson as an entrepreneur, see Green, *Selling the Race,* 84–59.

39. Stuart L. Goosman, *Group Harmony: The Black Urban Roots of Rhythm & Blues* (Philadelphia: University of Pennsylvania Press, 2005), 131.

40. Robert O. Carlson to Paul F. Lazarsfeld, "Interim Report on BMI Field Study," memorandum, November 25, 1952, B0470, CU-BASR.

41. "Hungry DJs a Growing Headache"; Herb Abramson quoted in Deffaa, *Blue Rhythms,* 37; "Payola Deejays Jeopardize Licensees," *Billboard,* December 11, 1948; "Tax Note," *Billboard,* August 5, 1950; editors' note in "Deejay Org Airs Payola Reply," *Billboard,* February 19, 1949; Jerry Wexler quoted in Warren Zanes, *Dusty in Memphis* (New York: Continuum, 2003), 45. On the moral issues arising from the Hollywood blacklist, see

Victor S. Navasky, *Naming Names* (New York: Hill and Wang, 2003); Green, *Selling the Race*, 87.

42. BMI Program Clinics ad, *Billboard*, April 26, 1952; Glenn Dolberg, speech at the BMI Clinic, Gainsville, Fl., March 26, 1951, tape 311, LAB-BMI.

43. Hugh Smith, speech at the BMI Clinic, Salt Lake City, Utah, February 11, 1951, tape 409, LAB-BMI; Fred Robbins to *Billboard*, December 4, 1948, 20; Robert Pruter, *Chicago Soul* (Champaign-Urbana: University of Illinois Press, 1992), 24 (Vivian Carter).

44. "Roy Milton Hollers Loud On Tune Piracy," *New York Amsterdam News*, February 21, 1948; Dolberg, BMI Clinic speech.

45. Dick Redmond, speech at the BMI Clinic, Harrisburg, Pa., August 20, 1951, tape 355, LAB-BMI; "Storm Rages in Cincy over DJ 'Exclusives,'" *Billboard*, March 7, 1953; "Broadcasters, DJs Plagued by New Law," *Billboard*, January 31, 1953.

46. On Top 40, see Eric W. Rothenbuhler and Tom McCourt, "Radio Redefines Itself, 1947–1962," in *Radio Reader: Essays in the Cultural History of Radio*, ed. Michele Hilmes and Jason Loviglio (New York: Routledge, 2002), 367–87; and McCourt and Rothenbuhler, "Burnishing the Brand."

Epilogue

1. David Pogue, "The Generational Divide in Copyright Morality," *NYT*, December 20, 2007, http://www.nytimes.com/2007/12/20/ technology/personaltech/20pogue-email.html; "Protest Suit of WEAF," *New Jersey Evening Journal*, March 1924. See, for example, Sarah F. Brosnana and Frans B. M. de Waal, "Monkeys Reject Unequal Pay," *Nature*, September 18, 2003; Ernst Fehr and Simon Gachter, "Fairness and Retaliation: The Economics of Reciprocity," *Journal of Economic Perspectives* 14, no. 3 (Summer 2000): 159–81; Marc Hauser, *Moral Minds: How Nature Designed Our Universal Sense of Right and Wrong* (New York: Ecco, 2006); International Intellectual Property Alliance, *2010 Special 301 Report*, http://www.iipa.com/2010_SPEC301_TOC.htm; Patrick Barkham, "Britons Set Another Technological Lead—in Pirating TV Shows," *Guardian* (London), February 19, 2005, http://www.guardian.co.uk/technology/2005/feb/19/media.broadcasting; International Intellectual Property Alliance, *2010 Special 301 Report*, February 18, 2010, 174, http://www.iipa.com/2010_SPEC301_TOC.htm.

2. Siva Vaidhyanathan, *Copyrights and Copywrongs: The Rise of Intellectual Property and How it Threatens Creativity* (New York: New York University Press, 2003); Siva Vaidhyanathan, *The Anarchist In The Library: How the Clash Between Freedom and Control Is Hacking the Real World and Crashing the System* (New York: Basic Books, 2005); Tarleton Gillespie, *Wired Shut: Copyright and the Shape of Digital Culture* (Cambridge, Mass.: MIT Press, 2007); Lawrence Lessig, *Code: Version 2.0*, 2nd ed. (New York: Basic Books, 2006); Lawrence Lessig, *Free Culture: How Big Media Uses Technology and the Law to Lock Down Culture and Control Creativity* (New York: Penguin Press, 2004); Lawrence Lessig, *The Future of Ideas: The Fate of the Commons in a Connected World* (New York: Random House, 2001); Bill Glahn, "The New Mo-

rality of Capitalism," *Counterpunch*, October 22, 2003, http://www.counterpunch.org/glahn10222003.html (radio commentator).

3. Yochai Benkler, *The Wealth of Networks: How Social Production Transforms Markets and Freedom* (New Haven, Conn.: Yale University Press, 2006); Christopher Kelty, *Two Bits: The Cultural Significance of Free Software* (Durham, N.C.: Duke University Press, 2008); Steven Levy, *Hackers: Heroes of the Computer Revolution* (New York: O'Reilly Media, 2010); Gabriella Coleman and Alex Golub, "Hacker Practice: Moral Genres and the Cultural Articulation of Liberalism," *Anthropological Theory* 8, no. 3 (September 2008): 255–77; Gabriella Coleman and Mao Hill, "The Social Production of Ethics in Debian and Free Software Communities," in *Free and Open Source Software Development*, ed. Stephan Koch (Hershey, Pa., and London: Idea Group, 2004); For two in-depth overviews of digital culture as an interdisciplinary field of study, see Gabriella Coleman, "Ethnographic Approaches to Digital Media," *Annual Review of Anthropology* 39 (2010): 1–19; and Siva Vaidhyanathan, "Afterword: Critical Information Studies," *Cultural Studies* 20, no. 2 (May 2006): 292–315.

4. Jason Schultz, "File Sharing Must Be Made Legal," *Salon*, September 2003, http://www.salon.com/technology/feature/2003/09/12/file_sharing_two (EFF statement); "File Sharing," *EFF*, http://www.eff.org/issues/file-sharing (campaign launched in 2003); IIPA, *2010 Special 301 Report* (see n. 1); for analyses of this and an earlier IIPA report, see Michael Geist, "US Copyright Lobby Out-of-Touch," *BBC*, February 20, 2007, http://news.bbc.co.uk/2/hi/technology/6379309.stm; *Intellectual Property: Observations on Efforts to Quantify the Economic Effects of Counterfeit and Pirated Goods* (Washington, D.C.: U.S. Government Accountability Office, April 2010); on the pharmaceutical industry, see Jacqui Cheng, "Human Rights Groups Slam Special 301 Report," *Ars Technica*, July 20, 2010, http://arstechnica.com/tech-policy/news/2010/07/groups-say-special-301-report-denies-countries-life-saving-drugs.ars; for a useful general history of piracy and intellectual property, see Adrian Johns, *Piracy: The Intellectual Property Wars from Gutenberg to Gates* (Chicago: University of Chicago Press, 2009).

5. Barkham, "Britons Set Another Technological Lead"; Michael Pollitt, "Science and Technology: Small-Screen Bounty," *Independent* (London), February 19, 2005, 11; Ciar Byrne, "New Twist in Internet Piracy as Britons Rush to Download TV," *Independent* (London), February 19, 2005; Ernesto, "Top 10 Most Pirated TV-Shows of 2009," *TorrentFreak*, December 31, 2009, http://torrentfreak.com/top-10-most-pirated-tv-shows-of-2009-091231.

6. Henry Jenkins, *Convergence Culture: Where Old and New Media Collide* (New York: New York University Press, 2006); Henry Jenkins, *Textual Poachers: Television Fans and Participatory Culture* (New York: Routledge, 1992); John Tullock and Henry Jenkins, *Science Fiction Audiences: Watching Doctor Who and Star Trek* (London and New York: Routledge, 1995); Elana Shefrin, "Lord of the Rings, Star Wars, and Participatory Fandom: Mapping New Congruencies between the Internet and Media Entertainment Culture," *Critical Studies in Media Communication* 21, no. 3 (September 2004): 261–81.

7. "Creative Commons," http://creativecommons.org/; "The Rise, Rise and Rise of

the Downfall Hitler Parody," *BBC*, April 13, 2010, http://news.bbc.co.uk/2/hi/8617454.
stm; "Constantin Films Pulls Hitler," http://www.youtube.com/watch?v=DvJqZ3SDwNc;
Lucas Hilderbrand, "Youtube: Where Cultural Memory and Copyright Converge," *Film
Quarterly* 61, no. 1 (September 2007): 48–57.

8. Randall Stross, "First It Was Song Downloads. Now It's Organic Chemistry," *NYT*,
July 27, 2008, http://www.nytimes.com/2008/07/27/technology/27digi.html (student
anger and Textbook Torrents); Public Library of Science, http://www.plos.org/; Connex-
ions, http://cnx.org/; Kelty, *Two Bits*; IIPA, *2010 Special 301 Report*, 174.

9. James A. Evans and Jacob Reimer, "Open Access and Global Participation in Science," *Science* 323, no. 5917 (February 20, 2009): 1025; Adrian Johns, *Piracy: The Intellectual Property Wars from Gutenberg to Gates* (Chicago: University of Chicago Press, 2009),
427–28 (Heaviside); Sylvia Nasar and David Gruber, "Manifold Destiny," *New Yorker*, August 28, 2006, http://www.newyorker.com/archive/2006/08/28/060828fa_fact2.

10. "FSF Free Software Licensing and Compliance Lab," *Free Software Foundation*,
n.d., http://www.fsf.org/licensing; "Creative Commons," http://creativecommons.org/; On
Richard Stallman and recursive publics, see Kelty, *Two Bits*; Gabriella Coleman, "Code Is
Speech: Legal Tinkering, Expertise, and Protest Among Free and Open Source Software
Developers," *Cultural Anthropology* 24, no. 3 (2009): 432–33 (Lessig consulted free software programmers); Lessig, *The Future of Ideas*; Lessig, *Code 2.0*; Lessig, *Free Culture*; Oliver Wendell Holmes, Jr., *The Common Law* (London: Macmillan, 1881), 1 (quote); Oliver
Wendell Holmes, Jr., "The Path of the Law," *Harvard Law Review* 110, no. 5 (March 1997):
991–1009.

11. "The Betamax Case," *Electronic Frontier Foundation*, http://w2.eff.org/legal/cases/
betamax/. On *Universal v. Sony*, see James Lardner, *Fast Forward: Hollywood, the Japanese,
and the Onslaught of the VCR* (New York: Norton, 1987) and Lucas Hilderbrand, *Inherent
Vice: Bootleg Histories of Videotape and Copyright* (Durham, N.C.: Duke University Press,
2009). On early video stores, see Joshua M Greenberg, *From BetaMax to Blockbuster: Video
Stores and the Invention of Movies on Video* (Cambridge, Mass: MIT Press, 2007).

12. "MGM Studios v Grokster," *U.S. Copyright Office*, http://www.copyright.gov/docs/
mgm/; Hilderbrand, *Inherent Vice*; Coleman, "Code Is Speech;" "EFF Wins New Legal
Protections for Video Artists, Cell Phone Jailbreakers, and Unlockers," *Electronic Frontier
Foundation*, July 26, 2010, https://www.eff.org/press/archives/2010/07/26.

13. IIPA, *2010 Special 301 Report*; "When Using Open Source Makes You an Enemy
of the State," *Guardian* (London), February 23, 2010, http://www.guardian.co.uk/technol-
ogy/blog/2010/feb/23/opensource-intellectual-property; Jeffrey S. Juris, *Networking Fu-
tures: The Movements against Corporate Globalization* (Durham, N.C.: Duke University
Press, 2008); Clifford J. Levy, "Russia Uses Microsoft to Suppress Dissent," *NYT*, September 11, 2010; Levy, "Microsoft Changes Policy Over Russian Crackdown," *NYT*, September 13, 2010; Levy, "Microsoft Expands Effort to Protect Nonprofit Groups," *NYT*, October
16, 2010; Ashlee Vance, "Microsoft vs. Software Piracy: Inside the War Room," *NYT*, November 6, 2010.

14. Raffi Khatchadourian, "WikiLeaks and Julian Paul Assange," *New Yorker*, June 7,

2010, http://www.newyorker.com/reporting/2010/06/07/100607fa_fact_khatchadourian (excellent early account of Wikileaks); "Wikileaks' Afghanistan Log: Wikileaks' 10 Greatest Scoops," *Telegraph*, July 26, 2010, http://www.telegraph.co.uk/news/worldnews/asia/ afghanistan/7911036/Wikileaks-Afghanistan-log-Wikileaks-10-greatest-scoops.html (Kenya and global warming). My account of Wikileaks 2010 disclosures is based on coverage of the Wikileaks controversy from April to December 2010 in the following sources: *New York Times*, http://nytimes.com; *Guardian* (London), http://www.guardian.co.uk/; Glenn Greenwald's blog, *Salon*, http://www.salon.com/news/opinion/glenn_greenwald/ index.html; and Greg Mitchell's "Media Fix" blog, *Nation*, http://www.thenation.com/ blogs/media-fix. (In December each source provided nearly daily coverage.)

15. As of this writing, Wikileaks is at http://213.251.145.96; Afghan War Logs app, *OWNI*, http://app.owni.fr/warlogs/; Iraq War Logs app, *OWNI*, http://warlogs.owni.fr/; State Logs app, *OWNI*, http://statelogs.owni.fr/; Cable Search Beta, *European Center of Computer Assisted Reporting*, http://cablessearch.org; Charles Arthur, "Openleaks? Brusselsleaks? Tradeleaks? The Market's Getting Crowded," *Guardian* (London), December 16, 2010, http://www.guardian.co.uk/media/pda/2010/dec/16/openleaks-brusselsleaks tradeleaks-whistleblowing.

16. W. W., "After Secrets: Missing the Point of Wikileaks," *Economist*, December 1, 2010, http://www.economist.com/blogs/democracyinamerica/2010/12/after_secrets.

Index

Acknowledgments

Since I began working on *The Listener's Voice*, many friends, colleagues, and teachers have shared their knowledge, experience, ideas, and companionship. My first and deepest thanks go to my mentor, Roy Rosenzweig. His life exemplifies what doing history means intellectually and politically. This book is dedicated to his memory. From the earliest stages of this project, Roy and Mike O'Malley were always available to read multiple drafts and suggest better ways to interpret, organize, and articulate my work. Charles McGovern shared with me his vast knowledge of consumer culture and his unflinching optimism about the future of his students. Cynthia Fuchs taught me how to think and write simultaneously as a historian, theorist, and critic.

My research and writing would not have been as much fun if I had not encountered many brilliant and generous people in my migration from Russia to the United States and then Canada. At Berkeley, Liz Hasse, Tom Luddy, Edith Kramer, and Lawrence Levine and, at New York University, Ellen Noonan, Karl Miller, Tricia Rose, and Walter Johnson helped me to appreciate my initial years in the United States. At George Mason University, I received valuable advice from Alison Landsberg, Jim Sparrow, Lisa Breglia, Alan Gevinson, Ellen Todd, Deborah Kaplan, Matt Karush, Steve Barnes, Dan Kerr, Suzy Smith, and John Cheng. At the National Museum of American History, I shared chapters, ideas, and drinks with Pete Daniel, David Suisman, Steve Garabedian, John Troutman, Matt Wray, Alex Russo, Laura Schiavo, David Hernandez, Todd Uhlman, and Lauren Sklaroff. I also learned from fellows at the Smithsonian American Art Museum—Jason Weems, Emily Shapiro, Deidre Murphy, Meredith Paige Davis, and Jobyl Boone. I benefited from conversations with media scholars Susan Smulyan, Derek Vaillant, David Goodman, Jason Loviglio, Kathleen Battles, Michele Hilmes, Mary Vipond, Jonathan Sterne, Mike Socolow, and Kathy Newman. I participated in a community of Washington, D.C., scholars including Lisa Gitelman, Lisa Lynch, Erik Dussere, Stephanie Hartman, Michael Sappol, Gayle Wald, and Joseph Chaves. Several colleagues helped me to relate my work to the new field of digital humanities: at the Center for History and New Media, Dan Cohen, Tom Scheinfeld, Josh Greenberg, Sharon Leon, Amanda Shuman, Stephanie Hurter, Jeremy Boggs, and Sheila Brennan; at the American Social History Project, Josh Brown, Steve Brier, Pennee Bender, and Andrea Vásquez; and at Concordia University in Montreal, Canada, Steve High, Ron Rudin, Shannon McSheffrey, Sean Gurd, Bart Simon, Jason Camlot, Jason Lewis, and Lynn Hughes. In Montreal, Andrew Ivaska, Rachel Berger, Wilson Jacob, Anya Zilberstein, Ted McCormick, Theresa Ventura, Michelle Hartman, Yumna Siddiqi, Lara Braitstein, Shahin Parhami, Khalid Medani, Setrag Manoukian, Laila Parsons, Joseph Chaves, Danielle Bobker, Omar Dewachi, Gavin Taylor, Meredith Evans, Nick Dew, Ceren Belge, Leander Schneider, Heloisa Marone, Nora Jaffary, and Zohar Kfir helped me to rethink my research in transnational and interdisciplinary contexts.

This work could not have been completed without the financial assistance of a Smithsonian Institution Fellowship, American Heritage Center Travel Grant, and several fellowships and research grants from George Mason University and Concordia University in Montreal. A version of Chapter 6 was previously published in *American Quarterly*; I am grateful to Johns Hopkins University Press for permitting me to reprint it here. Many librarians and archivists aided me in my research and in obtaining illustrations for the book. I am particularly grateful to Sam Brylawski, Janet McKee, and Bryan Cornell of the Recorded Sound Reference Center of the Library of Congress; Chuck Howell and Michael Henry of the Library of American Broadcasting; Alexander Magoun of the David Sarnoff Library; Dee Anna Grimsrud and Lisa Marine of the Wisconsin Historical Society; Kay Peterson of the Archives Center, National Museum of American History, Smithsonian Institution; John Waggener of the American Heritage Center at the University of Wyoming; and other archivists at the Library of Congress, at the Cinema and Television Library, University of Southern California, and at the Thousand Oaks Library in Thousand Oaks, California. Maureen Walthers of the *Ridgewood Times*, Queens, New York, graciously allowed me to peruse her private collection on radio station WHN. Special thanks go to my editor, Bob Lockhart, for his infinite patience in waiting for this manuscript to be completed, as well as to Erica Ginsburg, Julia Rose Roberts, and the staff of the University of Pennsylvania Press for their assistance in preparing the manuscript.

Finally, I extend particular thanks to my parents, my sisters, and my entire extended family. I can always rely on their wit and wisdom.